OWEN GLYNDWR

AND THE LAST STRUGGLE FOR WELSH INDEPENDENCE

WITH A BRIEF SKETCH OF WELSH HISTORY

BY

ARTHUR GRANVILLE BRADLEY

AUTHOR OF "HIGHWAYS AND BYWAYS IN NORTH WALES," "SKETCHES FROM OLD VIRGINIA," "THE FIGHT WITH FRANCE FOR NORTH AMERICA," ETC.

G. P. PUTNAM'S SONS

NEW YORK — LONDON

27 WEST TWENTY-THIRD STREET — 24 BEDFORD STREET, STRAND

The Knickerbocker Press

1902

Heroes of the Nations

EDITED BY

Evelyn Abbott, M.A.

FELLOW OF BALLIOL COLLEGE, OXFORD

FACTA DUCIS VIVENT, OPEROSAQUE GLORIA RERUM.—OVID, IN LIVIAM 265.

THE HERO'S DEEDS AND HARD-WON FAME SHALL LIVE.

OWEN GLYNDWR

 Miss Walker.

GLYNDWR'S MOUNT, GLYNDYFRDWY.

Frontispiece

PREFACE

IF this little book purported to be a biography in the ordinary sense of the word, the scantiness of purely personal detail relating to its hero might be a fair subject of criticism. But men of the Glyndwr type live in history rather by their deeds, and the deeds of those they lead and inspire. This is peculiarly the case with the last and the most celebrated among the soldier patriots of Wales. Though so little remains to tell us of the actual man himself, this very fact has thrown a certain glamour and mystery about his name even in the Principality. While numbers of well-informed Englishmen are inclined to regard him, so far as they regard him at all, as a semi-mythical hero under obligations to Shakespeare for such measure of renown and immortality as he enjoys, if the shade of Henry the Fourth could be called up as a witness it would tell a very different story. It is at any rate quite certain that for the first few years of the fifteenth century, both to England and to Wales, to friends and to foes, Owen was in very truth a sufficiently real personality. What we do know of him, apart from his work, might well suggest infinite possibilities to the novelist and the poet. It is my business, however, to deal only with facts or to record legends and traditions for what they are worth, as illustrating the men and the time.

Glyndwr is without doubt the national hero of the majority of Welshmen. Precisely why he takes precedence of warrior princes who before his day struggled so bravely with the Anglo-Norman power and often with more permanent success, is not now to the point. My readers will be able to form some opinion of their own as to the soundness of the Welsh verdict. But these are matters, after all, outside logic and argument. It is a question of sentiment which has its roots perhaps in sound reasons now forgotten. There are in existence several brief and more or less accurate accounts of Glyndwr's rising. Those of Thomas, written early in this century, and of Pennant, embodied in his well known *Tours in Wales*, are the most noteworthy,—while one or two interesting papers represent all the recent contributions to the subject. There has not hitherto, however, been any attempt to collect in book form all that is known of this celebrated Welshman and the movement he headed. I have, therefore, good reason to believe that the mere collection and arrangement of this in one accessible and handy volume will not be unwelcome, to Welsh readers especially. Thus much at least I think I have achieved, and the thought will be some consolation, at any rate, if I have failed in the not very easy task of presenting the narrative in sufficiently popular and readable guise. But I hope also to engage the interest of readers other than Welshmen in the story of Glyndwr and his times. If one were to say that the attitude of nearly all Englishmen towards Wales in an historical sense is represented by a total blank, I feel quite sure that the statement would neither be denied nor resented.

Under this assumption it was thought well to attempt a somewhat fuller picture of Wales than that presented by the Glyndwr period alone, and to lead up to this by an outline sketch of Welsh history. The earlier part, particularly, of this contains much contentious matter. But in such a rapid, superficial survey as will fully answer our purpose here, there has scarcely been occasion to go below those salient features that are pretty generally agreed upon by historians. The kind manner in which my *Highways and Byways of North Wales* was received, not only by English readers but by Welsh friends and the Welsh press, makes me venture to hope that my presumption as a Saxon in making this more serious excursion into the domain of Welsh history will be overlooked in consideration of the subject dealt with.

A continuous intimacy of many years with the Glyndyfrdwy region begat a natural interest in the notable personage who had once owned it, and this gradually ripened into a desire to fill, however inadequately, what seemed to me an obvious want. Before venturing on the task I took some pains to ascertain whether any Welsh writer had the matter in contemplation, and so far as information gathered in the most authoritative quarters could be effective it was in the negative. As this was at a time when the Welsh people were considering some form of National memorial to Glyndwr, the absence both in fact and in prospect of any accessible memoir of him overcame what diffidence on racial grounds I had naturally felt and encouraged me in my desire to supply the want.

A full list of the authorities I have consulted in the preparation of this work would, I have reason to understand, be too ponderous a supplement to a volume of this kind. Before noting any of them, however, I must first acknowledge the very great obligations I am under to Mr. Wylie for his invaluable and exhaustive history of Henry IV.; not merely for the information contained in the text of his book, but for his copious notes which have been most helpful in indicating many sources of information connected with the persons and events of the time. The following are some of the chief works consulted: Dr. Powell's translation of Humphrey Lloyd's *History of Wales* from the chronicle of Caradoc of Llancarvan, Ellis' original letters, *Annales Cambriæ*, Rymer's *Fœdera*, Williams' *History of Wales*, Warrington's *History of Wales*, Tyler's *Henry V.*, Adam of Usk, Matthew of Paris, Hardyng's and other chronicles, Giraldus Cambrensis, the historians Carte, Walsingham, and Holinshed, Bridgeman's *Princes of South Wales*, Lloyd's *History of the Princes of Powys Fadog*, the Iolo MSS., Owen's *Ancient Laws and Institutions of Wales*, *Archæologia Cambrensis*, the Brut, and, of course, the Rolls series. Among living writers who have been helpful in various ways and have my best thanks are

Mr. Robert Owen, of Welshpool, the author of *Powysland*, the Revd. W. G. Dymock Fletcher, of Shrewsbury, who has made a special study of the neighbouring battle-field; Professor Tout, who has published an interesting lecture on Glyndwr and some instructive maps connected with the period; and Mr. Henry Owen, the well known authority on Pembrokeshire and author of *Gerald the Welshman*; nor must I omit a word of thanks to Mr. Owen Edwards, whose kind encouragement materially influenced my decision to undertake this book.

I am under most particular obligations to that well known Welsh scholar, Mr. T. Marchant Williams, for suggestions and criticisms when the book was still in manuscript, and also to my lamented friend, the late Mr. St. John Boddington, of Huntington Court, Herefordshire, for assistance of a somewhat similar nature.

I am also greatly indebted to Miss Walker, of Corwen, for several photographic scenes in Glyndyfrdwy, which she most kindly took with an especial view to reproduction in these pages, and to Messrs. H. H. Hughes and W. D. Haydon, both of Shrewsbury, who rendered a like service in the matter of Glyndwr's other residence at Sycherth.

ERRATA.

Page 19, line 7. *For* March *read* Marsh.

Page 46. Footnote should be omitted.

Page 47, line 26. *For* Hereford *read* Brecon.

Page 52, line 5 from bottom. *For* Strata Florada *read* Strata Florida.

Page 56, line 11. *For* Llugwy *read* Lledr.

Page 100, line 9. *Omit the words*, Gryffydd Llwyd, much better known by his bardic name of.

Pages 101, 102, 103, 104, 120, 128, 183, 190, 306. *For* Sycherth *read* Sycharth.

Page 103, line 21. *For* the house *read* it.

Page 110, line 4 from bottom. *Omit the words*, the "Castell y Gwern Loch."

Page 116, line 3. *For* Sir Thomas *read* Sir Henry.

Page 123, line 22. *For* Cwmwrth *read* Cymarth.

Page 150. Add footnote as follows: Cayo is a parish on the Carmarthenshire side of the Teify, ten miles from Lampeter,—the place which Lewis Glyncothi, a native of the district, "loved like a beaver for its festivities, its music, etc."

Page 171, line 15. *For* Rhys ap Gethin *read* Rhys Gethin.

Page 190, line 23. *For* Jankyn Hanard *read* Jankyn Havard.

Page 190, line 31, and page 289, line 22. *For* Cardiganshire *read* Carmarthenshire.

Page 216, line 31. *For* Langhame *read* Laughame; *and for* Crickhowl *read* Crickhowel.

Page 225, line 20. *For* Tudor Trevor *read* John Trevor.

Page 232, line 11. *For* Maelgywn *read* Maelgwy.
Line 13. *For* Colwyn *read* Collwyn.
Line 17. *For* Sinion *read* Einion.

Page 234, line 7. *For* Ystymtegid *read* Ystymcegid.

Page 275, line 6. *For* Cedmore *read* Codnor.

Page 280, line 20. *For* Dysanni *read* Dysynni.
Line 6 from bottom. *For* A quite recently published manuscript from, *read* A manuscript in.
Omit footnote.

Page 297, line 4 from bottom, and first two lines on page 298. *For present wording read* "out with Glyndwr," while, as has been already related, he rewarded his more faithful lieges in the borough of Welshpool by a wide extension of their corporation limits.

Page 302, line 3. *For* grandfather *read* uncle; *and before* ancestor *insert* collateral.

Page 304, line 1. *For* Poitiers *read* Agincourt.

Page 325, lines 12–15. *Omit* previously only a few, *etc.*, *to close of sentence.*

CONTENTS

CHAPTER I

CHAPTER II

CHAPTER III

CHAPTER IV

CHAPTER V

CHAPTER VI

CHAPTER VII

CHAPTER VIII

CHAPTER XII

APPENDIX

ILLUSTRATIONS

[1] Copyright, Miss Walker.
[2] Copyright, W. Davis.
[3] Copyright, F. Frith & Co.
[4] Copyright, C. H. Young.
[5] Copyright, W. D. Hayson.
[6] Copyright, J. Bartlett.

[1] Copyright, Miss Walker.
[2] Copyright, F. Frith & Co.
[3] Copyright, C. H. Young.
[4] Copyright, R. St. John Boddington.
[5] Copyright, H. H. Hughes.
[6] Copyright, Marion & Co.
[7] Copyright, J. Bartlett.
[8] Copyright, W. H. Bustin.

---

[1] Copyright, Mrs. Leather.
[2] Copyright, F. Frith & Co.
[3] Copyright, W. H. Bustin.

OWEN GLYNDWR

CHAPTER I

INTRODUCTORY SKETCH OF WELSH HISTORY FROM THE SAXON CONQUEST OF ENGLAND TO THE RISING OF GLYNDWR

400–1400

THE main subject of this book is the man whose memory, above that of all other men, the Welsh as a people delight to honour, and that period of Welsh history which he made so stormy and so memorable. But having what there is some reason to regard as a well founded opinion that (to the vast majority of English readers) the story of Wales is practically a blank, it seems to me desirable to prepare the way in some sort for the advent of my hero upon this, the closing scene of Cambrian glory. I shall therefore begin with a rapid sketch of those nine centuries which, ending with Glyndwr's rising, constitute roughly in a political and military sense the era of Welsh nationality. It is an audacious venture, I am very well aware, and more especially so when brought within the compass of a single chapter.

Among the many difficulties that present themselves in contemplating an outline sketch of Welsh history, a doubt as to the best period for beginning it can hardly be included. Unless one is prepared to take excursions into the realms of pure conjecture and speculation, which in these pages would be altogether out of place, the only possible epoch at which to open such a chapter is the Saxon conquest of England. And I lay some stress on the word England, because the fact of Wales resisting both Saxon conquest and even Saxon influence to any appreciable extent, at this early period, is the keynote to its history.

What the British tribes were like, who, prior to this fifth century, lived under Roman rule in the country we now call Wales, no man may know. We do know, however, that the Romans were as firmly seated there as in most parts of Britain. From their strong garrisons at Chester, Uriconium, Caerleon, and elsewhere they kept the country to the westward quiet by means of numerous smaller posts. That their legions moved freely about the country we have evidence enough in the metalled causeways that can still be traced in almost every locality beneath the mountain sod. The traces, too, of their mining industry are still obvious enough in the bowels of the mountains and even beneath the sea, to say nothing of surface evidence yet more elaborate. That their soldiers fell here freely in the cause of order or of conquest is written plainly enough in the names and epitaphs on mortuary stones that in districts even now remote have been exposed by the spade or plough. But how much of Christianity, how much of Roman civilisation, these primitive Britons of the West had absorbed in the four centuries of Roman occupation is a matter quite outside the scope of these elementary remarks. Of civilisation beyond the influence of the garrisons there was probably little or none. As regards Christianity, its echoes from the more civilised parts of the island had probably found their way there, and affected the indigenous paganism of the mountains to an extent that is even yet a fruitful source of disagreement among experts. Lastly, as it seems probable that the population of what is now called Wales was then much more sparse in proportion to the rest of the island than in subsequent periods, its condition becomes a matter of less interest, which is fortunate, seeing we know so little about it.

With the opening of the fifth century the Romans evacuated Britain. By the middle of it the Saxon influx, encouraged, as every schoolboy knows, by the Britons themselves in their weakness, had commenced. Before its close the object of the new-comers had developed and the "Making of England" was in full operation.

For these same conquered Britons many of us, I think, started life with some tinge of contempt, mingled with the pity that beyond all doubt they fully merit. Mr. Green has protested in strong terms against so unjustifiable an attitude. He asks us to consider the condition of a people, who in a fiercely warlike age, had been for many generations forbidden to bear arms; who were protected by an alien army from all fear of molestation, and encouraged, moreover, to apply themselves zealously to the arts of peace. That men thus enervated made a resistance so prolonged is the wonder, not that they eventually gave way. If this nation, which resisted for a hundred years, is a fit subject for criticism, what can be said of their conquerors who, five centuries later, in the full enjoyment of warlike habits and civil liberty, were completely crushed in seven by a no more formidable foe?

While the pagan Saxons were slowly fighting their way across England towards the Severn and the Dee, the country about and behind these rivers had been galvanised by various influences into an altogether new importance.

After the departure of the Romans, the Welsh tribes, less enervated probably than their more Romanised fellow-countrymen to the east, found in the Scots of Ireland rather than the Picts of the North their deadliest foes. It was against these western rovers that the indigenous natives of what for brevity's sake we are calling Wales, relearnt in the fifth century the art of war, and the traces of their conflicts are strewn thick along the regions that face the Irish Sea. But while these contests were still in progress, three powerful tides of influence of a sort wholly different poured into Wales and contributed towards its solidity, its importance, its defensive power, and its moral elevation.

(1) Out of the north, from Cumbria and Strathclyde, came the great prince and warrior Cunedda, whose family seem to have taken possession, with or without resistance, of large tracts of Wales, Merioneth, Cardigan, and many other districts deriving their names in fact from his sons. His progeny and their belongings became in some sort a ruling caste; a faint reflection of what the Normans were in later days to England.

400-500, Cunedda.

Cunedda is said to have held his Court at Carlisle, and to have wielded immense power in the north and north-west of Britain. If he did not go to Wales in person he undoubtedly planted in it his numerous and warlike offspring, who, with their following, are usually regarded as the founders of the later tribal fabric of Wales, the remote ancestors, in theory at any rate, of the Welsh landed gentry of to-day; but this is a perilous and complex subject.

(2) In this century, too, came the first wave of a real and effective Christianity, with its troops of missionaries from Brittany and Ireland, in the front rank of which stand the names of St. David and Germanus or Garmon, Bishop of Auxerre. The latter is generally credited with the organisation of the Welsh Church, hitherto so vague and undefined. It was, at any rate, during this period, that the Church assumed definite territorial form, and that the Welsh diocese and the Welsh parish, their boundaries roughly approximating to the present ones, came into existence. Through the fifth, sixth, and well into the seventh century, church building and religious activity of all kinds flourished

Christianity.

marvellously in Wales; while Christianity was being steadily and ruthlessly stamped out over the rest of Britain by the advancing pagans, native chieftains vied with foreign ecclesiastics in building churches, cathedrals, and cells; and great monastic houses arose, of which Bangor Iscoed, on the Dee, with its two or three thousand inmates, was the most notable. The mountainous region that in former days had been among those least influenced by it was now the hope of the island, the seat of religious fervour, the goal of the foreign missionary and the wandering saint.

(3) The third, and perhaps not the least powerful, factor in the making of Wales was the advance of the Saxons. After their great victory of Deorham they destroyed the British strongholds of Bath, Gloucester, and Cirencester, and about the year 577, or 130 years after their first landing in Britain, they appeared on the Severn. The exact fate or disposal of the natives, whom with ceaseless fighting they thus drove before them, is a matter of perennial controversy. The ferocity of the conquerors, aggravated, no doubt, by the stubborn resistance of the conquered, is a fact beyond all question and should be emphasised, since its direful memories had much to do with the inextinguishable hatred that was felt for so many centuries, and to a certain degree is still felt, by many Welshmen towards their Saxon foes. It may fairly be assumed that the extirpation (though the term is much too strong) of the native stock was most marked in the eastern parts of Britain, and that as the tide of

Arrival of the Saxons, 577.

conquest swept westward its results in this particular were much modified. But however great the slaughter or however considerable the native element that was retained upon the soil by its conquerors, it is quite certain that the influx of British refugees into Wales throughout the sixth century must have been very large. Among them, too, no doubt, went numbers of men and women of learning, of piety, and sometimes perhaps even of wealth, for one need not suppose that every Briton waited to be driven from his home at the spear's point.

British refugees in sixth century.

A fierce onslaught in great force brought the invaders to the walls of the Roman-British city of Uriconium, where Cynddylan, Prince of Powys, with all the power of Central Wales, made a vain but gallant effort to arrest the ruin:

Cynddylan at Uriconium and Shrewsbury.

> Cynddylan with heart like the ice of winter.
> Cynddylan with heart like the fire of spring.

He and his brothers were at length all slain, and his armies routed. Uriconium or Tren was sacked, and higher up the valley the royal palace at Pengwern, as Shrewsbury was then called, was destroyed.

These terrible scenes are described for us by Llywarch Hên, one of the earliest British bards, himself an actor in them, who thus laments over the wreck of Pengwern:

> "The Hall of Cynddylan is dark
> To-night, without fire, without bed;
> I 'll weep awhile, afterwards I shall be silent.

"The Hall of Cynddylan is gloomy
To-night, without fire, without songs;
Tears are running down my cheeks.

"The Hall of Cynddylan, it pierces my heart
To see it roofless, fireless;
Dead is my chief, yet I am living."

or again, on the destruction of Tren:

"The eagle of Pengwern screamed aloud to-night
For the blood of men he watched;
Tren may indeed be called a ruined town.

"Slain were my comrades all at once
Cynan, Cynddylan, Cyncraith,
Defending Tren the wasted city."

In a few years the Saxons were beaten back, and Pengwern, with the surrounding country, once more became British, and remained so till the days of Offa, King of Mercia.

By the close of the sixth century Christianity had been introduced by Augustine into the south-eastern corner of England, and there is no more suggestive scene in Welsh history than the famous meeting of the great missionary with the Welsh bishops on the banks of the Severn. It accentuates in a striking manner the cleavage between the Eastern or the Latin Church, and that of the West and of the Welsh. Augustine, about the year 601, fresh from his victories over paganism among the Kentish Saxons, and having journeyed far through still heathen regions, approaches these Western Christians with a kindly

Augustine and the Welsh bishops, 601.

but somewhat supercilious and superior air. The seven Welsh bishops — or so-called bishops, for the full development of the office as understood later was not yet completed — were ready waiting for him on the banks of the lower Severn. They were a deputation of the Welsh Church, and, seeming already to scent patronage in the air, were fully prepared to resent any sign of it in the Roman missionary. The latter, it appears, knew very little about the Western Church, with its roots in Ireland, Armorica, and Gaul, and what he did know he did not like.

The arrogance of Augustine fully justified the Welshmen's suspicions, and he still further roused their indignation by hinting that they should take their instructions and receive their consecration from Canterbury, as representing Rome. Coming from a man who appeared to them but the missionary bishop of a handful of recently converted barbarians, this was a little too much for ecclesiastics who had behind them three or four centuries of Christianity, and knew nothing whatever of the Latin Church. Augustine, too, spoke disparagingly of their customs, and with particular severity of the absence of celibacy in their Church. This must have touched them to the quick, seeing that numbers of the offices and benefices in the Western Church were more or less hereditary, and that even saintship was frequently a matter of family, the tribal sentiment being predominant. All these things, together with their difference in Easter observance and in shaving the head, horrified Augustine, and he spoke so freely as to put all hope of combination out of the question. Indeed, the Welsh divines were so offended that they refused even to break bread beneath the same roof as the Roman saint. At a second conference Augustine, seeing he had gone too far, proposed that, even if they could not conform to each other's customs, they should at least combine in efforts to convert the rest of England. Such endeavours did not commend themselves in the least to the Welshmen. Whatever missionary zeal may have existed among Welsh churchmen it did not include the slightest anxiety about the souls of the accursed conquerors of Britain, the ruthless ravagers and destroyers of their once civilised and Christian country. It is probable that Augustine did not realise the fierce hate of the despoiled Celt towards the Saxon. At any rate his patience at length gave way, and as a parting shot he in effect told the Welshmen that since they shewed themselves so criminally careless about Saxons' souls, they should of a surety feel the prick of Saxon spears. This random threat, for it could have been nothing more, was strangely fulfilled within a few years' time, when the victory of the pagan Ethelfred at Chester, which sundered the Britons of Wales from those of North-Western England, culminated in the sacking of Bangor Iscoed and the slaughter of twelve hundred monks.

This futile conference of 601 marks the beginning of the long struggle of the Welsh or Ancient Brit-
601. ish Church to keep clear of the authority of Canterbury, and it lasted for some five hundred years. Till the close of the eleventh

century the bishops of the four Welsh dioceses were, as a rule, consecrated by their own brethren. St. David's perhaps took rank as "primus inter pares" for choice, but not of necessity, for there was no recognised Welsh metropolitan. Ages afterwards, when Canterbury had insidiously encroached upon these privileges, the Welsh clergy were wont to soothe their wounded pride by the assurance that this transfer of consecration had come about as a matter of convenience rather than of right. Long, indeed, before the final conquest of Welshmen by Edward the First, their Church had been completely conquered, anomalous though such an inverted process seems, by Norman bishops. A Welshman, though his sword might still win him political recognition and respect, had little more chance of Church preferment in the thirteenth century than he had in the eighteenth or the first half of the nineteenth. As early indeed as 1180 that clerical aristocrat of royal Welsh and noble Norman blood, Giraldus Cambrensis, pertinently asks the same question which from generation to generation and from reign to reign through the Hanoverian period must have been on every native churchman's tongue in the Principality, "Is it a crime to be a Welshman?"

The Latin and British Churches.

There is no occasion to enlarge upon the subtle methods by which the Norman Church anticipated the Norman sword in Wales. Sleepless industry no doubt was one. Another was the agency of the newer monasteries, filled with Norman, English, and foreign monks and for the most part devoted to the Latin Church.

Persistent denial of the validity of St. David's in the matter of consecration may in time, too, like the continuous drip of water on a stone, have had its effect upon the Welsh, even against their better judgment. On one occasion we know that some of their princes and nobles, stung by what they regarded as excessive exactions on the part of the Church, stooped so far as to throw in the faces of their prelates the taunt that their consecration was invalid. Such an attitude did not tend to lighten the immense pressure which was exercised in favour of the supremacy of Canterbury; and long before Welsh princes had begun to take orders from Norman kings, Welsh bishops were seeking consecration from Canterbury, unless indeed their thrones were already filled by Norman priests.

It is not only the ecclesiastical but also the secular divisions of Wales, that in a great measure date from these fifth and sixth centuries. The three chief Kingdoms, or Principalities, into which the country was apportioned, stand out from these days with consistent clearness till they are gradually broken into fragments by the Norman power: On the north was Gwynedd; in the centre, Powys; on the south, Deheubarth or South Wales. As St. David's was the premier see of the four Welsh dioceses, so Gwynedd was even more markedly the first among the three Welsh Kingdoms. Its ruler, when a sufficiently strong man to enforce it, had a recognised right to the title of "Pendragon" and the lip homage of his brother princes. When a weak one, however, filled the precarious throne, any

Divisions of Wales.

attempt to exact even such an empty tribute would have been a signal for a general outbreak.

Gwynedd included the present counties* of Flint, Anglesey, Carnarvon, and most of Merioneth, together with the northern part of Denbighshire.

Powys cannot be so readily defined in a line or two, but, roughly speaking, it was a triangle or wedge driven through Central Wales to a point on the sea, with a wide base resting on the English border, the present county of Montgomery representing its chief bulk. Its capital was Pengwern or Shrewsbury, till the eighth century, when Offa, King of Mercia, enraged at the inroads of the Welsh, gathered together his whole strength and thrust them permanently back from the plains of Shropshire to the rampart of hills along whose crests he made the famous Dyke that bears his name. Thenceforward Mathraval, and subsequently Welshpool, became the abode of the Princes of Powys.

Powys.

* The present counties of Wales were not in existence as such till after the final conquest by Edward I. Even then, as we shall see, only six were created; the larger part of the Principality retaining its feudal lordships until the reign of Henry VIII. There were ancient subdivisions of the three Welsh Kingdoms ruled over by petty Princes owing allegiance to their immediate overlord; and their names still survive in those of modern counties or districts. Ceredigion, for instance, remains as Cardigan, Morganwg as Glamorgan, while the vale of Edeyrnion and the county of Merioneth still preserve the memory of two sons of the conquering Cunedda. But the units of old Welsh delimitation were the "Cantrefs" and the "Commotes," which even to this day are often used for purposes of description, as well as occasionally for ecclesiastical and political divisions. Of Cantrefs there would be something like three to the modern county, while each "Cantref" again consisted of two "Commotes."

The Southern Kingdom, or Deheubarth, was also something of a triangle, but reversely placed to that of Powys, its point lying on the English border, and its broad base stretching along the Irish Sea from the mouth of the Dovey to the capes of Pembroke.

Deheubarth.

Of these three divisions, Powys, as will be obvious even from the brief and crude description of its boundaries here given, had the greatest difficulty in holding its own against both Saxon and Norman. South Wales, on the other hand, was the thorniest crown, for it included to a greater degree than the others semi-independent chieftains, such as those of Morganwg and Cardigan, who were inclined to pay their tribute and their homage only when their overlord, who held his Court at Dynevor on the Towy, was strong enough to enforce them.

Thus for nearly seven centuries there were separate sources of strife in Wales, and three distinct classes of warfare. First there came the meritorious defence of the country against Saxon, Dane, and Norman, in which, upon the whole, there was much creditable unanimity. Secondly, during the lulls from foreign invasion, there was almost constant strife between North and South, Powys holding as it were the balance of power between them. Lastly there were the purely provincial quarrels, when heady chieftains fell out with their superiors, a form of entertainment to which South Wales, as I have already remarked, was peculiarly prone.

Warfare in Wales.

But, after all, it is not quite accurate to give such

emphasis to the existence and definition of the three Kingdoms till the death of Roderic the Great in 877. Several kings had essayed with varying success to rule all Wales, but it was Roderic who with scanty foresight finally divided the country between his three sons, laying particular stress on the suzerainty of Gwynedd. The prevalent custom of gavelkind worked admirably, no doubt, in private life among the primitive Welsh, but when applied to principalities and to ambitious and bloodthirsty princelings the effect was usually disastrous. To mitigate the dangers of his unwise partition, Roderic ordained a scheme which would have proved of undoubted excellence if the practice had only been equal to the theory. This was to the effect that if any two of the Princes of Wales quarrelled, all three were to meet in conclave in the wild pass of Bwlch-y-Pawl, through which the present rough road from Bala to Lake Vyrnwy painfully toils. Here they were to settle their difficulties peacefully; and as it was presumed that only two would be parties to the quarrel, the third was to act as arbiter. For some centuries after this we know very well that the successive rulers of the three Kingdoms drenched Wales in blood with their quarrels, but no tradition remains of a single conference at this wild spot among the hills, where the infant Vyrnwy plunges down through heathery glens and woods of birch and oak to the most beautiful artificial lake perhaps in Christendom.

Roderic divides Wales, 877.

The sins of omission must of necessity be infinite in dealing with so vast a subject in so compressed a space, and sins of omission, if not confessed in detail, sometimes affect the accuracy of the whole. Something, for instance, ought to be said of the pastoral character, even in these early days, of all Wales, except perhaps Anglesey and West Carnarvon; of the tribal organisation and the laws of gavelkind; of the domestic and family nature of the Church, whose minor benefices at any rate were largely hereditary, and whose traditions were intensely averse to centralisation. Among other things to be noted, too, is that Cadvan, who flourished in the seventh century, is generally regarded as the first genuine King of Wales, just as Roderic, nearly three hundred years later, was the great decentraliser.

Cadvan.

Another important date is that of 815, when a Saxon victory in Cornwall destroyed the last vestige of British independence in England. For hitherto the Britons of Wales had by no means regarded themselves as the mere defenders of the soil they occupied. Steeped in the prophecies of Merlin and his contemporaries, which assured them of the ultimate reconquest of the whole island of Britain, they still cherished dreams which may seem to us by the light of history vain enough, but in the opening of the ninth century they still fired the fancy of a proud, romantic, and warlike race.

815. Saxons conquer Cornwall.

Amid the conflicting evidence of rival chroniclers, Saxon and Welsh, it is not often easy to select the victors in the long series of bloody combats that continued throughout the centuries preceding the Norman Conquest. What-

Saxons made little way.

ever victories the Saxons gained, they were not much less barren than their defeats. Nominal conquests were sometimes made of the more vulnerable districts, but they were not long maintained. At the next upheaval such loose allegiance as had been wrung from the provincial ruler was repudiated without a moment's thought, and often indeed the Saxons beyond the border found themselves in their turn fighting for hearth and home.

In the ninth century the Danes appeared upon the scene. Though they harried Wales from time to time, both in the interior and on the coast, their doings in England were so incomparably more serious that their Welsh exploits almost escape our notice. About the year 890, Danish outposts were established beneath the Breiddon hills, that noble gateway of mid-Wales, through which the Severn comes surging out into the Shropshire plains. Hither four years later came that formidable Danish leader, Hastings, with the Anglo-Danish forces of East Anglia and the north behind him. King Alfred, who was in the west, hastened to the scene and contributed to this strange spectacle of Saxons and Cymry fighting side by side. A decisive victory at Buttington, near Welshpool, rewarded their efforts, and though the struggle between Dane and Saxon was of great service to Wales by bringing a long immunity from the attacks of her hereditary foe, the Danish name calls for little more notice in Welsh annals.

The Danes, 890.

Seeing that vague dreams of reconquest still lingered among the Welsh, England's difficulty, to apply a familiar modern aphorism, should have been Cambria's opportunity. But readily as the three Welsh Princes, when their common country was in danger, were accustomed to combine, and efficiently as they raided in independent fashion across the English border, cohesion for a serious aggressive movement was almost hopeless. The moment that they were safe, they turned their arms against each other. The whole history of Wales, from the days of Roderic to those of Edward, with a few brief intervals, is one long tale of bloody strife.

Nor were the Princes of Gwynedd, Powys, and Deheubarth always content to fight their quarrels out alone. As time went on they grew more accustomed to their Saxon neighbours, even if they did not love them more. Occasional amenities became possible. Intermarriages between the two aristocracies were not unknown, and when they had progressed thus far a Prince of Powys would scarcely have been human if he had not occasionally been tempted to call in Saxon aid against his powerful rivals of Gwynedd or Deheubarth. But in spite of this dangerous game, played often enough and in later Norman days so fatal, the soil of Wales, so far as any serious occupation or dominion is implied, remained inviolate throughout the whole Saxon period.

No Saxon settlement.

Strathclyde Britons occupy the Vale of Clwyd.

One very narrow escape from a permanent lodgment of Saxons, of which the Welsh chronicle tells us, should not perhaps be passed over. It occurred in the days when Anarawd, one of the sons of Roderic, was ruling over North Wales, at the close of the ninth century. More than a hundred years before, the Mercians, under Offa, had driven the Welsh finally from Shropshire and pressed them back behind the famous Dyke, whose clearly marked course still preserves the name of their warlike monarch. The great Saxon victory on Rhuddlan Marsh, at the mouth of the Clwyd, had occurred soon afterwards, and the wail of the defeated is still sounded in one of the most notable of Welsh airs. But Offa's Dyke had been since then considerably overleaped, and the slaughter of Rhuddlan had been long avenged. When the descendants of these same Mercians poured once more into the pleasant country that lies upon the north shore between Chester and the Conway, the invaders of the "Perfeddwlad," as this region was then called (a term I shall use for convenience throughout this chapter), proved too powerful for Anarawd. He was driven back into Snowdonia and Anglesey, and the Saxons settled down in the Vale of Clwyd and upon either side of it, with a deliberation that, but for an opportune accident, would have probably converted a large slice of North Wales into a piece of England for all time. But just as the Strathclyde Britons in the days of Cunedda had brought to Wales in the time of her need after the Roman departure a valuable and warlike element, so their descendants, four centuries later, came just in time to save what are now the Celtic districts of Flint and northern Denbigh from becoming Saxon. These people, hard pressed in north Lancashire,

Saxon settlement prevented by Strathclyde Britons.

Cumberland, and even beyond, by Danes and Saxons, decided to seek a new home, and their thoughts naturally turned to Wales. They made overtures to Anarawd, begging that he would grant them of his abundance sufficient territory for their needs. But Anarawd's kingdom had, as we have seen, been sadly circumscribed, and his homeless subjects from the east of the Conway were already on his hands. A bright thought struck him, and he informed his Strathclyde kinsmen that if they could reconquer the Perfeddwlad they were welcome to it. Necessity, perhaps, nerved the arms of the wanderers, and the Saxons, who, as Dr. Powell quaintly puts it, "were not yet warm in their seats," were driven headlong out of Wales. The Mercians, however, were not the kind of men to sit quietly down after such an ignominious expulsion; they made vigorous preparations for taking their revenge, and retrieving their fortunes and their honour. The Strathclyde Britons sorely doubted their powers of resistance to the great force which now threatened them, so, carrying all their cattle and effects back again across the Conway, they begged Anarawd in his own interest as well as in theirs to support them. The Prince of Gwynedd rose nobly to the occasion and, joining all his forces to those of his immigrant kinsmen, they met the returning Saxon invaders near Conway, and in a pitched battle drove them back to the Dee with prodigious slaughter, never to return. So the country between the two rivers was preserved to the Cymric race and saved from becoming, as for the moment

Victory of Anarawd, 878.

looked extremely probable, another Cheshire or Shropshire.

Anarawd, however, could not rest content with his triumph over the Saxons. As an illustration of the thirst for war that seems to have been chronic with most of the Welsh Princes, it may be noted that, with the Saxons vowing vengeance on his borders, he did not hesitate to march into South Wales and make an unprovoked attack upon its Prince, his own brother.

But with the death of Anarawd and his brothers, various contingencies, which need not detain us here, made Howel Dda, or Howel the Good, both the heir and the acceptable ruler of all three provinces. His reign was unique in Welsh annals, for it was not only long, but almost peaceful. This excellent Prince turned his brilliant talents and force of character almost entirely to the civil and moral elevation of his people. He drew up his famous code of laws, which, as is sometimes asserted, unconsciously influence the legal instincts of remoter Wales even to this day. In the preparation of this great work he summoned his bishops and nobility and wise men to meet him at Ty Gwyn on the Towy, for it should be noted that this ruler of a temporarily united Wales was in the first instance Prince of Deheubarth.

Howel Dda, 940.

Here this select assembly spent the whole of Lent, fasting and praying for the Divine aid in their approaching task. Howel then picked out from among them the twelve most capable persons, with the Chancellor of Llandaff

The laws of Howel Dda enacted.

at their head, and proceeded to examine in exhaustive fashion all the laws of the Cymry. Of these they eliminated the bad, retained the good, and amended others to suit present requirements. This new code was then ratified by the entire assembly before it dispersed. Three copies were made, and it is significant of the change already creeping over the Welsh Church, that Howel and his four bishops are said to have journeyed to Rome and submitted one of them to the Pope for his approval. The Laws of Howel Dda may be read to-day by anyone with access to a reference library. The rights of every class of person are herein clearly set forth, and the precise value of each man's life according to his rank, and of every animal's hide and carcase accurately defined. The tribal sanctity of land, too, is well illustrated by a law forbidding the owner of an estate to mortgage it to anyone but a kinsman. Books, harps, swords, and implements of livelihood were exempted from distraint, while among live stock horses were placed in the same category, as being necessary for defence. Suits in connection with land could not be heard between February and May, or between May and August, since these were the periods of seed-time and harvest, while all cases touching inheritance were to be heard by the King himself. The latter is pictured to us as sitting in his judicial chair above the rest of the Court, with an Elder upon either hand and the freeholders ranged upon his right and left. Immediately below the King sat the Chief Justice of the Province, with a priest upon one side of him and the Judge of the Commote upon the other.

After hearing witnesses and taking depositions, the two judges and the priest retired to consider the verdict. This done, the King took counsel with them, and, if he agreed, delivered judgment himself. If the case was too involved, however, for a satisfactory decision, the matter was settled by the simple expedient of single combat. A fixed price, as I have remarked, was set upon almost everything, both living and inanimate. One is surprised, for instance, to find an apple tree worth 60*d.*, and a tree planted for shelter worth 24*d.*, while a coracle is only worth 8*d.* A salmon net is appraised at just double the last amount, while a spade, again, is rated at a penny only. Though the skin of an ox or hart is fixed at 8*d.* the near extinction of the beaver is significantly shewn by its value of 120*d.* Dogs, too, vary most curiously on the list. A common cur is held at 4*d.*, a shepherd dog at 60*d.*, and the best sporting dogs at four times the latter sum. There is special mention, too, of chargers, hunters, roadsters, pack-horses, and draught-horses for carts and harrows. Horses are not to be broken till their third year; while three rides through a crowd is the legal test of "warranted broken." Cows and mares, too, are prohibited from ploughing. We learn also in this singular price-list the current value, among other things, of a battle-axe, a bow with twelve arrows, a white-hilted sword, a shield enamelled with blue and gold; of plaids, too, striped and chequered stuffs, mantles trimmed with fur, robes, coats, hose, buskins, shoes, gloves, caps, bonnets, girdles, and buckles.

Value of articles fixed by Howel Dda.

There are stringent laws against cruelty to animals and in favour of hospitality. Game laws existed of the strictest kind, classifying every animal of the chase and dealing with the management of hounds, and the etiquette of hunting. For their ardour in these pursuits, the Welsh were distinguished among nations, not being surpassed even by the Normans themselves.

The customs obtaining in the royal household are tabulated in Howel Dda's code with extraordinary minuteness, and the duties of every official, from highest to lowest, strictly defined; from the Chaplain, Steward, Judge, and Master of the Horse down to the porter and birdkeeper. The perquisites, it may be noted, of the Master of the Horse are all colts under two years old, taken in war, and all gold and silver spurs thus acquired; those of the porter, every billet of wood he could snatch from a passing load, with one hand, as he held the gate with the other, and any swine out of a herd that he could lift breast high by its bristles only!

Of the bards there is so much to be said elsewhere that we need only remark here that the duties of the Bardd Teulu, or Poet Laureate, were to follow the army and sing the "Unbennaeth Prydain" or "Monarchy of Britain" before, and if triumphant after, the battle; to perform at all times before the Court, and also privately to the Queen, only in so low a tone as not to disturb the King and his courtiers. This illustrious functionary was valued at 126 cows.

A remarkable official was the "Crier of Silence," who beat a particular pillar in the great hall with a rod when the noise became excessive, and had for his perquisites the fines that were exacted for any such undue boisterousness. Strangest by far of all was the King's "footholder," whose duty it was to sit under the table at meals and nurse his Majesty's foot, and to "scratch it when required."

Nor can we forget the "Pencerdd," the Chief of Song, who was of popular election and presided at the Bardic Gorsedd held every third year, and held only at Aberffraw in Anglesey, the royal residence of Gwynedd; for the Eisteddfodau were held by all the Welsh Princes apparently at will. The Pencerdd was expected to know by heart the prophetic song of Taliesin. He lodged in the quarters of the heir apparent, and was presented by the King with a harp and key.

Renewed conflicts, 950.

Howel the Good died about 950. With the divisions and disputes of his sons and nephews Wales quickly lost its unanimity, and once more the flame of war was lit from one end of the country to the other by these foolish broilers, in attempts to despoil each other of their respective portions. The question was at length settled for a while by a great battle at Llanrwst, where the men of North Wales utterly discomfited those of the South, pursuing them with fire and sword far beyond the northern boundaries of Deheubarth.

Growing intercourse between Welsh and Saxon.

Towards the close of the tenth century we begin to get glimpses of those amenities between Cymry and Saxon, which a now common religion, a common foe in the Danes, and considerable private intercourse, had rendered inevitable. We find King Eadgar himself, for instance, at Bangor, helping Iago ap Idwal, Prince of Gwynedd, against his nephew Howel ap Ievan. Everything, however, being amicably arranged, the Saxon King actually remains in friendly fashion at Bangor, and bestows gifts and endowments upon its see. Finally the two recent disputants return with Eadgar to Chester, and take an oar in that celebrated crew of kinglets which rowed the Saxon monarch upon the Dee. Gwaithvoed, Prince of Powys, who was invited to assist in this somewhat inglorious procession, seems to have been the only one of the Welsh *Reguli* who refused the honour. "Tell the King," said Gwaithvoed, "I cannot row a barge, and if I could, I would not do so, except to save a life, whether king's or vassal's." On being pressed by a second messenger from Eadgar, his brief answer was: "Say to the King, 'Fear him who fears not death.'"

Eadgar rowed by Welsh Princes on the Dee.

It is not easy to define the precise attitude of the Welsh Princes towards the King of England as the Saxon period drew towards its close. Though the ancient Britons had become crystallised into Welshmen, the old tradition of the island as a whole with an "Emperor" in London, and a general scheme of defence against foreign foes, was not yet dead. The Saxons, though little loved, had become an accepted fact, and there seems to have been no particular reluctance among the Welsh princes to pay lip homage, when relationships were not too strained, to the "King in London," and tribute, too, as representing the ancient contribution to "the defence of the island."

For the last hundred years prior to the Norman conquest, one follows the bloody path of Welsh history in vain efforts to find some breathing space, wherein rulers turned their attention to something besides the lust of power and the thirst for glory. It was about the year 1000 when the first of the three Llewelyns succeeded to the throne of North Wales. Under a King whose title was absolutely indisputable, and who possessed some force of character, it seemed as if the sword was now for a season, at any rate, to remain undrawn. But it was not to be; for in no long time the throne of South Wales fell vacant, and there was, unhappily, no direct heir. So the nobles of the Province, fearing, and with some reason, that Llewelyn would seize the opportunity to attach the Southern Kingdom to his other dominions, brought forward a creature of their own, a low-born adventurer, who claimed to be of the royal lineage. This precipitated the catastrophe which it was designed to prevent, and Llewelyn fell upon Deheubarth with the whole force of Gwynedd. The fight lasted through a whole day, and the slaughter was immense, but the Northerners again prevailed.

Llewelyn I., 1000.

But there were also years of peace under Llewelyn ap Seisyllt, and of conspicuous prosperity, so the chronicler tells us, in which "the earth brought forth double, the people prospered in all their affairs, and multiplied wonderfully. The cattle increased in great numbers, so that there was not a poor man in

Wales from the south to the north sea, but every man had plenty, every house a dweller, every town inhabited." Llewelyn fell ultimately before Carmarthen, and his throne was seized by Iago ap Idwal, a collateral relative. He in turn was quickly overthrown and slain by Llewelyn's warlike son Griffith, who enjoyed what from a purely military point of view might be called a successful reign.

Griffith ap Llewelyn.

The Danes at this time began again to make attacks on Wales, but were defeated in Anglesey, and again in the Severn valley.

Flushed with victory, and without a particle of excuse, Griffith now turned upon South Wales, ravaged it with fire and sword, and drove out its new Prince, Howel ap Edwy. Howel, however, came back with an army of Danes and Saxons, so had times changed in Wales, but only to meet with disaster and defeat at the hands of the vigorous Griffith. Yet again the indomitable Howel returned with a fresh army to try his luck, and so certain was he this time of victory that he brought his wife to witness it. But again disaster overtook him, and his wife, instead of sharing his triumph, was carried off to share his conqueror's bed.

Griffith ap Llewelyn attacks South Wales.

Thus rolls on the tumult and the turmoil of the old Welsh story. The wonder is when and how the laws of the wise and peaceful Howel Dda found scope for application, and we can only suppose that the partial nature of these fierce struggles atoned in some measure for their continuity. Yet through all this devastation Church property, of which there was now a considerable amount and of a tangible kind, seems to have been well respected. The Danes alone were regardless of shrines and monasteries; and we hear of them at St. David's and Llanbadarn and other sacred spots along the sea-coast doing wild work.

The twenty years preceding the battle of Hastings were busy years in Wales, and the foremost name of that epoch in England came to be perhaps more dreaded among the native Welsh 1040. than that of any other Saxon since the days of Offa. But Harold, Earl of the West Saxons and commander of the English armies, got much deeper into Wales than Offa had ever succeeded in doing, and indeed came much nearer than any of his predecessors to a conquest of the country. Griffith ap Llewelyn, Prince of Gwynedd by right, and of all Wales by force, was, as we have seen, no mean soldier. He was Harold's adversary, and the last Welsh Prince to face the Saxon power. This, the final quarrel of five centuries of strife, was, for a wonder, not of Griffith's seeking.

Harold and Griffith.

We have seen how greatly modified the cleavage between the two peoples had by now become. Intermarriages had taken place in the higher ranks, alliances had been formed, and Saxon influences in matters such as land tenure and Church government had been sensibly felt beyond the Severn and the Dee. So now, while the shadow of the Norman invasion was hanging over unconscious England, Algar, Earl of Chester, falling out with King Edward, did nothing particularly unusual when he fled to the warlike son of the first Llewelyn, and tried to embroil him in his quarrel. Griffith was peacefully hunting at his second residence at Aber near Bangor, and had indeed made good use of a few years of peace, but he was not the man to turn a deaf ear to any prospect of a fight. The upshot was a very serious war, in which Griffith and his ally were for a long time singularly successful. They defeated Edwin of Mercia in a great battle near Welshpool; they afterwards took Hereford, won a victory at Leominster, and penetrated as far as Wiltshire.

A brief truce ensued with Harold, who had been opposing them, and then the struggle began

Harold in Wales.

afresh. The tables were now completely turned. Harold's memorable invasion of Wales took place, in which he was assisted to success by the many enemies Griffith had made in his high-handed annexation of Deheubarth. The

Death of Griffith, 1061.

Welsh Prince, after a stirring reign of thirty-four years, perished during this campaign of 1061 at the hand of a hired assassin. His head, like that of many another Welsh leader, was sent across the border in a basket, and received at Gloucester by Harold with much demonstrative satisfaction. The latter, in the meantime, had marched to the Conway, and afterwards through South Wales. He had been victorious everywhere; and now nominated fresh rulers to the vacant thrones of Gwynedd and Deheubarth, under promise of vassalage to the English Crown.

The tenure of the three Welsh Princes was always

complicated and, indeed, liable to fluctuation with the balance of power, both in Wales and across the border. In theory, Powys and South Wales owed lip homage and a nominal tribute to the Prince of Gwynedd as "Pendragon." The latter, on behalf of Wales, owed a similar service to the King of England and, as I have mentioned before, was not inclined to dispute it so long as his independence was respected. Harold's so-called conquest only altered matters to the extent of making the three Welsh provinces theoretically equal and individually vassals of the English Crown. This paper arrangement would have probably remained a dead letter or would have been maintained just so long as there was an arm strong enough to maintain it. But a people were coming to eliminate the Saxon as an aggressive power, and to take his place,—a people who would not be satisfied with lip homage and occasional tribute.

The great struggle in England between Norman and Saxon seemed by the mere force of contagion to set the Welsh Princes once more by the ears. Some of them, however, in accordance with their generous tradition of loyalty to the soil of the Britain they had lost, joined the West Saxons in their resistance to this new and formidable foe. Others essayed to make use in their domestic quarrels of the crafty Norman, who was only too glad to get a finger so cheaply into the Welsh pie.

1066. Welsh and Normans.

The followers of William of Normandy, indeed, lost no time in turning their attention to Wales.

Within ten years of the battle of Hastings,—almost immediately, that is to say, after the completion of the conquest of England,—they began their marauding expeditions across the border, and were not unnaturally surprised at finding themselves confronted by a people so entirely different from those they had just subdued. But these initial successes taught the Welsh nothing, and they still continued their fatal internecine strife.

The first serious lodgments of the Normans were made at Montgomery, where a baron of that name built the castle, whose fragments still look down from their rocky throne upon the windings of the upper Severn. Rhuddlan, at the mouth of the Clwyd, the site of an even then ancient fortress, was next occupied and strengthened. Flushed with their easy conquest of England, the Normans had already begun to regard Wales as if it also belonged to them; and still the quarrelsome Welsh chieftains continued to engage these formidable new-comers in their disputes. At Chester, Hugh Lupus, its Earl of famous memory, and the nephew of the Conqueror, held in secure confinement the person of the Prince of Gwynedd whom he had seized by treachery. He then proceeded to farm out the realm of the captive prince, but as he only received £40 as rental the sum is more eloquent than any words would be to express the nature of the hold he had won over it. It is more than likely the contractors had a bad bargain even at that figure.

The Normans in Wales.

In the conspiracy of 1075, when William was on the continent, many of the Welsh nobles joined, and had consequently their share of the hanging and mutilating that followed its discovery. Lupus, however, marched an army through the North and built or rebuilt castles at Bangor, Carnarvon, and Anglesey. He was closely followed by the Conqueror himself, who with a large force proceeded with little apparent opposition through the turbulent South, received the homage of its king, Rhys ap Tudor, and its petty Princes, and then repaired with great pomp to the cathedral of St. David's, at whose altar he offered costly gifts. This kind of triumphal progress, as the Saxons well knew, though the Normans had yet to learn the fact, did not mean the conquest of Wales. King William in this single campaign seems to have imbibed some respect for Welshmen, for he spoke of them on his death-bed as a people with whom he had "held perilous conflicts."

Lupus, Earl of Chester, invades North Wales, 1075.

Infinitely more dangerous to Welsh liberty was the experiment next tried by a native Prince of acquiring Norman aid at the expense of territory. The story of the conquest and settlement of Glamorgan is such a luminous and significant incident in Welsh history, and was of such great future importance, that it must be briefly related.

The present county of Glamorgan was represented, roughly speaking, in ancient Wales by the subkingdom, or, to use a more appropriate term, the lordship of Morganwg. It had acquired its name in the ninth century through the martial deeds of its then proprietor, "Morgan Fawr," or "Morgan the Great."

Norman settlement in Glamorgan.

Morganwg, though part of Deheubarth, was at times strong enough to claim something like independence, and indeed the uncertain relationships of the smaller chieftains of South Wales to their overlord at Dynevor may well be the despair of any one attempting to combine tolerable accuracy with unavoidable brevity. But these remarks are only relevant for the purpose of emphasising the comparative importance at all times in Wales of the country we call Glamorgan; and this was due not only to its size and to its seacoast, but to its comparative smoothness and fertility. In the year 1091, in the reign of William Rufus, one Iestyn, a descendant of Morgan the Great, was ruling over Glamorgan, and as he was upon anything but friendly terms with his feudal superior, Rhys ap Tudor, Prince of South Wales, he bethought him of calling in alien aid, a habit then growing lamentably common among Welsh chieftains.

1091.

The Saxons had ceased to exist as a military power, and the Normans stood in their shoes. Iestyn knew nothing of Normans, but he had a friend named Einion who was reputed to have had much experience with them. To Einion, then, he repaired and promised him his daughter's hand, which presumably carried with it something substantial, if he would bring a band of Normans to his assistance in his dispute with Rhys. Einion consented to be his intermediary and without much difficulty secured the services of Robert Fitzhamon and twelve knightly adventurers who served under him. The Normans in due course arrived and

Iestyn and Einion.

rendered Iestyn invaluable assistance in resisting his lawful sovereign. They then, so runs the chronicle, having received their pay, quite contrary to Norman custom peacefully re-embarked at Cardiff and weighed anchor for home. But Iestyn, before they had well cleared the harbour, was injudicious enough to repudiate the promise of his daughter to Einion, whereupon the exasperated princeling put to sea, interviewed Fitzhamon, and persuaded him to return with his friends and his forces and eject the faithless Iestyn from his rich territory. One may well believe it did not take much to win over the Normans to so attractive and congenial an undertaking. At any rate they reversed their course with much alacrity, returned to Cardiff, ejected Iestyn, and after some fighting, assisted by Einion's people, divided the province among themselves, each building one or more great castles, whose ruins are notable features in Glamorganshire scenery to-day. The blood of Fitzhamon's knightly followers courses in the veins of many an ancient family of South Wales, and one of them at least is still directly represented in name as well as lineage. This conquest must be placed among the earliest in Wales, and it became the type of many future Norman settlements, though it was the outcome of an incident, while the others were for the most part deliberately planned. The reign of Rufus was memorable for these filibustering expeditions. They were executed under the sanction of the King, who found in them a cheap method of granting favours to his barons, particularly those who had perhaps not come out so

Fitzhamon.

well as they could have wished in the partition of England. They might, in short, take of Wales as much as they could keep, subject only to holding what they acquired as feudatories of the King. There will be more to say about these Marcher barons later on. In the meantime, Brecheiniog, or Brecon, had been also conquered by another Norman, Bernard de Newmarch, with a similar band of followers, and secured by a similar system of castle building. Montgomery and other points in North and South Wales had been occupied, but they were for the most part purely military outposts. The occupation of Brecon and Glamorgan by a Norman aristocracy is a salient and permanent factor in Welsh history. This does not, however, imply that such filibustering barons were allowed to settle quietly down in their seats. Before the end of the reign, indeed, they were driven out, and William Rufus himself, who marched through Wales more or less upon their behalf, had, after all, to retire discomfited: but they were soon back again. It was not wholly by brute force that they held their own. Life would hardly have been worth living upon such terms, and as a matter of fact, so far as one can read between the lines of these old chronicles, there does not seem to have been at first the same antipathy between Norman and Welshman as had formerly existed between Saxon and Welshman. Marriages carrying Welsh property with them seem to have been readily arranged. A singular and romantic instance of this was in the matter of Coity Castle, whose ruined walls still hold

William Rufus and Wales.

Marriages with Normans.

together near Bridgend, and of the Turbervilles who even yet, after all these centuries, retain their name and position in Glamorganshire. For Paine Turberville, one of Fitzhamon's twelve knights, having been by some mischance forgotten in the distribution of land, inquired of his chief where he was to look for his reward. "Here are arms and here are men," replied Fitzhamon; "go get it where you can." So Turberville went to Coity, which was still unconquered, and summoned Morgan, the Welsh lord, to surrender it into his hands. Whereupon Morgan came out leading his daughter, and passing through the army, with his sword in his right hand, came to Paine Turberville, and told him that if he would marry his daughter, and so come like an honest man into his castle, he would yield it to him; but if not, said he, "let not the blood of any of our men be lost, but let this sword and arm of mine and those of yours decide who shall call this castle his own." Upon that Paine Turberville drew his sword, took it by the blade in his left hand and gave it to Morgan, and with his right hand embraced his daughter. After settling matters to the satisfaction of all parties he went to church and married her, and so came to the lordship by true right of possession; and by the advice of his father-in-law kept under his command two thousand of the best of his Welsh soldiers.

Turberville at Coity.

Turberville, having now achieved so secure a position without the aid of Fitzhamon, very naturally refused to pay him tribute or own him as his overlord, but voluntarily recognised Caradoc, the son of the dispossessed Iestyn, as his chief. This caused unpleasantness, but Turberville, with his two thousand Welshmen and his father-in-law's help, was too strong for Fitzhamon, and he had his way. It must not, however, be supposed that these martial settlers as a class by any means followed the example of the later Norman adventurers in Ireland, and became "more Welsh than the Welsh themselves." They were too near their King, at whose will they held their lands, and not far enough removed from the centre of Anglo-Norman life, to throw off its interests and lose touch with their connections. Nevertheless the confusion of authority in South and Mid-Wales increased considerably as time went on; for not only did Norman barons marry Welsh heiresses, but occasionally a Welsh chieftain would win back a Norman-Welsh lordship by marriage, and present the anomalous spectacle of a Welshman holding Welsh land as a direct vassal of the King of England in entire independence of his district Prince. But these occasional amenities among the higher aristocracy but little affected the mass of the Welsh people, who stood aloof with lowering and uncompromising sullenness.

Welsh and Norman.

It was this intolerance of foreigners, bred in the bone and blood of Welshmen, or this excessive patriotism, call it what you will, that made possible their long and heroic resistance to the Norman yoke, and for so long upheld the tottering thrones of their not always honest, and always quarrelsome, Princes. They hugged their pedigrees and cherished their bards, who in turn played with tireless energy upon the chords of national sentiment and martial memories. No transfer of land to Normans, whether due to the sword or to more peaceful methods, was regarded as otherwise than temporary. As in parts of Ireland at the present day, generations of occupation by an alien stock commanded no respect beyond what belonged to the force of ownership. The original owners might be long extinct in fact, but in the mind they were the owners still. The Anglo-Saxon has a short memory; and is practical even in matters of sentiment. Four or five generations are sufficient to eliminate the memory of the humble or alien origin of the *parvenu*, and are quite enough to fill his cup of social reverence to the brim; perhaps fortunately so. The Celt, and particularly the Welsh Celt, is fashioned differently. With him the interloper remained an interloper far beyond his children's children, and this mental attitude had much to do with the facility with which a popular leader could at all times stir up strife in Wales, whatever might be the odds against success.

We have seen, then, the first wedge of alien occupation driven into this hitherto virgin refuge of the ancient British stock. For we must remember that, in spite of continual warfare, the Saxons had made no impression calling for notice in a brief survey like this. We must remember, also, that the Norman settlements were wholly military. The followers that came with these adventurers were just sufficient to garrison their castles. They were but handfuls, and lived within or under the protection of the Norman fortress: their influence upon the blood of the country may, I think, be put aside with certain reservations, as scarcely worth considering.

1105. Pembroke and the Flemings.

The severance of half the present county of Pembroke from Wales in the reign of Henry the First must by no means be passed over if one is to get a proper idea of what was meant by Wales at the time when this story opens. It was in this King's reign that a large body of Flemings were flooded out in the Low Countries by a great inundation, and despairing of finding a fresh home in their own crowded fatherland, they applied to the King of England to allot them territory out of his presumed abundance.* In their appeal the King saw another means of putting a bridle on the Welsh, at no expense to himself, to say nothing of the advantage of posing as a philanthropist. He granted therefore to the Flemings just so much of the south-western promontory of Wales as they could hold and conquer, together with the peninsula of Gower, which juts out from the coast of modern Glamorgan. Pembroke was the more important and populous colony of the two. The native inhabitants, it may be presumed, were few in the twelfth century; at any rate the Flemings had no difficulty in driving them inland and forming a permanent settlement. There was no assimilation with the natives; they were completely pushed back, and in a short time Normans came to the

*Some accounts say that Henry first received them in England, but got uneasy at the number which accumulated there and ordered them all into south-west Wales. Small lodgments of Normans and other aliens would seem to have preceded the Flemings.

CAREW CASTLE.

FROM OLD PRINT.

assistance of the Flemings. The great castles of Pembroke, Manorbier, Haverfordwest, and Tenby were built, and speaking broadly the south-western half of the modern county of Pembroke became as Teutonic, and in time as English, as Wiltshire or Suffolk. Continual fighting went on between the native Welsh and the intruders, keeping alive the animosity between the two races and laying the seeds of that remarkable cleavage which makes the county of Pembroke present to-day an ethnological curiosity without a parallel in the United Kingdom.

The Flemings, as English subjects and constantly reinforced by English arrivals, lost in time their nationality and their language, and became as thoroughly Anglo-Saxon as the most fervent Salopian or the most stolid Wiltshireman. They remain so, in a great measure, to this very day. Intermixture with the Celtic and Welsh-speaking part of the county has been rare. The isolated position of further Pembrokeshire makes this anomaly still more peculiar, cut off as it is from England by nearly a hundred miles of Welsh territory, and more particularly when the fact is remembered that for centuries there has been no religious or political friction to keep these two communities of a remote countryside apart. Somewhat parallel conditions in Derry or Donegal, though of much more recent origin, are far more explicable owing to the civil strife and religious hatred which are or have been rife there. Even so the mixture of Scotch-Irish Protestants with Celtic Catholics has, I fancy, been much greater in Ireland than that of the Anglo-

Fleming Protestants of further Pembroke and of Gower with their Welsh neighbours of the same faith "beyond the Rubicon" in the same counties.

These conquests may, however, be regarded as constituting for some time the extent of solid Norman occupation. The story of Wales is one long tale of continuous attempts by Norman barons on the territory of the Welsh Princes, varied by the serious invasions of English Kings, which were undertaken either directly or indirectly on behalf of their Norman-Welsh vassals. Upon the whole but slow headway was made. Anglo-Norman successes and acquisitions were frequently wiped out, for the time at any rate, by the unconquerable tenacity of the Welsh people, while every now and again some great warrior arose who rolled the whole tide of alien conquest, save always further Pembroke, back again pell-mell across the border, and restored Wales, panting, harried, and bloody, to the limits within which William the Norman found it.

One of these heroic leaders was Owen ap Griffith, Prince of Gwynedd, who arose in the time of Henry II. of England. Not only did he clear North Wales of Normans, but he so ruthlessly harried Cheshire and the Marches, and so frightened the Prince of Powys that the latter joined the Norman-Welsh nobles in a petition to the King of England begging him to come up in all haste with a strong force to their aid. Henry, under whom England was rapidly recovering strength and cohesion, now essayed that profitless and thorny path of Welsh

1156.

Henry II. and Owen Gwynedd.

invasion, which his predecessors, Norman and Saxon, had so often trodden, and his successors were so often and so vainly to tread.

He marched with a large army to Chester and, being there joined by the Prince of Powys and the Norman-Welsh barons, encamped on Saltney Marsh. Owen with the forces of North Wales had come out to meet him as far as Basingwerk, and as the vanguard of the royal army advanced against the Welsh through the wooded defile of Coed Eulo the sons of Owen fell suddenly upon it, and with great slaughter rolled it back upon the main force. The King, then taking the seashore route, made head for Rhuddlan at the mouth of the Clwyd. But near Flint, in another narrow pass, he met with even a worse disaster. For here his vanguard was again attacked, many of his knights and nobles slain, his standard overthrown, and he himself in danger of his life. Eventually he reached Rhuddlan, garrisoned it, came to terms with Owen, and went home again. But there were two fierce and uncontrollable Princes now in Wales: Owen himself, "Eryr Eryrod Eryri"—the "Eagle of the Eagles of Snowdon"—and Rhys ap Griffith, the scarcely less warlike ruler of South Wales. The period was one of continuous conflict in Wales and on the border, and it ended in something like a national movement against all the centres of Norman power, both royal and baronial, that were sprinkled over the country. This was in 1165, and Henry, vowing vengeance, advanced once more to the Welsh border. He had

Henry II. defeated by Owen Gwynedd.

Rhys ap Griffith.

learnt wisdom, however, in his former campaign, and moved cautiously to Rhuddlan in order to make a preliminary investigation of the state of affairs. It was evident that nothing but a great effort would be of any avail; so returning to England he gathered a large army and sat down at Chester. In the meantime Owen Gwynedd as suzerain or Pendragon of Wales, with Rhys, Prince of Deheubarth, and even the two Princes of vacillating Powysland, which had recently been split in half, and in fact with the whole strength of the Cymry, raised the dragon standard at Corwen on the Dee. The two armies met eventually upon the banks of the Ceiriog, just beneath the hill where the Castle of Chirk, then called Crogen,* now lifts its storied towers. The slopes of the Welsh mountains, even to Snowdon itself, were in those days sprinkled freely, if not thickly clad, with timber, and a feature of this expedition was some two thousand woodcutters employed to open the country for Henry's army and secure it against those ambuscades in which the Welsh were so terribly proficient. But Owen Gwynedd came down from the Berwyns this time to meet his foe and, as I have said, a long and fierce battle was waged in the deep valley of the Ceiriog. The Welsh were in the end forced to retreat, and recrossing the Berwyn they took post again at Corwen, and, as tradition has it, on the lofty British camp at Caer Drewyn on the north bank of the Dee. Henry followed and sat

Henry II. again in Wales, 1166.

Battle of Crogen.

* This was a Welsh fortress on or near the site of the present castle, whose origin will be spoken of in another chapter.

 W. Davis.

CORWEN AND PEN Y PIGIN, FROM THE DEE.

down with his army on the high ridge of the Berwyn, above Pen-y-pigin, the river flowing through what was then no doubt a swampy valley between the two positions. It was the old story, a wearisome enough one in the long strife between England and Wales. Henry dared not advance in the face of the difficult country before him and the Welshmen's superiority in hill and woodland fighting. Moreover his provisions had run out, and to make matters worse the weather broke up, so there was nothing to be done but to march his great army home again. The Welsh Princes now attacked and destroyed many of the King's castles in the North, and on the border recovered Flint or Tegengle, which Henry had nominally annexed, and in the South sorely pressed the Norman barons in Glamorgan, Brecon, and Gwent. But the old madness of greed and jealousy which in Welsh Princes seemed inseparable from success, now took possession of Rhys and Owen; they turned on their late allies of Powys, fickle ones, no doubt, and divided their inheritance between them.

Henry returns to England.

As for Owen Gwynedd, we must leave him and his deeds to the fame which, wherever Welshmen congregate, endures for ever, and pass on to a brief mention of his son Howel, who has earned immortality in a curiously different field. Amid the passions and storms of that fierce age in Wales, it is strange enough, not to find a poet-Prince, but to find one singing in such strains as did Howel ap Owen Gwynedd. Warlike ballads are readily conceivable in such an atmosphere as

Howel ap Owen Gwynedd.

that in which Howel lived, and of war and hunting he wrote. But he also wrote sonnets, many of which are extant, to the yellow bloom of the furze, the blossoms of the apple tree, the laugh of his bright-eyed sister, to fields of tender trefoil, and to nightingales singing in privet groves. He shared the fate of so many Welsh Princes and fell by the dagger, the assassins being his half-brothers. Both he and his famous father were buried in Bangor Cathedral.

It may be well to point out that one of the causes of this chronic strife between the Welsh Princes, besides the prevalent custom of gavelkind, was that of fostering out the children of the royal houses; for when the inevitable struggle for the succession ensued, each claimant was backed up and vigorously assisted by the whole interest of the family in which he had been reared.

To another son of Owen Gwynedd belongs a tale, notable in Welsh tradition at any rate, if not in serious history. Madoc, who had for his portion the country lying round the western base of Snowdon, found the struggle for the possession of it perhaps too wearisome, for he manned a small fleet and sailed out over the western seas for many months till he discovered a strange country, good in all things for the habitation of man. From this venture, so the legend runs, Madoc returned, and, collecting a following of three hundred men in North Wales, again safely crossed the Atlantic and there founded, in what is supposed to have been Mexico,*

Madoc ap Owen Gwynedd.

Madoc's colony in Mexico, 1169.

* If this were merely a fairy tale it would certainly be out of place

a colony of Welshmen, from whom sprang the royal dynasty of Montezuma.

Dafydd, the usurping half-brother and murderer of the poet-Prince Howel, had better luck than he deserved. King Henry, now bent on making friends with the Welsh, particularly the North Welsh as being the most formidable and homogeneous, gave him in marriage his sister Emma and with her the rich barony of Ellesmere. Troops from South Wales were already helping Henry in Ireland, and now Dafydd with a large force of his own people crossed to Normandy to fight the battles of his royal brother-in-law in that country. It is characteristic of Welsh politics that while Dafydd was in France, the only one of his brothers whom he had not killed or imprisoned took occasion to seize Anglesey and the four Cantrefs that now make Carnarvonshire.

Dafydd ap Owen Gwynedd, 1170.

Norman manners and customs seem about this time to have considerably infected the Welsh aristocracy. That celebrated ecclesiastic and author, Giraldus Cambrensis, comes upon the scene at this close of the twelfth century, and has much to tell us out of the fulness of his knowledge of Wales. He was of illustrious birth, half Welsh, half Norman, and Archdeacon of Brecon, though his mere office by no means suggests

Giraldus Cambrensis.

here; but as regards the Welsh colony it has been considered not wholly unworthy of the attention of some serious ethnologists. It may further be remarked, without comment, that a comparatively modern and (in the vulgar sense) popular short history of Wales treats the whole story as authentic fact without even a suggestion of any legendary attributes! There we will leave it.

his importance, much less the importance he attributed to himself. It is his entertaining descriptions of the Welsh life he knew so well that have immortalised him, and his mixed blood would seem to have endowed him with the impartiality which he professes. He was violently opposed among other things to the encroachments of the Norman Church in Wales; for the Pope, as I have stated, had now become recognised as omnipotent, and Canterbury as the source of all authority. Giraldus strove hard to get St. David's created an Archbishopric, and to persuade the Pope to send thither his pallium, the symbol of consecration. Though it is true he was himself burning to be installed at St. David's, Giraldus probably reflected the popular opinion of contemporary Welshmen in favour of recovering the old independence of the Welsh Church. The Crusades were now at their zenith, and Archbishop Baldwin undertook at this time his famous progress through Wales on behalf of the holy cause. Giraldus accompanied him as chaplain, interpreter, and friend on this protracted tour, and, happily for us, as special reporter too. The Archbishop's exhortations caused some passing enthusiasm throughout the country, though the practical results do not seem to have been considerable. Some say that Baldwin's main object was to hold high mass in St. David's Cathedral, and so put the coping-stone, as it were, on the annexation of the Welsh Church.

As regards the Crusades the Welsh in the Middle Ages do not seem to have been great rovers or much given to doing business on great waters;

always, of course, excepting Madoc ap Owen Gwynedd, the discoverer of America!

"These people," says Giraldus, alluding to the Welsh, "are light and active, hardy rather than strong, and entirely bred up to the use of arms; for not only the nobles, but all the people are trained to war, and when the trumpet sounds the husbandman rushes as eagerly from his plough as the courtier from his Court. They live more on flesh, milk and cheese than bread, pay little attention to commerce, shipping, or manufacture, and devote their leisure to the chase and martial exercises. They earnestly study the defence of their country, and their liberty. For these they fight, for these they undergo hardships, and for these willingly sacrifice their lives. They esteem it a disgrace to die in bed, an honour to die on the field of battle."

Giraldus on the Welsh people.

"Their arms and their coats of mail," he goes on to tell us, "are light, so also are their helmets, and shields, and greaves plated with iron. The higher class go to war on swift and well-bred steeds, but are ready at a moment's notice, should the nature of the ground require it, to fight on foot as do the mass of their people. In times of peace the young men by wandering in the dense forests and scaling the summits of the highest mountains inure themselves to the hardships of war when the necessity arrives."

They were addicted neither to gluttony nor drunkenness, and could readily go for two days without food, eating in any case but twice a day. They could lie out, moreover, all night in rain and storm, if an enemy had to be watched, or an ambush to be laid. There were whole bands of the better-born young men whose sole profession was arms, and to whom free quarters were given upon all occasions. The Welsh among other things were a clean-shaven race, reserving only their moustaches, and keeping the hair of their head short. The teeth of both sexes too were a special matter of pride. On this account they even abstained from hot meats, and rubbed their teeth constantly with green hazel till they shone like ivory. "They have powerful understandings, being much quicker at their studies than other Western nations, ready in speech and confident in expressing themselves, even to the lowest class." Their love of high birth and long pedigrees was then as now conspicuous, and the tribal system though rapidly modifying under Saxon and Norman influences encouraged them to think much of their ancestors, and to be quick in avenging insults to their blood. This custom, indeed, was carried to such lengths, that the Welshman's tendency to family quarrels, coupled with his sensitiveness for the family honour, was neatly satirised by an old proverb which affirmed that he "loved his brother better dead than alive."

Giraldus, who may be regarded as a well-informed neutral in the matter, criticises the injudicious manner in which war had hitherto been prosecuted against his countrymen. He deprecates, for instance, the use of heavy-armed soldiers and a profusion of cavalry, which the active Welshmen in their mountain country are easily able to elude and often to defeat. He declares that the only way to conquer

Wales would be by winter campaigns, when the leaves are off the trees and the pastures withered. "Then," he writes, "English troops must be pushed forward at all hazards, for even if the first are slaughtered any number of fresh ones can be purchased for money; whereas the Welsh are restricted in the number of their men." The question of commissariat, the crux of all Welsh campaigns in those days, seems to have escaped the notice of the clerical critic.

Giraldus on Welsh warfare.

Having thus descanted on their virtues, Giraldus now assumes the Anglo-Norman on the strength of his half blood, and enumerates their weak points.

"The Welsh are flighty," he tells us, "and readily undertake things which they have not the perseverance to carry out. They have little respect for oaths, and not much for the truth, and when a good opportunity occurs for attacking an enemy they regard neither truces nor treaties. In war they are very severe in their first attack, terrible by their clamour and looks, filling the air with horrid shouts and the deep-toned clangour of very long trumpets. Bold in the first onset they cannot bear a repulse, being easily thrown into confusion, as soon as they turn their backs. Yet though defeated and put to flight one day, they are ready to resume the combat on the next, neither dejected by their loss nor by their dishonour; easier in short to overcome in a single battle, than in a protracted war. Their great weakness after all," concludes Gerald, "lies in their internal jealousies. If they were inseparable, they would be insuperable, and above all, if instead of having three Princes they had but one, and that a good one!"

For their music this invaluable chronicler has nothing but enthusiasm, dwelling upon the sweetness of their instruments, the harp and the "crwth" (a primitive violin) in particular, and, above all, on their habit of singing in parts, and not, as most other nations do, in unison.

However distasteful the aggression of the Roman Church may have been to the mass of the Welsh people in the twelfth century, this period brought a great revival of religious fervour, even if it came largely from alien sources. The rude churches of wood or wickerwork that five and six centuries before had marked the dawn, not of Christianity, but of organised Christianity, now gave place to solid and sometimes beautiful specimens of early English or Norman art. Many of them, not greatly altered by the restorer's touch, still stand amid the grandeur of majestic mountains or the loneliness of surf-beaten shores, and seem in consequence to speak more eloquently of these far-off, mysterious times than their more imposing contemporaries, which are set amid tame and commonplace surroundings. In the twelfth and thirteenth centuries, too, the great Welsh abbeys were in their prime. Valle Crucis, whose graceful ruins still defy the ages amid the matchless beauties of the Vale of Llangollen, was the pride of Powys; Ystradfflur (*Strata Florada*) in Cardigan shared with the Cistercian House of Aber Conway the honour of recording and safeguarding the chronicles of the Principality and of giving burial to her most illustrious dead. In a wild Radnor valley

Religious fervour in the twelfth century.

Abbeys.

stood the great Cistercian abbey of Cwm Hir, while in the green meadows where the silver streams of the Mawddach and the Wnion meet in the shadow of Cader Idris, you may yet see the ivy clustering on the ruins of Cymmer, erected by the same order. Some centuries older than any of these, the most ancient of Welsh abbeys was still intact upon Ynys Enlli, the remote island of Bardsey, and served the churches that were so thickly sprinkled along the rugged coasts of Lleyn. It had been the "Rome of the Cymry." Thousands of pilgrims had annually turned thither their weary steps. It was accounted a good thing to go there, and still better to die there; and though divided from the main-land by three miles of water, whose tides rage with notorious violence, the dust of "twenty thousand saints" lies, as all good Welshmen know, beneath the sod of this narrow and stormy isle. These are but a few haphazard examples of the centres of religion, which, amid the fierce passions of the Celt and the restless greed of the Norman, struck at least one peaceful note in nearly every Cambrian valley.

We are now within less than a century of the final overthrow of Welsh independence. Enough has been said to show how gradually and with what hard fighting the disintegration of Wales was brought about, and still fiercer struggles were yet to come. The Princes of Powys, though liable to fitful attempts at independence, had now virtually submitted to the English King, and even ranged themselves at times against their countrymen. North Wales was still intact, always

Powys and the English power.

excepting that debatable land between the Dee and Conway, the Perfeddwlad, which was lost and retaken more times than it would be possible to take account of here. The great region of South Wales, however, from the edge of Hereford to Cardigan Bay, presented a rare confusion of authority. One scarcely ventures to touch the subject within such narrow limits as ours must needs be. Hardly as they were sometimes beset, even to the length of being driven from their lands and castles, the Norman adventurers steadily ate up bit by bit the old Kingdom of Deheubarth. Each man had just so much territory as he could win by the sword, and, what was more important, only so much as he could keep by it. They all held their lands, whose limits were but vaguely defined by charter or title-deed, since they were undefinable, direct from the King of England, and had by virtue of their office the right to sit in Parliament, and to support the royal canopy at coronations with silver spears.

Norman encroachments.

In their own domains they possessed absolute authority, so far as they could exercise it, even over the lives of their tenants. Small towns began to grow under the protection of their castle walls, and were occupied by their retainers. Courts were established in each lordship, and justice was administered to the Anglo-Norman minority after English custom and to the Welsh majority after the custom of old Welsh law, and in the native tongue. Let me repeat, I am but generalising. The condition of Wales at the opening of the thirteenth century was

 VALLE CRUCIS ABBEY. F. Frith & Co.

far too complex to admit of analytical treatment within such a brief space as this. The exceptions to every rule were numerous. The King of England himself, for example, owned many lordships and was represented in them by a Justiciar or Bailiff, and sometimes this functionary was actually a Welshman. Here and there again a Welsh noble held property as a Norman Baron from the King while occasionally a Norman did allegiance for his barony to a Welsh Prince, and posed as a Welshman.

Wales in the thirteenth century.

The landed system of Wales in the Middle Ages is still more hopeless for purposes of brief description. The indigenous tribal system, when land was held in families, or "gwelis," by the descendants of a privileged though perhaps a large class, had been steadily undergoing modification since the later Saxon period,* and in all directions it was honeycombed not only by encroaching Normans, with their feudal and manorial land laws, and by the monastic houses, but long before the twelfth century many Welsh princes and chieftains had felt the Saxon influence, and had drifted into the manorial system, so far at least as their own private possessions were concerned.

Landed system.

With the close of the twelfth century the most illustrious of all Welsh Princes, the only possible rival of Glyndwr, Llewelyn ap Iorwerth, comes upon the scene as a beardless boy; and in connection with this famous person it may fairly be said that though there was plenty of

Llewelyn the Great, 1195.

* See Seebohm's *Tribal Wales*.

fight left in the still unconquered moiety of South Wales, and a little even in Powys, it is with Gwynedd that the interest of the last century of Welsh resistance mainly rests. Son of Iorwerth the broken-nosed, who, though the rightful heir of Owen Gwynedd, was rejected on account of this disfigurement, Llewelyn the Great is supposed with good reason to have been born in the castle of Dolwyddelan, whose ruinous walls, perched high upon the wild foot-hills of Moel Siabod, still look down upon the infant Llugwy as it urges its buoyant streams through one of the most beautiful of North Welsh valleys.

Nurtured amid the clash of arms, the boy was only twelve years old when he asserted his right to the throne, and won it against his Norman-loving uncle, Dafydd, whom we left, it will be remembered, fighting in France. The young Prince, backed by a strong following in North Wales, and by the arms of Powys, deposed his uncle and commenced the long career which earned him that pre-eminent fame in warlike deeds which attaches to his name. By the time he was of age he was fully recognised as "Brenin holl Cymru," or Pendragon, by all that was left of Wales. John, who now occupied the English throne, so fully recognised the dawn of a new and formidable personal influence in his tributary realm that he bestowed upon Llewelyn in marriage his illegitimate daughter Joan, together with a handsome dower.

Llewelyn marries King John's daughter.

The first few years of the thirteenth century were fully occupied with ceaseless strife between the

Welsh Princes, their relatives, and the Norman nobles settled in their midst. It will be sufficient to say that Llewelyn, high-handed and autocratic, lost nothing of his importance in such congenial work, and by 1209 had left his mark upon the English borders so rudely that King John and his vigorous son-in-law at length came to blows. The former, collecting a large army, penetrated to the Conway River, behind which, in the mountains of Snowdonia, Llewelyn with all his people and all his movables defied attack.

John, with whom went many of the nobles of Powys, sat down at Deganwy Castle, one of the great strategic points of ancient Wales, and one whose scanty ruins are familiar to visitors at Llandudno and Conway. But the Welsh slipped behind them and cut off their supplies. Nor could the King move forward, for across the river rose the grim masses of the Snowdon mountains. His people were reduced to eating their horses, disease was ravaging their ranks, and there was nothing for it but to go back; so John returned to England with rage at his heart. Nothing daunted he returned again to the attack, marching this time by way of Oswestry and Corwen. He was now both more daring and more fortunate, seeing that he succeeded in throwing a portion of his forces into Bangor. This checkmated Llewelyn, and he sent his wife to see what terms could be exacted from her father. His reply indicated that the cession of the unfortunate Perfeddwlad, and a fine of twenty thousand head of

John invades Wales, 1209.

1212.

cattle was the least he could accept, and with these terms the Welsh Prince complied. The latter condition was probably inconvenient; the former was merely a question of might for the time being. Any territorial arrangement with John was likely to be of only temporary consequence, for that undesirable King was perpetually under the ban of the Church, and had none too many friends. So in 1212, when Pope Innocent absolved all John's feudatories from their allegiance, it furnished an admirable excuse for Llewelyn to reoccupy the whole of his ancient dominion of Gwynedd. When, two years later, John's own barons rose against him, they formed an alliance with the powerful Prince of Gwynedd, who captured Shrewsbury, and thereby contributed no little to the pressure which caused the signing of Magna Charta.

Llewelyn sides with the barons against John.

Llewelyn subsequently swept through both Mid- and South Wales, sacking and gutting many of the hated Norman castles, till he came to be regarded in the South with as much devotion as in his own province. Every dispute concerning territory or boundaries was submitted to his judgment. Even the Flemings of Pembroke for the first time since their occupation tendered their homage to a Welsh Prince.

But between the death of John and the accession of Henry III., the nobles of England forgot their obligations to Llewelyn, while the Marcher barons whose castles he had sacked were eager enough to turn this indifference into hostility. The result of all this was that Llewelyn found himself threatened by the whole power of England and of Anglo-Norman Wales in the event of his refusal to abandon his recent conquests. Llewelyn ap Iorwerth, wise in his generation, sought a personal interview with the young King, his brother-in-law, at which he undertook to do him homage; a formality which, I have more than once observed, Welsh Princes had no reluctance upon principle in conceding. On this occasion, moreover, Llewelyn's pride was fully gratified. He was officially recognised as Prince of all Gwynedd, with the second title of Lord of Snowdon, and his suzerainty over the other divisions of Wales was formally acknowledged. We find him emphasising this diplomatic triumph by granting that bone of contention, the Perfeddwlad, to his son Griffith, and the latter with the fatuity so common to his race returning this piece of parental affection by laying violent hands on Merioneth, another district within his father's Principality. This was a wholly outrageous proceeding and Llewelyn, finding remonstrance unavailing, hastened eastward with a strong force to chastise his incorrigible offspring. The latter was quite prepared to fight, and we have the edifying picture of father and son facing each other in arms in a cause wholly wanton, and as if there were no such thing as Normans and Saxons, to say nothing of South Welshmen, ever and always threatening their existence. A reconciliation was happily effected, but when Llewelyn found himself with most of the soldiery of his province around him in arms, the temptation

Llewelyn recognised by John as ruler of Wales.

Llewelyn's son rebels against him.

was too great, and throwing treaties to the winds, he fell upon the English border and harried it from Chester to Hereford. Drawn thence south-westwards by signs of restlessness on the part of that ever-rankling sore, the Anglo-Flemish colony of Pembroke, he swept through South Wales and fought a great battle on the confines of their territory, which the fall of night found still undecided.

From now onwards till 1234 there was little peace in Wales, and above the ceaseless din of arms the star of Llewelyn ap Iorwerth shone with ever increasing glory. Then came a confederation of Norman barons against King Henry, who, turning for support to Llewelyn, entered into a solemn league and covenant both with him and with his tributary princes. It was so strong a combination that Henry shrank from coping with it. It was the first occasion on which Anglo-Norman Barons and Welsh Princes on an important scale had formed a treaty of alliance with each other and, still more, had honourably observed it. Even more singular perhaps was the outcome, when, Henry being forced to a compromise, a Welsh Prince found himself in the unprecedented position of being able to exact conditions for the great Norman feudatories of Wales from a Norman King.

Continuous war, 1234.

Llewelyn, having buried his wife Joan in the abbey of Llanfaes near Beaumaris, himself died at Aber in the year 1240, after a stormy but, judged by the ethics of the time, a brilliant reign of over half a century. His triumphs were of course for the most part military ones. But no

Death of Llewelyn II., 1240.

Welsh Princes having regard to the decline of Cymric power had ever accomplished quite so much. He had forced his authority upon all Wales except the lordship Marches, but he had also been a sleepless patriot, driving the English arms back and greatly weakening the English influence throughout the whole Principality. With this scant notice of a long and eventful reign we must take leave of the warlike son of Iorwerth. He was buried at Aber Conway in the abbey he had founded; but his stone coffin was removed in later days to the beautiful church at Llanrwst, where amid the historic treasures of the Gwydir Chapel it still recalls to the memory of innumerable pilgrims "the eagle of men, who loved not to lie nor sleep, who towered above the rest of men with his long red lance and his red helmet of battle crested with a savage wolf, Llewelyn the Great."

Wales, though rapidly approaching the era of her political extinction, was now so unusually strong and even aggressive that the English King was compelled to watch the course of events there with a vigilant eye. From the Welsh point of view it was of vital importance that Llewelyn's successor in Gwynedd should be both acceptable to his people and strong in himself. Unhappily he was neither, unless indeed obstinacy may count for strength. Of Llewelyn's family two sons alone concern us here. Griffith, the elder of these by a Welsh mother, has been already alluded to as going to war in such wild fashion with his father. Rightly or wrongly he was regarded as illegitimate, though that circumstance, it may be remarked parenthetically, was not such a vital matter in Old Wales. But his father's marriage with an English King's daughter suggests the possibility of making too light of a former and less distinguished alliance. Be that as it may, the younger of the two, the son of the Princess Joan and nephew of Henry III., succeeded in seating himself on his father's throne, though not without protest from the Welsh nobility who did not by any means relish his English blood. Dafydd had all the English influence behind him, while his close connection with the King seemed to make for peace. But Griffith, the elder, in spite of his presumed illegitimacy, was the popular candidate, and Dafydd did not improve his own position by proceeding to strip his half-brother of his private property, and immuring his person in Criccieth Castle. All Wales protested. The Bishop of Bangor went so far as to excommunicate his temporal ruler, and King Henry himself on his distant throne expressed unmistakable disapproval of the whole business. But Dafydd cared neither for King nor Bishop. To the former he replied that if Griffith were at liberty there would be no peace in Wales, a possibility that seems by no means remote when one considers the performances of this young man in his father's lifetime. Henry was not to be thus put off, and approached the Marches with a strong army. This unmistakable procedure and the almost unanimous support it met with from the Welsh nobility frightened Dafydd into a promise of submission. But the upshot of all this was not precisely what Griffith's

Griffith sent to the Tower by Henry III.

Welsh friends had expected. He was released from Criccieth, it is true, but only to be transferred to the Tower of London pending Henry's decision as to his ultimate fate.

Much more important than this disposal of Griffith's person was the extraction from Dafydd by his uncle of one of the most humiliating treaties ever wrung from a Welsh Prince, a treaty which might well cause his father, the great Llewelyn, to turn in his grave beside the Conway. Every advantage that Llewelyn's strong arm had gained was tamely abandoned by his unworthy son. The Princes of Powys and South Wales were absolved from their oath of homage to the ruler of Gwynedd, which Principality shrank once more to the banks of the Conway. In the meantime Griffith with his young son Owen was left by Henry to languish in the Tower, till, filled with despair, he made a bold bid for freedom. Weaving ropes out of his bed-clothing he let himself down by night from his prison window; but, being a corpulent man, his weight was too much for such slender supports, and he fell from a great height to the ground, breaking his neck upon the spot.

Death of Griffith.

The Welsh were greatly exasperated at the news, laying the death of their favourite most naturally at Henry's door, and as the Marcher barons had been encouraged of late in their aggressions and tyrannies by the decline of Welsh strength, the time seemed ripe for another general rising. Dafydd now came out as a warrior and a patriot leader, and Wales rallied to his standard. He was, however, so appalled by the memory of the awful oaths of allegiance he had sworn to his royal uncle and the vengeance of Heaven he had invited in case of their non-observance, that he sent secretly a sum of money to the Pope,—all in fact he could scrape together,—begging for absolution. His Holiness granted this readily enough and professed to recognise his right to independence. But Henry, hearing of it, and disturbed by these manœuvres of the Vicar of God, secretly forwarded twice the amount of money sent by Dafydd to the Pope, who thereupon reversed all his previous decisions. We do not hear whether the Welsh Prince got his money back. He certainly got no value for it. So now in these years of 1244–45 war raged once more throughout Wales and the Marches, and Dafydd, though unendowed with his father's warlike talents, nevertheless by his patriotic action regained the affection of his people. Henry was busy in Scotland and it was nearly a year before he could get to Wales in person; when he did, he pushed his way, with only one brisk fight, to that time-honoured barrier, the Conway estuary, and sat down with a large army of English and Gascons on the green pastures around Deganwy Castle, where he gazed with inevitable helplessness at the Welsh forces crowding on the marsh across the river, or lining the outer ramparts of Snowdonia that frown behind it. The troubles of King John, and even worse, befell his son. Matthew of Paris has preserved for us a "letter from the front" written by a knight, who gives a graphic

Dafydd makes war on the English.

1244.

Henry III. in Wales.

description of the sufferings of the army, not forgetting himself in the narration of them. Cold, sickness, and hunger were their lot, varied by fierce skirmishes with the Welsh and desperate fights over the English provision boats, which made their way from Chester round the Orme's Head into the Conway. Aber Conway Abbey was ruthlessly sacked by the English soldiery, much to the regret, it should be said, of our "special correspondent" and greatly to the rage of the Welsh, who in revenge slaughtered every wounded Englishman they could lay hands on.

No definite result accrued from this war. Dafydd died a few months after this amid the regrets of his people, whose affection had been secured by his later deeds. He had atoned for his former pusillanimity by the stubborn resistance which marked the close of his life. His death made way for the last and, to Englishmen, the most illustrious of all the long line of Welsh Princes.

Dafydd left no heir. Strictly speaking, his legal successor was a Norman, Sir Ralph Mortimer, who had married Gwladys, a legitimate daughter of Llewelyn. Such a successor was of course out of the question, and, as Henry abstained from all interference, the nobles of North Wales naturally fell back on the illegitimate branch, that of Griffith, who perished in the moat of the Tower of London. This unfortunate Prince, whose body was about this time removed to Conway and buried with great pomp, had three sons, Llewelyn, Owen, and Dafydd. It would seem as if all past experiences were lost upon the nobles of Gwynedd, since they were fatuous enough to appoint the two elder of these Princes to the joint rulership of their province. The partnership survived an English invasion which Henry made on hearing that the chieftains of South Wales were calling on the new Princes of Gwynedd to aid them, in the belief that a diversion would be opportune.

Sons of Griffith appointed to joint rulership of N. Wales.

Once more the English appeared on the Conway. As usual, the Welsh with their stock and movables had slipped over the river into the impregnable wilds of Snowdonia, and the King returned as he went, burning St. Asaph's Cathedral on his march. There was now peace in Wales for some years; a lull, as it were, before the great conflict that was to be the end of all things. But peace and plenty, in the words of the chronicler, "begat war." For want of enemies the two brothers turned their arms against each other. Owen, the younger, was the aggressor in this instance, and he justly suffered for it, being overcome by Llewelyn and immured for the rest of his life in the lonely castle of Dolbadarn, whose ivy-mantled shell still stands by the Llanberis lakes.

Henry III. again in Wales.

Dafydd, the third brother, had supported Owen, and he, too, was seized and securely confined. Llewelyn, now supreme in North Wales, becomes the outstanding figure around which the closing scene of the long and heroic resistance of the Welsh henceforth gathers. South Wales was in a distracted state. The Lord Marchers and the King's Bailiffs, backed by English support, had taken fresh heart from Welsh dissensions

Llewelyn III. (or ap Griffith).

and were pressing hardly on those native chieftains who did not side with them. Every chieftain and noble in Wales whose patriotism had not been tampered with now took up arms. Llewelyn was universally recognised as the national leader, and the years 1257–58 were one long turmoil of war and battle in every part of Wales. 1257-58. Llewelyn had cleared off all recent aggression, fallen with heavy hand on the old settled barons, and smitten the traitors among his fellow-countrymen hip and thigh. A battle was fought on the Towy, which some chroniclers say was the bloodiest ever engaged in between Welsh and English, to the worsting of the latter and the loss of two thousand men.

King Henry attacks Llewelyn.

The Perfeddwlad had been granted to Prince Edward, then Earl of Chester. His agents there had distinguished themselves, even in those cruel times, for intolerable oppression. Llewelyn in his vengeance swept Edward's new property bare from the Conway to the Dee. The future conqueror and organiser of Wales was at this moment hardly pressed. His Welsh friends, like the then Prince of Powys, were heavily punished by Llewelyn and their lands laid waste. Edward sent to Ireland for succour, but the Irish ships were met at sea by those of Llewelyn and driven back. Henry now returned to his son's assistance, and, drawing together "the whole strength of England from St. Michael's Mount to the river Tweed," executed the familiar promenade across the wasted Perfeddwlad, and experienced the familiar sense of impotence upon the Conway with its well defended forts and frowning mountains alive with agile spearmen.

Once again the tide of battle rolled back to the English border, and the first serious punishment we hear of the Welsh receiving curiously enough was at the hands of some German cavalry imported and led by Lord Audley, whose large horses seem to have struck some terror into the mountaineers. But this is a detail. Llewelyn may almost be said to have repeated the exploits of his grandfather and reconquered Wales. Even Flemish Pembroke had been forced to its knees. His followers to the number of ten thousand had bound themselves by oath to die rather than submit, and these, being picked men and inured to war, were a formidable nucleus for the fighting strength of Wales to rally round. The revolt, too, of Simon de Montfort against Henry was all in favour of Llewelyn, who took the former's part and was able to render him considerable personal service in the decline of his success.

Through many years of intermittent strife and varying fortunes the balance of power remained with Llewelyn, till in 1267 a peace was made at Shrewsbury very greatly in his favour. By this agreement Henry in consideration of a sum of money undertook to recognise Llewelyn as Prince of all Wales and entitled to receive homage and fealty from every prince and noble in the country save the sadly shorn representatives of the old line of Deheubarth. But after two years' enjoyment of this contract the King's death and the succession of the

1267. Llewelyn makes peace and is recognised by Henry as Prince of all Wales.

strenuous Prince Edward threw everything once more into confusion.

It is true that Edward, who was in the Holy Land fighting Turks, took two years in finding his way home. But when he did so, in 1274, and was crowned King he threw his father's treaty with Llewelyn to the winds; an action for which, it is true, the latter gave him some excuse by refusing to attend at his coronation, not from recusancy, but from a well-grounded fear that his life would not be safe from certain Anglo-Norman nobles whose territory he would have to pass through.

Llewelyn and Edward I, 1275.

Now comes a passage in Llewelyn's stormy life that his admirers would fain forget, since it records how for love of a woman he reversed the indomitable front he had hitherto shown to the invading English, and submitted almost without a blow to the dictation of the returned Crusader, whom he had so often beaten of old in the Welsh Marches. It was perhaps the memory of these former rebuffs that made the proud and warlike Edward so vindictive towards Llewelyn. A weapon, too, was at this moment placed in his hands which was to assist him in a manner he had not dreamed of. The young daughter of the late Simon de Montfort, to whom the Welsh Prince was betrothed and whom he is said to have deeply loved, was sailing from France to become his bride. In anxiety to escape the English, the ship that bore her unluckily ran among some Bristol vessels off the Scilly Islands. The captains seized

Llewelyn's betrothed wife seized by the English.

the prospective bride and carried her at once to Edward, who was on the point of invading Wales with two armies. Four years of peace had doubtless weakened the strong Welsh league that had worked such wonders against Henry III. Numbers of his old friends at any rate failed to respond to Llewelyn's call. The Prince had now before him the alternatives of immediate union with his betrothed, or of war and chaos with a lukewarm or hostile South Wales and certainly a hostile Powys added to the power of England.

After being cooped up for some weeks in the Snowdon mountains by the royal army, Llewelyn signed at length a treaty with Edward, the conditions of which were as humiliating as if he had been crushed to the earth by a series of disastrous battles, whereas he was in truth the still recognised suzerain of all Wales. To put the case, or the gist of it, briefly: all Wales except the Snowdon lordships (the present Carnarvonshire) was to revert absolutely to the King of England, Welsh and alien lords alike becoming his tenants. Even Anglesey was to revert to the Crown in the event of Llewelyn's dying without issue. Nothing was to be left of Welsh independence but the "cantrefs," or lordships, constituting Snowdonia; and over this remnant Llewelyn's heirs were to be graciously permitted to reign in peace. The Prince's passion had proved greater than his patriotism; the treaty was signed at Conway, and King Edward, who had advanced unopposed to Cardiganshire, withdrew his troops.

Llewelyn makes peace with Edward I.

"The force of love," says the chronicler, groaning over this depressing episode, "docs indeed work wonders." Llewelyn, not long afterwards, was married in great pomp at Worcester in presence of the whole Court of England, the King himself giving the bride away, and the late ruler of all Wales and now lord merely of Snowdonia, with a life interest in Anglesey, retired to the obscurity of his contracted honours. Here, amid the Carnarvon mountains, he began ere long to feel the prickings of conscience, and remorse for the weak part he had played.

Llewelyn's marriage.

Edward, too, kept open the wound by frequently summoning him to this place or that on various pleas, and the Welsh Prince, dreading treachery and remembering his father, Griffith's, fate, as constantly refused to go without a guaranty of safety. The greater part of the present counties of Carmarthen and Cardigan were already King's ground. As forming part of the old Principality of South Wales, and therefore not Marcher property, they had come to Edward. A county court had before this been established at Carmarthen, and efforts to make this territory shire ground had been feebly made, but they were now vigorously renewed, and the Perfeddwlad was treated in savage fashion. Ferocity was the distinguishing mark of all the servants of Edward I.

From every part of Wales came the cry of despairing Welshmen ground to powder by the insensate tyrannies of the King's Bailiffs and the Lord Marchers, now left entirely to their own wild wills. Llewelyn's third brother,

Cruelty of Edward's government, 1281.

Dafydd, who had played the part of King's friend and traitor to his own people for most of his life, was rewarded by the Barony of Denbigh. It was the year 1281 and the time was now ripe for the last scene of the last act in this long, sanguinary struggle. Many of the chieftains of Wales, thinking, as they had often thought before, that death was preferable to the intolerable oppression from which the country now suffered, approached Dafydd at Denbigh and assured him that if he would even thus tardily be reconciled to his brother Llewelyn and lead them, they would strike yet one more blow for freedom. Dafydd, probably with their knowledge, was smarting under some real or fancied slight from his patron, King Edward, though maybe his heart was really touched at the extreme sufferings of his countrymen. At any rate he played the man to an extent that more than atoned for his unworthy past. Dafydd and his brother Llewelyn now met at the former's castle upon the high rock of Denbigh, and there the Welsh chieftains who had declared for death or freedom rallied to the standard raised by the grandsons of Llewelyn the Great, and held upon "the craggy hill in Rhos" the last formal council of either peace or war that was to be recorded in the pages of Welsh history. The news of the proposed rising had reached England before Llewelyn had left his palace at Aber, and had caused some consternation. Edward and his barons had regarded the Welsh question as settled, and thought that on the death of the now pacified and uxorious

Dafydd turns patriot.

Llewelyn and Dafydd unite for resistance.

Llewelyn the last vestige of independence would quietly lapse. The Archbishop of Canterbury was greatly distressed. He sent word to Llewelyn that he was coming to see him for the love he bore to Wales, and without the King's knowledge; and he then, in actual fact, travelled all the way to Aber and used every argument, persuasive and coercive, he could think of to turn the Welsh Prince from what seemed a mad and hopeless enterprise. He threatened him with the whole physical power of England, the whole spiritual power of Rome. Never did the last Llewelyn, or indeed any Llewelyn, show a nobler front than on this occasion. For himself, he was materially well provided for and beyond the reach of the persecution that pressed upon most of his fellow-countrymen. But they had called to him in their despair, and desperate as the risk might be he had resolved to stand or fall with them. A schedule of conditions was sent him from the English King and his council, under which everything was to be overlooked, if only he and his people would return to their allegiance. Among other things an English county, with a pension of £1000 a year, was offered him in lieu of Snowdon. Llewelyn replied with scorn that he wanted no English county, that his patrimony was lawfully his own by virtue of a long line of ancestors; that even if he himself were base enough to yield up the Snowdon lordships, his subjects there would never submit to a rule that was hateful to them and had brought such misery on their neighbours of the Perfeddwlad. It was better, he declared, to die with honour than to

Llewelyn rejects all terms.

live in slavery; and it may perhaps be repeated to his advantage that Llewelyn himself was only a sufferer so far as his proper pride was concerned, though it is possible he felt some pricks of conscience about the concessions made two years previously. At any rate he nobly atoned for them. There is evidence that admiration for the gallant stand made by this remnant of the Welsh was being kindled not only across the seas but even among Englishmen themselves. "Even Englishmen and foreigners," says Matthew of Paris, who was assuredly no Welshman, "were touched with pity and admiration."

Outside sympathy for Wales.

Prince Dafydd, who was offered his pardon on condition of immediately repairing to the Holy Land, was equally stubborn, though perhaps the temptation to be otherwise was not so great. He replied to the effect that he had no intention of undertaking a Crusade at the dictates of others. However admirable was this tardy patriotism, his past record from that point of view was wholly dishonourable, for he had been consistently a King's man. On the other hand, if, as was possibly the case with many Welsh nobles, he had sincerely believed that submission to English rule was the wisest thing for Welshmen, his abrupt repudiation of the man whose favours he had sought and received is not readily excusable. In this direction it is urged that the Anglo-Norman garrisons in these first years of Edward's reign had made life so intolerable that Dafydd was sufficiently touched by his countrymen's sufferings to risk everything and

Dafydd rejects Edward's terms.

join his gallant brother in so forlorn a hope. "It was better for the kingdom at large that Wales should be governed," wrote the brothers to Edward, "by her own Princes, paying that homage to the King of England which they had never refused, than by greedy strangers whose only thought was to oppress her people, despoil her churches, and advance their own private interests."

The fall of the curtain upon this remnant of Welsh independence was now but a matter of a few months. Edward's answer to the Princes was the despatch of a fleet to Anglesey, and of an army along the north coast route, containing large numbers of Gascons, and even some Spaniards. Edward himself went as far as Conway, meeting on the way with a heavy repulse and considerable loss in what was soon to be Flintshire. Dafydd, who was commanding in the north, was pushed into Snowdonia. The English army in Anglesey bridged the Menai with boats, and a strong detachment, crossing before the connection was complete, encountered the Welsh near Bangor. The invaders, however, were all cut off and slain in a fierce battle fought upon the shore, among them being many barons, knights, and squires.

Fighting on the Menai Straits.

These successes could only delay the end and exasperate the inevitable conquerors. Llewelyn, not wishing to be starved into surrender among the Snowdon mountains, had gone south to rouse the new shire land of Cardigan and Carmarthen, and the warlike Radnor tenants of the Mortimers. The Earl of Gloucester with another English army had meanwhile penetrated into South Wales and defeated a large force of Welsh patriots at Llandilo in the valley of the Towy.

Death of the last Llewelyn.

Llewelyn came up, fighting his way through Cardiganshire, and had reached Builth on the Wye, when, on December 11th, he met his fate. The story of his death is too much confused, and there is no space here for repeating the slightly varying versions of the tragedy, but it seems quite clear that he was tempted away from the main body of his army by treachery, and slain when he was without arms in his hands. His head was struck off and despatched at once to King Edward at Conway, who, receiving it with great joy, sent it immediately by sea to his army in Anglesey. Thence the gruesome trophy was forwarded to London, where crowds of people met it outside the city and placed upon the gory brows a wreath of ivy in mockery of the old Welsh prophecy that a Prince of Welsh blood should once more be crowned in London. It was then fixed upon the point of a lance and carried in triumph through the streets to the pillory, and from the pillory to its final resting-place above the gate of the Tower.

Llewelyn's head carried through London in triumph.

Thus perished the last representative of the long line of Welsh Princes that may be said to have had its rise with the sons of Cunedda eight centuries before. The last dim spark of Welsh independence flickered feebly for a few weeks, till the very recesses of Snowdonia, for almost the first time in history, gave back their echoes to the blast of English bugles, and the wild passes of Nant Francon and Llanberis felt the tramp of alien feet. Dafydd found himself alone, a hunted outlaw in the forests of the Vale of Clwyd. He was soon captured and taken to Shrewsbury, where a Parliament was then sitting. Llewelyn's remains had been treated with doubtful logic and poor chivalry as a traitor. What treatment he would have met with at Edward's hands as a prisoner we cannot know. But Dafydd could expect nothing but the worst and he received it. He was tried as an English baron at Shrewsbury and sentenced to be quartered, disembowelled, and beheaded. His quarters were distributed among four English cities, Winchester and York, it is said, quarrelling for the honour of his right shoulder, while his head was sent to moulder by his brother's over the gateway of the Tower of London. A story runs that while his entrails were being burned his heart leaped from the flames and struck the executioner who was feeding them.

Capture and execution of Dafydd.

All resistance worthy of mention was now over in Wales. The six centuries or thereabouts of its history as a separate nation in whole or in part had closed. A new epoch was to open, and Edward was the man to mark the division between the past and the future in emphatic fashion. Hitherto, though statesmanlike in his views, he had been in actual deed both cruel and unjust to Wales, and allowed his agents to be still more so; but now that resistance was crushed he dropped the warrior and tyrant and showed himself the statesman

1282. Edward settles the new government of Wales.

that he was. Most of the Welshmen that had remained in arms received their pardons, though a few took service abroad. The King exacted no sanguinary vengeance, but followed, rather, the more merciful and practical course of providing against the chance of his Welsh subjects requiring it in future. He went to Wales with his Court and remained there for nearly three years. He made Rhuddlan his principal headquarters, rebuilding its ancient castle; and at Conway, Harlech, and Carnarvon, besides some less formidable fortresses, he left those masterpieces of defensive construction that have been the admiration of all subsequent ages. From Rhuddlan in due course he issued the famous statutes called by its name, which proclaimed at once the death-knell of Old Wales and the fact of its territorial fusion with the realm of England. The details of the settlement were laborious, and the spectacle of an English Court spending in all nearly three busy years in Wales is evidence of the thoroughness with which Edward did his work.

The Statutes of Rhuddlan.

It is enough here to say that with the exception of modern Denbighshire, which was left in lordships, Edward carved North Wales into the present counties of Flint, Anglesey, Carnarvon, and Merioneth. Powys and South Wales being honeycombed with Anglo-Norman lordships and reconciled Welsh chieftains, he shrank probably from disentangling a confusion that brought no particular danger to himself, and from a course that would have embroiled him with the whole feudal interest of the Marches.

Copyright F. Frith & Co.

CONWAY CASTLE.

The still mainly Welsh districts, however, of Cardigan and Carmarthen, he had already, as we have seen, formed into counties. They were now, like those of the North, to be governed by lieutenants, sheriffs, and justices, and in all things to resemble English counties, except in the privilege of sending representatives to Parliament. Wales was kept separate from England, however, in so far as its immediate feudal lord was not the King of England, but the King's eldest son; and the Principality of Wales at this time, it must be remembered, meant only the royal counties.

Edward's laws for the conquered country were just and his intention not ungenerous. He reduced the rentals hitherto due to the Welsh Princes and listened patiently to the grievances of the people. He enacted that both in counties and lordships the old Welsh laws should be those of the Welsh so far as possible, and that justice should be administered in both languages, and he sent the Archbishop of Canterbury on a long visitation to take note of the destruction to churches perpetrated during the recent wars, and to arrange for their repair.

Edward's intentions just.

He was severe on the bards, it is true, but he did not slaughter them, as an old fiction asserts. Their wandering avocations were sternly repressed, and with the business that he had in hand it is not easy to see what other course he could have taken with men whose trade then chiefly consisted in recalling the wrongs of Wales and urging revenge. The whole business was concluded by a great tournament at Nevin, on the Carnarvon coast, which was attended by the flower of Welsh, English, and Gascon chivalry.

When the King returned to London after his long absence, he went with splendid ceremonial and a vast procession to the Tower and to Westminster Abbey, causing the regalia of the exterminated Welsh Princes and the skull of St. David to be borne before him. Nor must one omit mention of the immortal but grim joke which tradition says that he played upon the Welsh nobility before leaving the country. For does not every schoolboy know how, having promised them a Prince who was born in Wales and could speak no English, he sent Queen Eleanor to Carnarvon for the birth of Edward the Second?

The King's return to London.

A good deal can be said of the century that was to elapse before our story opens, but not much that is of vital import. In 1295, thirteen years after the conquest, Madoc ap Meredith, a connection of Llewelyn's, made a last attempt to rouse the Welsh. It proved abortive, but was serious enough to stop Edward from going to France, and to take him down to Conway, where it is said that on a certain occasion a high tide cut him off from his men, and nearly delivered him into the hands of the insurgents.

1295.

It would be too much to say that the next hundred years in Wales were those of peace and prosperity. But by comparison with the past they might not untruly be called so. No serious friction occurred between the two races; while the long wars with France and

Wales through the fourteenth century.

constant broils with Scotland engrossed the attention of the Welsh aristocracy, both Norman and native. Nor, again, was it only the nobles and gentry that found respite from their domestic quarrels in a combined activity upon the unfortunate soil of France. Welsh soldiers as well as Welsh gentlemen served by thousands in the armies of England, and few people remember that about a third of the victorious army at Cressy were Welshmen. This long companionship in arms and partnership in almost unparallelled glories must have done something to lessen the instinctive antipathy with which the two peoples had from time immemorial regarded each other. Yet how much of the ancient enmity survived, only requiring some spark to kindle it, will be evident enough as I proceed to the main part of my story, and the doings of the indomitable Welshman who is its hero.

CHAPTER II

BIRTH AND EARLY LIFE

1359–1399

"　　.　　.　　.　　.　　.　　At my birth
The front of heaven was full of fiery shapes;
The goats ran from the mountains, and the herds
Were strangely clamorous to the frighted fields.
These signs have marked me extraordinary,
And all the courses of my life do show,
I am not in the roll of common men."

IN these famous lines the Glyndwr of Shakespeare, though not, perhaps, a very faithful portrait of the true Glyndwr, tells us of those dread portents which heralded his birth. Thus far, however, tradition rings true enough in the lines of the great poet, and is even shorn of some of the most fearsome details it has sent down to us through various channels. Shakespeare's Glyndwr might, for instance, have told us, what all Welshmen of his day were well assured of, that on that memorable night the horses of Griffith Vychan, his father, were found standing in their stables up to their fetlocks in blood; and how he himself, while still an infant in his nurse's arms, was accustomed to greet with demonstrations of delight the sight of a sword or spear and allow those

 C. H. Young.

DOLGELLY AND CADER IDRIS.

around him no peace till the deadly weapon was placed in his baby hand.

There is great uncertainty as to the day, and some disagreement as to the exact year, wherein old earth thus shook in labour with so heroic a soul. This divergency of opinion extends over the period of ten years, from 1349 to 1359. The evidence that seems to give the latter date unquestionable preference will be alluded to shortly. In any case the point to be noted is that the hero of this story, judged by the standard of his time, was quite advanced in life when he began the long and arduous undertaking that has made his name immortal, and cherished by his countrymen as the most famous of all names in their history. For there is no shadow of a doubt that if the Welsh people were polled upon the subject, Owen Glyndwr would stand, by an overwhelming majority, at the head of the list of national heroes. Whether rightly or wrongly he holds the first place among Welsh warrior patriots in the affections of his countrymen.

It was the fortune, as I have endeavoured to make plain in the introductory chapter, of a long succession of Welsh chieftains, to find themselves at the head of a people struggling desperately against conquest and absorption. It is no wonder that with such opportunities ever present, century after century, the list of those who seized them and won distinction and some measure of success, and thereby preserved their names to posterity, is no short one. It is not to the point that the field of their exploits was a small one, and the people who cherish their memory a small people,—so much more, rather, the honour, seeing the odds against which they contended with such rare tenacity; nor, again, is it to their discredit that English historians have done as a rule scant justice to the vigour of the old Welsh warriors. "Good wine needs no bush." The surface and the tongue of Wales to-day are sufficient evidence to the vitality of its people and their martial prowess in the days of old. Their heroes have happily too long been dust to suffer in reputation at the hands of the modern destroyer of historic ideals. But above them all, this last and most recent of patriots, Owen ap Griffith Vychan of Glyndyfrdwy, distinctly towers. Precisely why this should be is not readily explicable, and to very many educated Welshmen the fact is not acceptable. But it is unnecessary to advance here any reasons or theories for the particular preference accorded to Glyndwr. Whether worthy or not, the fame is his, and though, curiously enough, uncommemorated in marble, stone, or brass, and recorded by the poet and historian in a fragmentary and disconnected fashion, it is fame that seems to grow no dimmer with the lapse of time. Genealogy has charms for few people, and Welsh genealogy, to the Saxon who has not served some kind of apprenticeship to it, is notoriously formidable. But there will be Welsh readers of an assuredly more sympathetic turn of mind who, not having at their fingers' ends, perhaps, the details of the national hero's origin, will be not ungrateful for them.

Owen of Glyndyfrdwy, commonly called Owen Glyndwr, came of the princely house of Powys, and was a direct descendant in the male line of the celebrated Bleddyn ap Cynvyn, Prince of Powys, and for a short time of Gwynedd also, whose reign almost exactly covered the period of the Norman conquest of England. The second in descent from Bleddyn was the last Prince of United Powys, and this was Madoc ap Meredith, who died in 1159. Readers of the introductory chapter will remember that Powys, between the upper millstone of Norman power and the nether one of North Welsh patriotism, began to temporise and give way long before the Edwardian conquest. Its Princes would have been more than mortal if their politics had not been of an unsteady kind. They frankly accepted the Norman as "Emperor in London" somewhat early, thus accepting the inevitable, but could not resist the temptation when Welsh affairs were prospering to break away to the national side. While gaining at this cost some immunity from Norman greed and a measure of semi-independence, the Powys Princes were not wholly trusted by either party, and sometimes felt the vengeance of both. In 1159 Powysland fell in half; Powys Uchaf, or, roughly speaking, Montgomeryshire, being given to Madoc's famous nephew, Owen Cyfeiliog, warrior, poet, founder of Strata Marcella Abbey, and author of *The Hirlâs Horn*; Lower Powys, or Powys Fadog, the country of the Dee and Ceiriog, fell to Madoc's son, Griffith ap Madoc. This last was followed by another Madoc, who in 1200 founded the splendid Abbey of Valle Crucis, whose ruins, standing as they do in the loveliest nook of the Vale of Llangollen, are justly celebrated as presenting one of the most exquisite pictures of the kind in Britain. Beneath its grass-grown aisles lies the dust of the chieftain of this line of Powys. To a height of eight hundred feet above its crumbled walls and gables, still graceful in their decay, springs an isolated cone-shaped hill, on whose sharp crown stands a pile of ragged, splintered ruins placed in weird, suggestive fashion against a background of sky. This is Dinas Brân, the most proudly perched mediæval fortress in Wales, perhaps in all Britain. Here in this eagle's nest, swung betwixt earth and heaven, lived the Princes of Powys Fadog; and no more fitting refuge could be imagined for men who, like them, had sometimes to look eastward for their foes and sometimes to the west. It was in 1270, close to the final conquest, that Madoc's son Griffith died, after dividing his life between friendship with the English King and repentant alliances with his own race. He had married Emma, daughter of James, Lord Audley, who had done great service for Henry III. against the Welsh with a body of German cavalry. The death of this Griffith ap Madoc is the last event recorded in the Welsh Chronicle. It is supposed that the monks of Conway and Ystradfflur, who conjointly compiled it, could not bring themselves to put on record the sad events of the next twelve years, the last years of Welsh independence. Griffith's son, another Madoc, followed, and died in seven years, leaving two young sons, and dividing his inheritance between them. The elder, Llewelyn, had Dinas Brân with Yale and Bromfield,

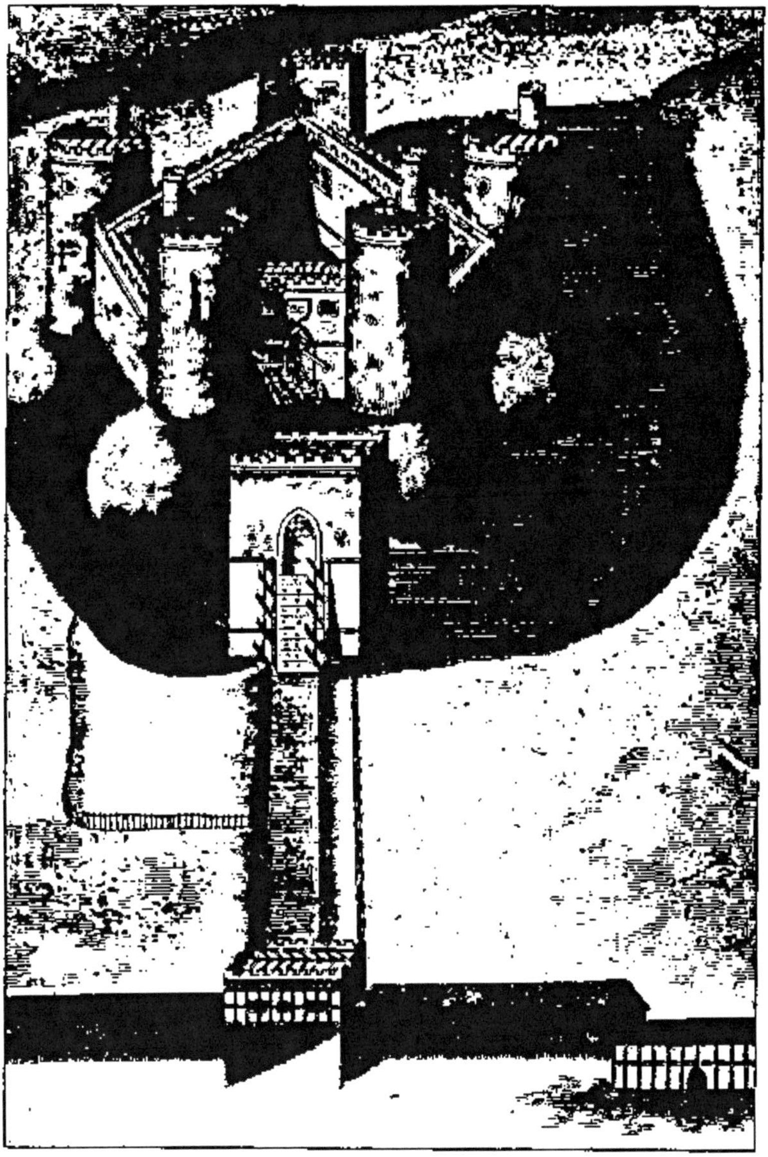

HOLT CASTLE.

FROM OLD PRINT.

while Griffith had Chirk and the territory attached to it. The orphan boys, their father having been tenant *in capite* of Edward the First, became that monarch's wards. Edward, as was customary, handed them over to the guardianship of two of his nobles, selecting in this case the great Marcher barons, Warren and Roger Mortimer. Trusteeships were not in those days, even under favourable conditions, the thankless and unprofitable affairs they are now. Warren had Llewelyn and Dinas Brân; Roger Mortimer, Griffith and Chirk. A Welsh ward in the hands of a Norman Lord Marcher must have been a lamb among wolves indeed; and as every one, no doubt, expected, under conditions so painfully tempting, the two boys in due course disappeared and were no more seen, while two magnificent castles arose at Chirk and Holt respectively, with a view to securing to these unjust stewards their ill-gotten territory. A black tale, which posterity has accepted, crept steadily about, to the effect that a deep pool in the Dee beneath Holt Castle could tell of a midnight tragedy therein enacted. The two boys at any rate disappeared, and the Earls, according to custom, succeeded to their estates. Nor is it very likely that the King, who himself had a slice of them in that outlying fragment of Flint still conspicuous on the map of England, asked many questions.

It seems that such conscience as Earl Warren possessed was smitten with compunction as years went on, and these twinges he thought to allay by restoring a fragment of the property to the family he had so outraged. When the King was sitting at Rhuddlan in 1282 the remorseful Earl petitioned that the manors of Glyndyfrdwy on the Dee beyond Llangollen and of Cynllaeth a few miles to the south of it, should be restored to Griffith, an uncle of the two boys whose fate weighed, let us hope, upon his soul.

In this manner Griffith succeeded to these estates and was known as Y Baron Gwyn, or "the White Baron," Lord of Glyndyfrdwy in Yale, dying about 1300. Fourth in direct descent from him and occupying the same position was Owen Glyndwr's father, Griffith Vychan (*i. e.*, "the little" or "the younger"), the preceding owner having been a Griffith too. To him succeeded Owen, as eldest son, holding his two manors, like his fathers before him, direct from the King. On his mother's side Owen's descent was quite as distinguished,—even more so if one is to believe that his mother, Elen, was a great-granddaughter of Catherine, the daughter of the last Llewelyn. Putting this aside, however, as mere tradition, it will be enough to say that Griffith Vychan's wife came from South Wales and was a daughter of Thomas ap Llewelyn ap Rhys, a descendant of the Princes of Deheubarth, Lord of Iscoede Vchirwen in Cardigan and of Trefgarn in the parish of Brawdy, Pembrokeshire. He had two daughters, co-heiresses, the elder of whom, Elen, married Owen's father, while the younger became the wife of Tudor ap Gronow of Penmynydd, the grandfather of the famous Owen Tudor. It will be seen, therefore, that Thomas ap Llewelyn was the ancestor both of Glyndwr and of our present King.

Owen was actually born in the South Welsh home

of his mother's family and inherited property from her which no doubt added to his wealth and consequence. Trefgarn Owen, Trefgarn West (or "*castel*"), still exists as a farmhouse, and the tradition that Owen was born in it is likely long to outlast the edifice itself. This event occurred probably in the year 1359, in the heyday of the successful wars in France, so that it is quite possible that Griffith Vychan may have been among the crowd of Welsh gentlemen who followed the banners of Edward the Black Prince across the Channel. This would quite account for the presence of Owen's mother at such a time in the home of her fathers; and as we know nothing of his childhood, it is perhaps permissible to indulge in conjectures that have about them some reasonable probability.

Of Owen's early manhood and domestic life, however, quite enough is known to dissipate the notion engendered by Shakespeare, and but faintly discouraged by English historians, that he was a wild Welsh chieftain, a sort of picturesque mountaineer. On the contrary, he was a man accustomed to courts and camps, and, judged by the standard of his time, an educated and polished gentleman. The first actual record we have of him is on September 3, 1386, when he gave evidence at Chester as a witness in the greatest and most prolonged lawsuit that had ever, in England, filled the public eye. This was the celebrated case of Scrope and Grosvenor, the point in dispute relating solely to a coat of arms. It lasted four years and nearly every prominent person in the country at one time or another gave evidence.

Among these appears the name of "*Oweyn Sire de Glendore de age XXVII ans et pluis*," also that of "*Tudor de Glindore*," his brother, who was some three years younger than Owen, and fell ultimately in his service. Of the nature of his evidence we know nothing. The entry is only valuable as giving weight to the year 1359 as the most likely date of his birth.

In the social economy of Wales, Owen's forbears, since they lost at the Edwardian conquest, in the manner related, the chieftainship of Powys Fadog, had been simply minor barons or private gentlemen of fair estate. They had nothing like the official position, the wealth, or the power of the Lord Marchers. Still they owed no allegiance, as did many of the lesser nobility, to any great Marcher baron, but held their estates in North Wales direct from the King himself. And we may well suppose that with the long memories of the Welsh no Marcher baron, no Mortimer, nor Gray, nor Talbot, whether in peace or war, was in their eyes so great a man as simple Owen of Glyndyfrdwy, on whose modest patrimony the vast estates of these interlopers encroached. As, in the ancient tribal laws of Wales, it took nine generations for an alien or servile family to qualify for admission to full rights, so it was equally difficult to make a medieval Welshman realise that the ejected landowners and princes of their own race were other than temporary sufferers. They could not believe that Providence intended to perpetuate so great an outrage. They recognised in their hearts no other owner but the old stock, whatever the exigencies of the times might compel them to do with their lips, and even their spears and bows, while every vagrant bard and minstrel helped to fix the sentiment more firmly in their breasts.

Owen himself, as a man of the world, had, of course, no such delusions. No one, however, when the time was ripe, knew better than he how to work upon the feelings of those who had. A family grievance of his own, as we have shown, he might justifiably have nursed, but there is no reason to suppose that he was on bad terms with the houses either of Warren or Mortimer. Indeed, he is said to have been esquire at one time to the Earl of Arundel. His local quarrels lay, as we shall see, to the north and rested wholly on personal grounds, having no relation whatever to the wrongs of his great-great-grandfather.

In the only signature extant of Owen previous to his assumption of princely honours, we find him describing himself as "Oweyn ap Griffith, Dominus de Glyn D'wfrdwy." To dwell upon the innumerable ways in which his name and title were spelt by Norman and Celtic writers, contemporary and otherwise, in times when writers' pens vaguely followed their ears, would be, of course, absurd. The somewhat formidable sounding name of Glyndyfrdwy simply means the Glen of the Dwrfdwy or Dyfrdwy, which in turn is the original and still the Welsh name for the river Dee. About the first syllable of this word philologists have no scope for disagreement, "Dwr" or "Dwfr" signifying water; but concerning the terminal syllable there is room for some difference of opinion. It will be sufficient for us here to say that the derivations which seem to the eye most obvious are not so much in favour as that from "Diw," sacred or divine. This attribute at any rate has been bestowed on the chief and most beautiful of North Welsh rivers by English and Welsh poets from Spenser to Tennyson and, according to the former, "by Britons long ygone."

In regard, however, to the pronunciation of the name of Owen's patrimony, when I have said that the very natives of the historic hamlet slur the name into something like Glyndowdy,—a rare luxury among the Welsh,—it is not surprising that Anglo-Norman chroniclers and others have made havoc of it with their phonetic spelling. Even Welsh writers have been unsteady upon the point. And Owen of Glyndyfrdwy probably figures under more designations than any hero who ever lived: Glendour, Glindor, Glindore, Glendurdy, Glyndurdu, and Glendowerdy, are but a few selected specimens.

English historians, with characteristic contempt of Welsh detail, have selected the last and the most unlikely of them all. In his own country Owen was generally known during his later life and ever since his death as Glyndwr, the spelling to which I have adhered in these pages. It may perhaps not be out of place to note that the Welsh "w" is equivalent to a "o͞o," and by a Welsh tongue the terminal "r" is, of course, strongly marked.

Of the early youth of Glyndwr history tells us nothing, nor, again, is it known what age he had reached when his father died and the estate came into his possession. It is supposed that like so many

POWYS CASTLE.

FROM AN OLD ENGRAVING FROM PAINTING BY W. DANIELLS.

Welshmen of his time he went to Oxford; but this, after all, must be mere surmise, though, judging by the bent of his life at that period, we seem to have good grounds for it. In such case it is likely enough that he took a leading part in the ferocious faction fights with which the jealousies of English, Welsh, and Irish students so often enlivened the cramped streets of medieval Oxford. It is quite certain, however, that Owen went to London and became a student of the Inns of Court, a course virtually confined in those times to the sons of the wealthy and well-born. There is something very natural in the desire of a large Welsh landowner of that time to familiarise himself with English law, for the two codes, Welsh and English, to say nothing of compromises between them, existed side by side over nearly all Wales, and one can well understand the importance of some knowledge of Anglo-Norman jurisprudence to a leading Welshman like Glyndwr, who must have had much to do, both directly and indirectly, with both kinds of courts. That he was no wild Welsh squire has been already shown, and it was not unnatural that a youth of handsome person, high lineage, and good estate should drift, when his law studies were completed, into the profession of arms and to the English Court. Here he soon found considerable favour and in course of time became squire of the body, or "scutiger," not, as most Welsh authorities have persisted, and still persist, to King Richard the Second, but to his cousin of Bolingbroke, the future Henry the Fourth. This latter view is certainly supported by the only documentary evidence extant, as Mr. Wylie in his able and exhaustive history of that monarch points out. "Regi moderno ante susceptum regnum," is the sentence in the *Annales* describing Glyndwr's position in this matter, and it surely removes any doubt that Bolingbroke is the King alluded to. In such case Owen must have shared those perils and adventures by land and sea in which the restless Henry engaged. It is strange enough, too, that men linked together in a relationship so intimate should have spent the last fifteen years of their lives in a struggle so persistent and so memorable as did these two. Bolingbroke began this series of adventures soon after the loss of his wife, about the year 1390, and we may therefore, with a fair probability of truth, picture Glyndwr at that grand tournament at Calais where Henry so distinguished himself, and poor Richard by comparison showed to such small advantage. He may also have been present at the capture of Tunis, where English and French to the wonder of all men fought side by side without friction or jealousy; or again with Bolingbroke on his long journey in 1393 to Jerusalem, or rather towards it, for he never got there. There were adventures, too, which Owen may have shared, with German knights upon the Baltic, and last, though by no means least, with Sigismund, King of Hungary, at that memorable scene upon the Danube when he was forced into his ships by the victorious Turks.

Yet the tradition is so strong that Glyndwr was in the personal service of Richard during the close of that unfortunate monarch's reign, that one hesitates to brush it aside from mere lack of written evidence. Nor indeed does the fact of his having been Henry's esquire constitute any valid reason for doing so. It is not very likely that, when the latter in 1398 was so unjustly banished by Richard to an uneventful sojourn in France, Glyndwr, with the cares of a family and estate growing upon him, would have been eager to share his exile. On the other hand, he must have been by that time well known to Richard, and with his Pembrokeshire property and connections may well, like so many Welshmen, have been tempted later on to embark in that ill-fated Irish expedition which promised plunder and glory, but turned out to be incidentally the cause of Richard's undoing. That this feckless monarch possessed some peculiar charm and a capacity for endearing individuals to his person seems tolerably evident, however strange. That the Welsh were devoted to him we know, so that perhaps the loyalty to Richard with which most Welsh writers credit Glyndwr arose from such personal service rendered after the departure of Bolingbroke for France. And it is quite possible that he went, as they assert, with the King on that last ill-timed campaign which cost him his crown.

Some declare that he was among the small knot of faithful followers who, when his army abandoned the slothful Richard on his return to Pembrokeshire from Ireland, rode across country with him to Conway, where Salisbury in despair had just been compelled to disband his freshly mustered Welshmen for lack of food and pay. If this is true, Glyndwr, who most certainly never lost battles from sloth or timidity when he became in one sense a king, must have witnessed with much sympathy the lamentations of the faithful Salisbury:

> "O, call back yesterday, bid time return,
> And thou shalt have ten thousand fighting men;
> To-day, to-day, unhappy day too late,
> O'erthrows thy joys, friends, fortune, and thy state."

All this occurred in September of the year 1399. Henry, taking advantage of Richard's absence, had landed, it will be remembered, at Ravenspur in Yorkshire some two months earlier. He found discontent with the existing state of affairs everywhere prevalent and the recognised heir to the throne but lately dead. The situation was tempting to a degree. Bolingbroke's first intention had almost certainly aimed at nothing more than the recovery of his own immense estates of which he had been most unjustly and unscrupulously deprived by his royal cousin. But unexpected temptations confronted him. He was met on landing by the Percys and soon afterwards by other great nobles, who, from what motives it matters little, encouraged him to seize the throne. To make a short story of a famous episode in English history, Bolingbroke found himself by September, when Richard was returning with fatal tardiness from Ireland, not indeed actually crowned, but in full possession of London and other districts and virtually acknowledged as King. In the same month he was heading a triumphant march by way of Bristol at the head of a great and gathering army towards North Wales, where Richard lay, as we

 F. Frith & Co.

LLANGOLLEN AND DINAS BRÂN.

have seen, at Conway, helplessly wringing his hands and cursing the fate he had brought upon himself.

According to the Welsh version, Glyndwr must have been present when Percy, Earl of Northumberland, who in years to come was to be so vitally bound up with his fortunes, entered the great hall of Conway Castle, to all appearances a friendly and unarmed envoy of Henry of Bolingbroke. We all remember his soft speech and how with the utmost deference and humility he told King Richard that all his dear cousin required of him was to ride back by his side to London and there summon a Parliament, and bring to justice certain persons, who, for the past few years, had been his evil counsellors. If Glyndwr was in truth there, he must almost certainly have seen these two illustrious personages commit that astounding piece of perjury and sacrilege in Conway church, when they knelt side by side and swore before the altar and upon the sacred elements that their intentions towards each other were wholly friendly and without guile. He must then, too, have heard King Richard, when scarcely off his knees, swear that if only he could get his dear cousin of Bolingbroke into his hands he would put him to such a cruel death it should be long spoken of even in Turkey. Perhaps it was the memory of the spectacle that decided Glyndwr on certain occasions in his after life to show a curious reluctance to "put his trust in princes," however loyal in the abstract he might be to their memory. If we follow the Welsh tradition, he saw this game of duplicity to the bitter end and made one of the small band of horsemen who crossed the estuary of the Conway in the dawn of an autumn morning with the puling king on their way to Rhuddlan Castle, whose ivy-mantled ruins still make such a charming picture amid the meadows where the Clwyd winds its tidal course towards the sea. Long before Richard got there, and while still surmounting the steep headland of Rhos above Old Colwyn, he caught sight of the troops which the crafty Northumberland had left there in concealment. It was too late to retreat. The waves roared far beneath him and rocky crags towered high above his head. He saw that he was undone and read in the situation the black treachery he would have himself dealt out with scant scruple to anyone lingering in the path of self-indulgence, which he had so long trodden.

> "O that I were as great
> As is my grief, or greater than my name,
> Or that I could forget what I have been,
> Or not remember what I must be now."

Amid faces from which the friendly mask had already half fallen and spears that may well have had an ominous glitter in his eyes, the disheartened King passed on to Rhuddlan and from Rhuddlan to the strong castle of Flint. Here in the morning came to him his cousin of Bolingbroke, inquiring, among other things, whether he had broken his fast, for he had a long ride before him. Whereat Richard demanded what great army was that which darkened the sands of Dee below the castle walls. Henry replied curtly that they were Londoners for the most part, and that they had come to take him prisoner to the Tower, and nothing else would satisfy them. If Glyndwr were indeed present it must have been a strange enough sight for him, this meeting of his former patron and his present master, under such sinister circumstances, in the gloomy chambers of Flint Castle. If he were still here it may be safely assumed that, like the rest of Richard's escort, he went no farther. Even if he were absent, quietly hawking and hunting at Glyndyfrdwy, there would be nothing irrelevant in calling to the reader's recollection a famous episode, the chief actors in which had so far-reaching an influence on the Welsh hero's life; how all semblance of respect for the King's person was dropped; how, mounted of design upon a sorry nag, he was led with many indignities along the weary road to London and there made to read his own abdication in favour of his captor and cousin; and how he was hurried from fortress to fortress, till at Pontefract he ended his misspent life in a manner that to this day remains a mystery—all this is a matter of historic notoriety. Whether the unfortunate Richard died of grief, failing health, and lack of attention, or whether he was the victim of deliberate foul play, only concerns us here from the fact of his name occurring so frequently in our story as a rallying-cry for Henry's enemies, and from the mystery attaching to the manner of his death being for years a genuine grievance among the rank and file of the disaffected, and a handy weapon for their more designing leaders.

How much of his life Glyndwr had so far spent in his native valleys of the Dee or Cynllaeth it is impossible to guess. Perhaps at odd times a good deal of it; seeing that he was now over forty, had found time to marry a wife, a lady of the neighbourhood, by whom he had become the father of a numerous family, and to win for himself great popularity and a name for hospitality. The famous Welsh poet, Gryffydd Llwyd, much better known by his bardic name of "Iolo Goch," or the Red Iolo, was his constant friend and companion at this time, and became, later on, the Laureate of his Court and of his cause. In the thick volume which the extant works of Iolo fill he has left us a graphic though somewhat fantastic picture of Glyndwr's domestic life. I have already shown how the Welsh chieftain owned the two estates of Glyndyfrdwy and Sycherth or Cynllaeth in his native district, while from his mother he inherited property in Pembroke. The two former places were near together. If the mountain fringes of Glyndyfrdwy, which ran east and west, did not actually touch the Sycherth estate, which ran north and south with the waters of the Cynllaeth brook, there could have been little but the deep Vale of the Ceiriog to divide them. There were mansions upon both estates, and, though Glyndyfrdwy was the more important property, it was in the less striking but still charming valley down which the Cynllaeth babbles to meet the Tanat beneath the woodlands of Llangedwyn, that Sycherth or Sychnant, the more imposing of Glyndwr's two houses, was situated. This valley lies snugly tucked away behind the first

Copyright W. D. Haydon.

SYCHARTH, FROM THE SOUTH.

ridge of hills which rises abruptly behind Oswestry and so conspicuously marks the Welsh frontier. It practically skirts the English border, and Offa's Dyke trails its still obvious course along the lofty summit of its eastern boundary. Scarcely anywhere, indeed, does the Principality begin in a social sense with such striking abruptness. Once over the hill from Shropshire, and within a short hour's drive from Oswestry, and you are for every practical purpose in the heart of Celtic Wales. Few travellers come this way, for it is on the road to nowhere that the outside world takes count of, and few strangers but an occasional antiquary ever see the well-defined and flat-topped tumulus on which the manor house of the most famous of all Welshmen stood. It lies in a meadow between a wooded hill and the Cynllaeth brook, not far from Llansilin, and is very conspicuous from the road leading up the valley to the little hamlet, whose churchyard holds the dust of another famous Welshman, the seventeenth-century poet, Huw Morris. The inner and the outer moat of Sycherth are still more or less perfect, and there are even yet, or were not long ago, plain traces of stonework beneath the turf. It will be well, however, to let Iolo, who was there so much and knew it so well, tell us what it looked like in his time, five hundred years ago.

There was a gate-house, he says, a strong tower, and a moat. The house contained nine halls, each furnished with a wardrobe filled with the raiment of Owen's retainers. Near the house on a verdant bank was a wooden building supported upon posts and roofed with tiles. Here were eight apartments in which the guests slept. There was a church, too, in the form of a cross, and several chapels. The mansion was surrounded with every convenience and every essential for maintaining a profuse hospitality: a park, warren and pigeon-house, mill, orchards, and vineyard; a fish-pond well stocked with "gwyniads" from Bala Lake, a heronry, and plenty of game of all sorts. The cook, Iolo declares with much enthusiasm, was one of the very best; and the hospitality of the establishment so unstinted that the office of gate porter was a sinecure. Our bard indeed makes his poetic lips literally smack over the good things beneath which Glyndwr's table groaned. Nor does he forget his hostess:

> "The best of wives,
> Happy am I in her wine and metheglyn;
> Eminent woman of a knightly family,
> Honourable, beneficent, noble,
> Her children come forward two by two,
> A beautiful nest of chieftains."

Charming, however, as is the site of Sycharth, nestling beneath its wooded hill and looking out towards the great masses of the Berwyn Mountains, it would ill compare with that almost matchless gem of Welsh scenery, where the vales of Edeyrnion and Llangollen meet among the mantling woodlands and sounding gorges of Glyndyfrdwy. It is a curiously apt coincidence that one of the most romantic spots in Wales should have been the cradle of the man who is without doubt the most romantic personage in

Welsh history. Scarcely anyone, as I have said, ever finds his way to Sycharth; but thousands of travellers every summer follow by road or rail that delightful route which, hugging the Dee from Ruabon almost to its source beyond Bala Lake, reveals new beauties at every turn. Such being the case I would venture to ask any intending traveller from Ruabon to Bala and Dolgelly to take special note of a spot just five minutes to the westward of Glyndyfrdwy station, where the wide torrent of the Dee, after clinging to the railroad for some distance, takes a sudden bend to the north. Precisely here, but perched high upon the other side of the railroad and so nearly overhanging it as not to be readily visible, is a green tumulus crowned by a group of wind-swept fir trees. This is locally known as "Glyndwr's Mount," not because, as was probably the case at Sycharth, it was erected as a foundation for the chieftain's house,—since this one here is evidently prehistoric,—but merely from the fact that the house stood at its foot. Vague traces of it are still visible beneath the turf of the narrow meadow that lies squeezed in between the Holyhead Road on the upper side and the river and railroad on the lower side.* Whether Sycharth was Owen's favourite home in peace or not, Glyndyfrdwy was most certainly his more natural headquarters in war, while in his own

* A friend of the writer, who lived to an advanced age, was told in his youth by old men in the neighbourhood that they could remember when there was a good deal of stonework to be seen lying about. Now, however, there is little to mark the spot but the suggestive undulations of the turf.

district. Both, however, were burnt down by Prince Henry, as we shall see later on, in one of his expeditions against the Welsh. As for the mound, it is a notable landmark, being one of a series which are sprinkled along the Dee valley in such fashion as to indicate beyond a doubt that if they were indeed the tombs of dead warriors, they were also most admirable signal-stations for living ones. But whatever the origin of this one it had at any rate no connection with times so recent as those of Glyndwr. The only surviving relic of that hero's residence is a long, narrow oaken table of prodigious thickness, which is yet treasured in a neighbouring farmhouse. A meadow below is still called "Parliament field," while the massive old stone homestead of Pen-y-bont, half a mile up the valley, contains a portion of the walls which formed, it is believed, Glyndwr's stables, or, more probably, his farm buildings. But as many of these local points will come up in the course of my story, it is time to say something of the lady who, so entirely blest in her earlier years, was to spend her later ones amid such stress and storm, and to share so precarious a crown.

This lady bountiful of Sycharth and Glyndyfrdwy, so extolled by Iolo, came of a notable Flintshire house. She was the daughter of Sir David Hanmer of Hanmer, a family long settled in that detached fragment of Flint known then as Maelor Seisnig, or "English Maelor." Sir David had been appointed by Richard the Second one of the Justices of the King's Bench and at the same time knighted. There are Hanmers even yet in those parts; till comparatively lately there were still Hanmers of Hanmer. More enduring than a human stock, there are monuments in stone and brass that tell the story, common enough in England, of a family that for centuries were great in their own district without ever making their name a familiar one to the average British ear. The Hanmers, too, were a fair specimen of many families in the Welsh Marches who had both English and Welsh blood in their veins, and whose sympathies were divided when social animosities took a warlike turn. It was very much so indeed with the Hanmers when Glyndwr's war by degrees forced everyone to take a side in self-defence. Of Glyndwr's sons only two are directly mentioned, Griffith and Meredith, both of whom we shall find fighting by his side, but at such an advanced stage of the struggle that it seems probable they were but boys when hostilities broke out. We hear dimly of three more, Madoc, Thomas, and John. Of the daughters somewhat more is known; and they must for the most part have been older, since it seems that three were married before the troubles began. The eldest, Isabel, became the wife of a Welshman, Adda ab Iorwerth Ddu. The second, Elizabeth, married Sir John Scudamore of Kent Church and Holme Lacy in Herefordshire, whose descendants still retain the name and the first of these historic manors. Another, Janet, was given to John Crofts of Croft Castle in the same county, and the youngest, Margaret, called after her mother, took another Herefordshire gentleman, Roger Monnington of Monnington. The most celebrated was the fourth daughter, Jane, whom we shall find being united under romantic circumstances to her father's illustrious captive and subsequent ally, Sir Edmund Mortimer. She it is, of course, whom Shakespeare brings upon his stage and, in her song to Hotspur and Mortimer,

> "Makes Welsh as sweet as ditties highly penned,
> Sung by a fair queen in a summer's bower."

The Commote of Glyndyfrdwy, which formed Owen's Dee property, lay in the then newly formed county of Merioneth, though it was wedged in by the Marcher lordships of Chirk, Bromfield, and Yale on the east; while to the north, Denbighshire as yet having no existence, it touched the Norman lordships of Ruthin and Denbigh in the Vale of Clwyd. But Glyndwr held his estates direct from the King, having manor courts of his own, and resorting in more important matters to the assize towns of Dolgelly and Harlech. Corwen must have been actually on his property but, though a notable gathering-spot in war time, it had no corporate existence, and was probably even more insignificant in size than the other Merioneth towns. The Welsh did not herd together in towns or villages. Each individual or group of individuals dwelt on their small homesteads scattered about the hillsides or cut out of the forests which then covered so much of the country and had contributed so greatly to its defence.

Owen in his home life must have been something of an unique personality. He was the equal in breeding and in knowledge of the world of the great barons around him,—the Greys, Talbots, and Charltons,—and of sufficient estate to be himself a grand seigneur. Yet his hospitable house must have offered a remarkable contrast in the eyes of the natives to the grim fortresses of Chirk, or Dinas Brân, or Ruthin, whose owners' mission in life, so far as the Welsh were concerned, was to make themselves unpleasant. Their claws, it is true, had been considerably cut down by Edward the First, but the same blood was there; and the habit of former years, which looked upon the killing of a Welshman as a meritorious action, only wanted an opportunity to reassert itself.

Owen's rent-roll was about two hundred pounds a year, and some slight mental effort is required to realise that this was a very large one, both actually when judged by the contemporary value of money, and relatively as regards the financial standing of private landowners, particularly in Wales, where this was low. Owen was probably one of the richest native Welshmen of his day. Few if any in the north had such an opportunity of showing the contrast between the simple and profuse hospitality of a native aristocrat, and the stiff, contemptuous solemnity of the lord of a Norman fortress. It was easy enough for the descendant of Madoc ap Griffith to make himself popular upon the the banks of the upper Dee, and Owen seems to have added a desire to do so to the personal magnetism that the whole story of his life shows him to have possessed in a very high degree. All the bards of his own time and that immediately following unite in this praise of his hospitality.

Amid much fanciful exaggeration, such for instance as that which compares Sycherth to "Westminster Abbey and Cheapside," there is no doubt about the esteem and admiration in which Owen was held by the Welsh and particularly by the bards who lived at free quarters in his roomy halls. But all this began before he had any idea of utilising his position and popularity in the manner that has made him immortal. There is really no authority at all for making him a follower of Richard. All Wales and Cheshire were indignant at the King's deposition and treatment, and Glyndwr, even supposing his Irish expedition to have been mythical, may well have shared this indignation. But in such a case his antecedents were, from private attachments, wholly Lancastrian. Not only had he been Bolingbroke's squire, but his former master, the Earl of Arundel, had been a pronounced foe of the late King. Discontent and turbulence were brooding everywhere, but we have no reason to suppose that Glyndwr at this date, the last year of the century, had any excuse whatever for entering into dynastic quarrels. On the contrary, unless the story of his recent connection with Richard be true, he had much reason to be contented with Bolingbroke's accession. At this moment he was in all probability living quietly at Sycherth, hunting deer amid the birchen woods and bracken glades of the Berwyn and hawking in the meadows of Llansilin. Amid all the pleasures, however, which filled his rural life there rankled one deep and bitter grievance, and this concerned the upland tract of Croesau that lay upon the north-western fringe of his Glyndyfrdwy manor, over which he and his powerful neighbour, Reginald Grey, Lord of Ruthin, had been falling out this many a long day. The details of this quarrel, the primary cause of that decade of strife which desolated Wales and profoundly influenced the reign and embittered the life of Henry of Bolingbroke, must be reserved for another chapter.

CHAPTER III

GLYNDWR AND LORD GREY OF RUTHIN

1400–1401

REGINALD, LORD GREY, of Ruthin, the prime cause of all the wars that devastated Wales and the English Marches throughout the first ten years of the fifteenth century, was a typical Lord Marcher, and was perhaps the worst of a fierce, unscrupulous, and pitiless class. His ancestors had been in the Vale of Clwyd for over a hundred years. At Edward's conquest the first Earl had been planted by the King at Ruthin to overawe the Welsh of what is now northern Denbighshire and of the two recently created counties of Flint and Carnarvon which lay upon either side. There were other Lord Marchers and other English garrisons between Chester and Carnarvon, but at the time this story opens the Greys were beyond a doubt the most ardent and conspicuous props of the English Crown. The great Red Castle at Ruthin had risen in Edward's time beside the upper waters of the Clwyd, and its ample ruins still cluster round the modern

RUTHIN CASTLE.

FROM OLD PRINT.

towers where the successors of the fierce Lord Marchers exercise a more peaceful sway.

Around Ruthin Castle, as at Denbigh, Conway, and Carnarvon, a group of English adventurers—soldiers, tradesmen, clerks, and gentlemen—had gathered together and built for themselves habitations, aided by favourable charters from the King, and still greater favours from their lord, who leant upon their services in times of danger. They led profitable, if sometimes anxious lives. Welsh and English alike pleaded before the lordship courts, whose records may still be read by the curious in such matters. Both Welsh and English laws, theoretically at any rate, were administered within the lordship, but as the Lord Marcher was, within his own domain, a law unto himself, the state of affairs that existed at Ruthin and similar places was complicated and is not immediately pertinent to this story. It will be quite accurate enough for present purposes to describe Grey as surrounded and supported by armed burghers and other dependents, mainly but not wholly of English blood, while the mass of the Welsh within his lordship, gentle and simple, remained obedient to his rule from fear and not from love. I need not trouble the reader with the limitations of his territory, but merely remark that it bordered upon that of Owen.

Now, upon the wild upland between the Dee valley and the watershed of the Clwyd, lay the common of Croesau, whose disputed ownership eventually set Wales and England by the ears. This strip of land had originally belonged to Owen's estate of

Glyndyfrdwy. Lord Grey, however, in Richard the Second's time, had, in high-handed fashion, appropriated it to himself on the sole and poor excuse that it marched with his own domain. Glyndwr, being at that time probably no match for Grey at the game of physical force, possessed his fiery soul in patience, and carried the dispute in a peaceful and orderly manner to the King's court in London. Here the justice of his claim was recognised; he won his suit and Lord Grey was compelled to withdraw his people from the disputed territory, cherishing, we may well believe, an undying grudge against the Welshman who, before the eyes of all the world and in an English court of justice, had got the better of him.

Now, however, a new King was upon the throne, and Owen apparently out of favour. The opportunity was too good an one to be missed by the grasping Norman, who, driving Owen's people off the disputed territory, annexed it once more to his own estate. Glyndwr nevertheless, whatever the cause may have been, proved himself even under this further provocation a law-abiding person, and, refraining from all retaliation, carried his suit once more to London and laid it before the Parliament which Henry summoned in the spring of 1400, six months after he had seized the throne. But Owen, though he had been esquire to the King, was now wholly out of favour, so much so as greatly to support the tradition that he had served the unfortunate Richard in a like capacity. His suit was not even accorded the compliment of a hearing, but was dismissed with contemptuous brevity. Trevor, Bishop of St. Asaph, who was then about the King's person and deeply in his confidence, protested in vain against the unjust and ill-advised course. As a Welshman, familiar with the condition of his own country, he solemnly warned the authorities against provoking a man who, though of only moderate estate, was so powerful and so popular among his own people.

The Bishop's pleadings were of no avail. "What care we for the barefooted rascals?" was the scornful reply. The Welsh were in fact already in an electrical condition. In spite of their general discontent with English rule, they had been attached to Richard, and with that strength of personal loyalty which in a Celtic race so often outweighs reason, they resented with heartfelt indignation the usurpation of Bolingbroke. They were very far from sure that Richard was even dead. If he were, then Henry had killed him, which made matters worse. But if in truth he actually still lived, they were inclined to murmur as loudly and with as much show of reason at his dethronement. Richard, it will be remembered, after having been compelled publicly and formally to abdicate the throne, had been imprisoned for a time in the Tower, and then secretly conveyed from castle to castle till he reached Pontefract, where he ended his wretched life. The manner of his death remains to this day a mystery, as has been intimated already. Whether he was murdered by Henry's orders or whether his weakened constitution succumbed to sorrow and confinement or bad treatment, no one will ever know. But his body, at any rate, was brought to London and there exposed in St. Paul's Cathedral for the space of three days, that all the world might see that he was in truth dead. The men of Wales and the North and West of England had to take all this on hearsay, and were readily persuaded that some trickery had been played on the Londoners and that some substitute for Richard had been exposed to their credulous gaze. For years it was the policy of Henry's enemies to circulate reports that Richard was still alive, and, as we shall see in due course, his ghost was not actually laid till the battle of Shrewsbury had been fought and won by Henry. Indeed, so late as 1406 the old Earl of Northumberland alleged, in a letter, the possibility of his being alive, while even seven years after this Sir John Oldcastle declared he would never acknowledge Parliament so long as his master, King Richard, still lived.

Glyndwr, after the insults that he had received in London, returned home, as may well be conceived, not in the best of tempers; Grey, however, was to perpetrate even a worse outrage upon him than that of which he had already been guilty and of a still more treacherous nature. It so happened that at this time the King was preparing for that expedition against the Scots which started in July, 1400. Among the nobility and gentry whom he summoned to his standard was Glyndwr, and there is no reason to assume that the Welshman would have failed to answer the call. The summons, however, was sent through Lord Grey, in his capacity of chief

Marcher in North Wales; and Grey, with incredibly poor spite, kept Owen in ignorance of it till it was too late for him either to join the King's army or to forward an explanation. Glyndwr was on this account credited at Court with being a malcontent and a rebel; and as there had been some brawling and turbulence upon the Welsh border the future chieftain's name was included among those whom it was Grey's duty, as it was his delight, to punish. There is no evidence that Owen had stirred. It is possible he might have made himself disagreeable to Grey upon the marches of their respective properties. It would be strange if he had not. There is no mention, however, of his name in the trifling racial disturbances that were natural to so feverish a time.

It seems pretty evident that if the malicious Lord Marcher had rested content with his plunder and let sleeping dogs lie, Owen, and consequently Wales, would never have risen. This ill-advised baron, however, was by no means content. He applied for further powers in a letter which is now extant, and got leave to proceed in force against Owen, among others, as a rebel, and to proclaim his estates, having an eye, no doubt, to their convenient propinquity in the event of confiscation.

But before Owen comes upon the scene, and during this same summer, a most characteristic and entertaining correspondence was being carried on between the irascible Lord Grey and a defiant gentleman of North Wales, Griffith ap Dafydd ap Griffith, the "strengest thief in Wales," Grey calls him, which is to say that he accuses him of carrying off some horses from his park at Ruthin. The letters, which are in Sir Thomas Ellis's collection, are much too long to reproduce, but they show unmistakably and not without humour, the relations which existed between Lord Grey and some of his Welsh neighbours, who, already turbulent, were later on to follow Glyndwr into the field of battle. The King, before starting for Scotland and before getting Grey's letters, had commanded his Lord Marchers to use conciliation to all dissatisfied Welshmen and to offer free pardons to any who were openly defying his authority.

Griffith ap Dafydd, it seems, had been prominent among these restive souls, but under a promise, he declares in his letter, of being made the Master Forester and "Keyshat" of Chirkeland under the King's charter, he had presented himself at Oswestry and claimed both the pardon and the office. In the last matter his claim was scouted, according to his own account, with scandalous breach of faith, and even his bodily safety did not seem wholly secure from the King's friends. He narrates at some length the story of his wrongs, and tells Grey that he has heard of his intention to burn and slay in whatever country he [Griffith] is in. "Without doubt," he continues "as many men as ye slay and as many houses as ye burn for my sake, as many will I burn and slay for your sake," and "doute not that I will have bredde and ale of the best that is in your Lordschip." There is something delightfully inconsequent in Griffith's method of ending this fire-breathing epistle: "Wretten in grete haste at the Park of Brunkiffe the XIth day of June. I can no more, but God kepe your Worschipful estate in prosperity."

Grey of Ruthin was filled with wrath at this impudence and replied to the "strengest thief in Wales" at great length, reserving his true sentiments, however, for the conclusion, where he bursts into rhyme: "But we hoope we shall do thee a pryve thyng: A roope, a ladder and a ring, heigh in a gallowes for to heng. And thus shall be your endyng. And he that made the be ther to helpyng. And we on our behalf shall be well willing for thy letter is knowlechyng."

It is quite evident that the Greys had not lived, aliens though they were, in the land of bards for five generations for nothing. Full of wrath, and by no means free from panic, Grey writes off in all haste to the young Prince Henry, who is acting as regent during his father's absence in the north. He encloses a duplicate of his answer to the "strengest thief in Wales" and advises the Prince of the "Misgovernance and riote which is beginning heer in the Marches of North Wales." He begs for a fuller commission to act against the rebels, one that will enable him to pursue and take them in the "Kyng's ground"; in the counties, that is to say, where the King's writ runs, and not merely in the lordships which covered what are now the counties of Denbigh and Montgomery. "But worshipful and gracious Lorde, ye most comaunden the Kynge's officers in every Cuntree to do the same." Grey goes on to declare that there are many officers, some in the King's shires, others in the lordships of Mortimer at Denbigh and of Arundel at Dinas Brân and in Powys-land, that are "kin unto these men that be risen, and tyll ye putte these officers in better governance this Countrie of North Wales shall nevere have peese." He enclosed also the letter of the "strengest thief," and begs the Prince to read it and judge for himself what sort of people he has to face. He urges him to listen carefully to the full tidings that his poor messenger and esquire Richard Donne will give him, and to take counsel with the King for providing some more sufficient means of curbing the turbulent Welshmen than he now has at his disposal. "Else trewly hitt will be an unruly Cuntree within short time."

About the same time similar despatches to the Prince sitting in Council were flying across Wales penned by one of the King's own officers, the Chamberlain of Carnarvon. These informed the authorities, among other things, that the Constable of Harlech had trustworthy evidence of a certain Meredith ap Owen, under whose protection it may be mentioned Griffith ap Dafydd, Grey's correspondent, lived, being in secret negotiation with the men of the outer isles ("owt yles") of Scotland, "through letters in and owt," that these Scottish Celts were to land suddenly at Abermaw (Barmouth), and that Meredith had warned his friends to be in readiness with horses and harness against the appointed time. It was also rumoured from this same source upon the Merioneth coast that men were buying and even stealing horses, and providing themselves with saddles, bows, arrows, and armour. "Recheles men of divers Countries," too, were assembling in desolate and wild places and meeting privily, though their councils were still kept secret, and by these means the young men of Wales were being greatly demoralised.

No special notice seems to have been taken of these urgent warnings by those whom the King during his absence in the north had left to guard his interests. Tumults and disturbances continued both in Wales and on the Marches throughout the summer, but nothing in the shape of a general rising took place till the luckless Grey, armed perhaps with the fresh powers he had sought for, singled out Glyndwr again as the object of his vengeance. Glyndwr had shown no signs as yet of giving trouble. His name is not mentioned in the correspondence of this summer, although he was the leading and most influential Welshman upon the northern Marches. He or his people may have given Grey some annoyance, or been individually troublesome along the boundaries of the property of which he had robbed them. But the Lord Marcher in all likelihood was merely following up his old grudge in singling out Owen for his first operations, though it is possible that, having regard to the latter's great influence and the seething state of Wales, he thought it politic to remove a man who, smarting under a sense of injustice, might recommend himself for every reason as a capable leader to his countrymen. One would have supposed that the "strengest thief in Wales" would have claimed Grey's first attention, but Griffith ap

Dafydd, who dates his letter from "Brunkiffe,"* a name that baffles identification, was very likely out of ordinary reach. However that may be, the Lord of Ruthin, collecting his forces and joining them to those of his brother Marcher, Earl Talbot of Chirk, moved so swiftly and unexpectedly upon Owen that he had only just time to escape from his house and seek safety in the neighbouring woodlands before it was surrounded by his enemies. Whether this notable incident, so fraught with weighty consequences, took place upon the Dee or the Cynllaeth—at Glyndyfrdwy, that is to say, or at Sycherth—is uncertain; conjecture certainly favours the latter supposition, since Sycherth was beyond a doubt the most important of Owen's mansions, as well as his favourite residence. Nearly all historians have hopelessly confounded these two places, which are seven or eight miles apart as the crow flies and cut off from each other by the intervening masses of the Berwyn Mountains. Seeing, however, that Pennant, the Welshman of topographical and archeological renown, falls into this curious mistake and never penetrated to the real Sycherth or seemed aware of its existence, it is not surprising that most English and even Welsh writers have followed suit.

It is of no importance to our story which of the two manors was the scene of Owen's escape and his enemy's disappointment, but the attack upon him filled the Welshman's cup of bitterness to the brim. It was the last straw upon a load of foolish and wanton insult; and of a truth it was an evil day for

*Possibly Brynkir near Criccieth.

Copyright J. Bartlett.

AN OLD STREET, SHREWSBURY.

Grey of Ruthin, and for his master, Henry, that saw this lion hunted from his lair; and an evil day perhaps for Wales, for, though it gave her the hero she most cherishes, it gave her at the same time a decade of utter misery and clouded the whole of the fifteenth century with its disastrous effects.

Henry was very anxious to conciliate the Welsh. Sore and angry as they were at the deposition of their favourite Richard, the desultory lawlessness which smouldered on throughout the summer would to a certainty have died out, or remained utterly impotent for serious mischief, before the conciliatory mood of the King, had no leader for the Welsh been found during his absence in the north. Henry had beyond question abetted his council in their contemptuous treatment of his old esquire's suit against Grey. But he may not unnaturally have had some personal grievance himself against Owen as a sympathiser with Richard; a soreness, moreover, which must have been still further aggravated if the tradition of his taking service under the late King be a true one. Of the attachment of the Welsh to Richard, and their resentment at Henry's usurpation, we get an interesting glimpse from an independent source in the manuscript of M. Creton, a French knight who fought with Richard in Ireland and remained for some time after his depositition at the English Court. He was present at the coronation of young Prince Henry as Prince of Wales, which took place early in this year. "Then arose Duke Henry," he says, "the King's eldest son, who humbly knelt before him, and he made him Prince of Wales and gave him the land. But I think he must conquer it if he will have it, for in my opinion the Welsh would on no account allow him to be their lord, for the sorrow, evil, and disgrace which the English together with his father had brought on King Richard."

The Welsh had now found a leader indeed and a chief after their own heart. Owen was forty-one, handsome, brave, and, as events were soon to prove, as able as he was courageous. Above all, the blood of Powys and of Llewelyn ab Iorwerth flowed in his veins. He was just the man, not only to lead them but to arouse the enthusiasm and stir up the long-crushed patriotism of an emotional and martial race. He seems to have stept at once to the front, and to have been hailed with acclamation by all the restless spirits that had been making the lives of the Lord Marchers a burden to them throughout the summer, and a host of others who had hitherto had no thought of a serious appeal to arms. His standard, the ancient red dragon of Wales upon a white ground, was raised either at, or in the neighbourhood of, his second estate of Glyndyfrdwy, possibly at Corwen, where many valleys that were populous even then draw together, and where the ancient British camp of Caer Drewyn, lifted many hundred feet above the Dee, suggests a rare post both for outlook, rendezvous, and defence. Hither flocked the hardy mountaineers with their bows and spears, not "ragged barefoots," as English historians, on the strength of a single word, *nudepedibus*, used by an Englishman in London, have called them in careless and offhand fashion, but men in great part well armed, as became a people accustomed to war both at home and abroad, and well clad, as became a peasantry who were as yet prosperous and had never known domestic slavery. From the vales of Edeyrnion and Llangollen; from the wild uplands, too, of Yale and Bryn Eglwys; from the fertile banks of the Ceiriog and the sources of the Clwyd; and from the farther shores of Bala Lake, where beneath the shadow of the Arans and Arenig fawr population clustered thick even in those distant days, came pouring forth the tough and warlike sons of Wales. In the van of all came the bards, carrying not only their harps but the bent bow, symbol of war. It was to them, indeed, that Glyndwr owed in great measure the swift and universal recognition that made him at once the man of the hour. Of all classes of Welshmen the bardic orders were the most passionately patriotic. For an hundred years their calling had been a proscribed one. Prior to Edward the First's conquest a regular tax, the "cymarth," had been laid upon the people for their support. Since then they had slunk about, if not, as is sometimes said, in terror of their lives, yet dependent always for their support on private charity and doles.

But no laws could have repressed song in Wales, and indeed this period seems a singularly prolific one both in poets and minstrels. They persuaded themselves that their deliverance from the Saxon grip was at hand, and saw in the valiant figure of Owain of Glyndyfrdwy the fulfilment of the ancient prophecies that a Welsh prince should once again wear the crown of Britain. Glyndwr well knew that the sympathy of the bards would prove to him a tower of strength, and he met them more than half way. If he was not superstitious himself he understood how to play upon the superstition and romantic nature of his countrymen. The old prophecies were ransacked, portents were rife in sea and sky. The most ordinary occurrences of nature were full of significant meaning for Owen's followers and for all Welshmen at that moment, whether they followed him or not; and in the month of August Owen declared himself, and by an already formidable body of followers was declared, "Prince of Wales." His friend and laureate, Iolo Goch, was by his side and ready for the great occasion.

"Cambria's princely Eagle, hail,
Of Gryffydd Vychan's noble blood;
Thy high renown shall never fail,
Owain Glyndwr great and good,
Lord of Dwrdwy's fertile Vale,
Warlike high born Owain, hail!"

Glyndwr would hardly have been human if he had not made his first move upon his relentless enemy, Lord Grey of Ruthin. There is no evidence whether the latter was himself at home or not, but Owen fell upon the little town on a Fair day and made a clean sweep of the stock and valuables therein collected. Thence he passed eastwards, harrying and burning the property of English settlers or English sympathisers. Crossing the English border and spreading panic everywhere, he invaded western Shropshire, capturing castles and burning houses and threatening even Shrewsbury.

The King, who had effected nothing in the North, was pulled up sharply by the grave news from Wales and prepared to hasten southwards. By September 3rd he had retraced his steps as far as Durham, and passing through Pontefract, Doncaster, and Leicester arrived at Northampton about the 14th of the same month. Here fuller details reached him, and he deemed it necessary to postpone the Parliament which he had proposed to hold at Westminster in September, till the beginning of the following year, 1401. From Northampton Henry issued summons to the sheriffs of the midland and border counties that they were to join him instantly with their levies, and that he was proceeding without delay to quell the insurrection that had broken out in North Wales. He wrote also to the people of Shrewsbury, warning them to be prepared against all attacks, and to provide against the treachery of any Welshmen that might be residing within the town. Then, moving rapidly forward and taking his son, the young Prince Henry, with him, he reached Shrewsbury about the 24th of the month.

Henry's crown had hitherto been a thorny one and he had derived but little satisfaction from it. The previous winter had witnessed the desperate plot from which he only saved himself by his rapid ride to London from Windsor, and the subsequent capture and execution of the Earls of Salisbury,

Kent, and Huntington, who had been the ringleaders. From his unsteady throne he saw both France and Scotland awaiting only an opportune moment to strike him. The whole spring had been passed in diplomatic endeavours to keep them quiet till he was sure of his own subjects. Isabella, the daughter of the King of France and child-widow of the late King Richard, had brought with her a considerable dower, and the hope of getting a part of this back, together with the young Queen herself, had kept the French quiet. But Scotland, that ill-governed and turbulent country, had been chafing under ten years of peace; and its people, or rather the restless barons who governed them, were getting hungry for the plunder of their richer neighbours in the South, and, refusing all terms, were already crossing the border. Under ordinary circumstances an English king might have left such matters in the hands of his northern nobles. But it seemed desirable to Henry that he should, on the first occasion, show both to the Scotch and his own people of what mettle he was made. He was also angered at the lack of decent excuse for their aggressions. So he hurried northward, as we have seen, and having hurled the invaders back over the border as far as Edinburgh, he had for lack of food just returned to Newcastle when the bad news from Wales arrived. He was now at Shrewsbury, within striking distance, as it seemed, of the Welsh rebels and their arch-leader, his old esquire, Glyndwr. Neither Henry nor his soldiers knew anything of Welsh campaigning or of Welsh tactics, for five generations had passed away since Englishmen had marched and fought in that formidable country and against their ancient and agile foes. Henry the Fourth, so far as we can judge, regarded the task before him with a light heart. At any rate he wasted some little time at Shrewsbury, making an example of the first Welshman of importance and mischievous tendencies that fell into his hands. This was one Grenowe ap Tudor, whose quarters, after he had been executed with much ceremony, were sent to ornament the gates of Bristol, Hereford, Ludlow, and Chester, respectively. The King then moved into Wales with all his forces, thinking, no doubt, to crush Glyndwr and his irregular levies in a short time and without much difficulty. This was the first of his many luckless campaigns in pursuit of his indomitable and wily foe, and perhaps it was the least disastrous. For though he effected nothing against the Welsh troops and did not even get a sight of them, he at least got out of the country without feeling the prick of their spears, which is more than can be said of almost any of his later ventures. His invasion of Wales, in fact, upon this occasion was a promenade and is described as such in contemporary records. He reached Anglesey without incident, and there for the sake of example drove out the Minorite friars from the Abbey of Llanfaes near Beaumaris, on the plea that they were friends of Owen. The plea seems to have been a sound one, for the Franciscans were without doubt the one order of the clergy that favoured Welsh independence. But Henry, not content with this, plundered their abbey, an inexcusable act, and one for which in after years some restitution appears to have been made. Bad weather and lack of supplies, as on all after occasions, proved the King's worst enemies. Glyndwr and his people lay snug within the Snowdon mountains, and by October 17th, Henry, having set free at Shrewsbury a few prisoners he brought with him, was back at Worcester. Here he declared the estates of Owen to be confiscated and bestowed them on his own half-brother, Beaufort, Earl of Somerset. He little thought at that time how many years would elapse before an English nobleman could venture to take actual possession of Sycherth or Glyndyfrdwy.

Upon November 20th a general pardon was offered to all Welsh rebels who would come in and report themselves at Shrewsbury or Chester, the now notorious Owen always excepted, and on this occasion Griffith Hanmer, his brother-in-law, and one of the famous Norman-Welsh family of Pulestone had the honour of being fellow-outlaws with their chief. Their lands also were confiscated and bestowed on two of the King's friends. It is significant, however, of the anxiety regarding the future which Glyndwr's movement had inspired, that the grantee of the Hanmer estates, which all lay in Flint, was very glad to come to terms with a member of the family and take a trifling annuity instead of the doubtful privilege of residence and rent collecting. The castle of Carnarvon was strongly garrisoned. Henry, Prince of Wales, then only in his fourteenth year, was left at Chester with a suitable council and full powers of exercising clemency toward all Welshmen lately in arms, other than the three notable exceptions already mentioned, who should petition for it. Few, however, if any, seem to have taken the trouble to do even thus much. And in the meantime the King, still holding the Welsh rebellion as of no great moment, spent the winter in London entertaining the Greek Emperor and haggling with the King of France about the return of the money paid to Richard as the dower of his child-queen, Isabella who was still detained in London as in some sort a hostage.

Parliament sat early in 1401 and was by no means as confident as Henry seemed to be regarding the state of Wales, a subject which formed the chief burden of their debate. Even here, perhaps, the gravity of the Welsh movement was not entirely realised; the authorities were angry but scarcely alarmed; no one remembered the old Welsh wars or the traditional defensive tactics of the Welsh, and the fact of Henry having swept through the Principality unopposed gave rise to misconceptions. There was no question, however, about their hostility towards Wales, and in the early spring of this year the following ordinances for the future government of the Principality were published.

(1) All lords of castles in Wales were to have them properly secured against assault on pain of forfeiture.

(2) No Welshman in future was to be a Justice, Chamberlain, Chancellor, Seneschal, Receiver, Chief Forester, Sheriff, Escheator, Constable of a castle, or Keeper of rolls or records. All these offices were to be held by Englishmen, who were to reside at their posts.

(3) The people of a district were to be held responsible for all breaches of the peace in their neighbourhood and were to be answerable in their own persons for all felons, robbers, and trespassers found therein.

(4) All felons and evildoers were to be immediately handed over to justice and might not be sheltered on any pretext by any lord in any castle.

(5) The Welsh people were to be taxed and charged with the expense of repairing and maintaining walls, gates, and castles in North Wales when wilfully destroyed, and for refurnishing them and keeping them in order, at the discretion of the owner, for a term not exceeding three years, except under special orders from the King.

(6) No meetings of Welsh were to be held without the permission of the chief officers of the lordship, who were to be held responsible for any damage or riot that ensued.

The gifts called "Cwmwrth," too, exacted by collection for the maintenance of the bards or minstrels, were strictly interdicted. Adam of Usk, one of the few lay chroniclers of this period, was himself present at the Parliament of 1401 and heard "many harsh things" to be put in force against the Welsh: among others, "that they should not marry with English, nor get them wealth, nor dwell in England." Also that the men of the Marches "might use reprisals against Welshmen who were their debtors or who had injured them," a truce for a week being first granted to give them the opportunity of making amends.

It was much easier, however, to issue commands

Copyright Miss Walker.

CARCHARDY OWAIN, GLYNDWR'S PRISON HOUSE AT LLANSANTFFRAID.

and instructions than to carry them out. The King seems to have felt this, and leant strongly towards a greater show of clemency. But there was sufficient panic in parts of England to override the royal scruples or common sense, and so far as intentions went the Welsh were to be shown little mercy.

Owen all this time had been lying quietly in the valley of the upper Dee, preparing for still further endeavours. The short days and the long nights of winter saw the constant passing to and fro of innumerable sympathisers through the valleys and over the hills of both North and South Wales, and a hundred harps, that had long been faint or silent, were sounding high to the glories of the unforgotten heroes of Old Wales. Mere hatred of Henry and tenderness for Richard's memory were giving place to ancient dreams of Cambrian independence and a fresh burst of hatred for the Saxon yoke. Owen, too strong now to fear anything from isolated efforts of Lord Marchers, seems to have held high festival at Glyndyfrdwy during the winter, and with the assumption of princely rank to have kept up something of the nature of princely state. With the exception of Grey to the north and the lords of Chirk upon the east, it is probable that nearly everyone around him was by now either his friend or in wholesome dread of his displeasure.

Shropshire was panic-stricken for the time. Hotspur was busy at Denbigh, and Glyndwr, among his native hills, had it, no doubt, very much his own way during the winter months, and made full use of them to push forward his interests. His property, it will be remembered, had been confiscated. But so far from anyone venturing to take possession of Glyndyfrdwy, its halls, we are told, at this time rang with revelry and song, while Owen, in the intervals of laying his plans and organising his campaign for the ensuing summer, received the homage of the bards who flocked from every part of the principality to throw their potent influence into the scale. However much Glyndwr's vanity and ambition may have been stirred by the enthusiasm which surged around him, and the somewhat premature exultation that with wild rhapsody hailed him as the restorer of Welsh independence, he never for a moment lost sight of the stern issues he had to face, or allowed himself to be flattered into overconfidence. Courage and coolness, perseverance and sagacity, were his leading attributes. He well knew that the enthusiasm of the bards was of vital consequence to the first success of his undertaking. It is of little moment whether he shared the superstitions of those who sang of the glorious destiny for which fate had marked him or of those who listened to the singing. It is not likely that a man who showed himself so able and so cool a leader would fail to take full advantage of forces which at this early stage were so supremely valuable.

He knew his countrymen and he knew the world, and when Wales was quivering with excitement beneath the interpretation of ancient prophecies bruited hither and thither and enlarged upon by poetic and patriotic fancy, Glyndwr was certainly not the man to damp their ardour by any display of criticism.

Already the great news from Wales had thrilled the heart of many a Welshman poring over his books at the university, or following the plough-tail over English fallows. They heard of friends and relatives selling their stock to buy arms and harness, and in numbers that yet more increased as the year advanced, began to steal home again, all filled with a rekindled glow of patriotism that a hundred years of union and, in their cases, long mingling with the Saxon had not quenched. Oxford, particularly, sent many recruits to Owen, and this is not surprising, seeing how combative was the Oxford student of that time and how clannish his proclivities. Adam of Usk, who has told us a good deal about Glyndwr's insurrection, was himself an undergraduate some dozen years before it broke out, and has given us a brief and vivid picture of the ferocious fights upon more or less racial lines, in which the Welsh chronicler not only figured prominently himself, but was an actual leader of his countrymen; "was indicted," he tells us, "for felonious riot and narrowly escaped conviction, being tried by a jury empanelled before a King's Judge. After this I feared the King hitherto unknown to me and put hooks in my jaws." These particular riots were so formidable that the scholars for the most part, after several had been slain, departed to their respective countries.

In the very next year, however, "Thomas Speke, Chaplain, with a multitude of other malefactors, appointing captains among them, rose up against the peace of the King and sought after all the Welshmen abiding and studying in Oxford, shooting arrows after them in divers streets and lanes as they went, crying out, 'War! war! war! Sle Sle Sle the Welsh doggys and her whelpys; ho so looketh out of his house he shall in good sooth be dead,' and certain persons they slew and others they grievously wounded, and some of the Welshmen, who bowed their knees to abjure the town," they led to the gates with certain indignities not to be repeated to ears polite. We may also read the names of the different halls which were broken into, and of Welsh scholars who were robbed of their books and chattels, including in some instances their harps.

It is not altogether surprising, therefore, that Welsh Oxonians should have hailed the opportunity of Owen's rising to pay off old scores. We have the names of some of those who joined him in an original paper, in the Rolls of Parliament, which fully corroborates the notice of this event; Howel Kethin (Gethin) "bachelor of law, duelling in Myghell Hall, Oxenford," was one of them; "Maister Morres Stove, of the College of Excestre," was another, while David Brith, John Lloid, and several others are mentioned by name. One David Leget seems to have been regarded as such an addition that Owen himself sent a special summons that he "schuld com till hym and be his man." So things in Wales went from bad to worse; Glyndwr's forces gaining rapidly in strength and numbers, and actively preparing in various quarters for the operations that marked the open season of 1401.

CHAPTER IV

OWEN AND THE PERCYS

1401

NORTH WALES, as already mentioned, was being now administered by the young Prince Henry, with the help of a council whose headquarters were at Chester. Under their orders, and their most active agent at this time, was Henry Percy, the famous Hotspur, eldest son of the Earl of Northumberland. He was Justice of North Wales and Constable of the castles of Chester, Flint, Conway, Denbigh, and Carnarvon, and had recently been granted the whole island of Anglesey. Hotspur, for obvious reasons, made his headquarters at the high-perched and conveniently situated fortress of Denbigh, which Lacy, Earl of Lincoln, had built at the Edwardian conquest. Its purpose was to overawe the lower portion of the Vale of Clwyd, which had fallen to Lacy's share at the great division of plunder that signalised the downfall of the last of the Welsh native Princes. The lordship of Denbigh, it may be remarked parenthetically, since the fact becomes one of some significance later on, belonged at this time to the Mortimers, into which famous family Henry Percy had married. The latter, to whose house the King was under such great obligations, was the leading exponent of his master's policy in Wales, both in matters of peace and war, and had been sufficiently loaded with favours to at least equalise the balance of mutual indebtedness between the houses of Northumberland and Lancaster.

Shakespeare's fancy and dramatic instinct has played sad havoc in most people's minds with the mutual attitude of some of the leading figures of this stormy period. It has been sufficiently disproved by his biographers, if not, indeed, by the facts of general history, that Henry of Monmouth was no more the dissipated, light-headed trifler and heartless brawler than was Glyndwr the half-barbarous and wholly boastful personage that Shakespeare has placed upon his stage. The King, it will be remembered, is depicted, in the play that bears his name, as bewailing with embittered eloquence the contrast between the characters of Hotspur and his own son, and making vain laments that the infants had not been changed while they lay side by side in their cradles. It is something of a shock to recall the fact that Henry Percy was a little older than the distraught father himself, and a contemporary, not of the Prince, but of the King, who was now about thirty-five, and many years younger than Glyndwr.

Prince Henry, even now, though not yet fourteen, seems to have had a mind of his own. He had, in truth, to face early the stern facts and hard realities of a life such as would have sobered and matured a less naturally precocious and intelligent nature than his. His youth was not spent in frivolity and debauchery in London, but upon the Welsh border, for the most part, amid the clash of arms or the more trying strain of political responsibility, aggravated by constant want of funds. One might almost say that Henry of Monmouth's whole early manhood was devoted to a fierce and ceaseless struggle with Glyndwr for that allegiance of the Welsh people to which both laid claim. In later years, as we shall see, it was the tenacity and soldier-like qualities of the Prince that succeeded where veteran warriors had failed, and that ultimately broke the back of Glyndwr's long and fierce resistance. The King, far from deploring the conduct or character of his valiant son, always treated him with the utmost confidence, and invariably speaks of him in his correspondence with unreserved affection and pride. He was of "spare make," say the chroniclers who knew him, "tall and well proportioned, exceeding the stature of men, beautiful of visage, and small of bone." He was of "marvellous strength, pliant and passing swift of limb; and so trained to feats of agility by discipline and exercise, that with one or two of his lords he could on foot readily give chase to a deer without hounds, bow, or sling, and catch the fleetest of the herd."

Either from a feeling that Hotspur was too strong, or that popular fervour had perhaps been sufficiently aroused to the north of the Dovey, Glyndwr now turned his attention to the southern and midland districts of the country. But before following him there I must say something of the incident which was of chief importance at the opening of this year's operations.

Conway will probably be more familiar to the general reader than any other scene of conflict we shall visit in this volume, from the fact of its being so notable a landmark on the highway between England and Ireland. The massive towers and walls of the great castle which Edward the First's architect, Henry de Elfreton, raised here at the conquest of Wales, still throw their shadows on the broad tidal river that laps their feet. The little town which lies beneath its ramparts and against the shore is still bound fast within a girdle of high, embattled walls, strengthened at measured intervals by nearly thirty towers, and presenting a complete picture of medieval times such as in all Britain is unapproached, while immediately above it, if anything were needed to give further distinction to a scene in itself so eloquent of a storied past, rise to heaven the northern bulwarks of the Snowdon range. Here, in the early spring of this year, within the castle, lay a royal garrison closely beset by the two brothers, William and Rhys ap Tudor, of the ever famous stock of Penmynydd in Anglesey. They had both been excluded from the King's pardon, together with Glyndwr, among whose lieutenants they were to prove themselves at this period the most formidable to the English power.

Conway Castle, as may readily be believed by those familiar with it, was practically impregnable, so long as a score or two of armed men with sufficient to sustain life and strength remained inside it. The Tudors, however, achieved by stealth what the force at their command could not at that time have accomplished by other means. For while the garrison were at church, a partisan of the Glyndwr faction was introduced into the castle in the disguise of a carpenter, and after killing the warders he admitted William ap Tudor and some forty men. They found a fair stock of provisions within the castle, though, as will be seen, it proved in the end insufficient. The main body of the besiegers retired under Rhys ap Tudor to the hills overlooking the town to await developments. They were not long left in suspense, for the news of the seizure of the castle roused Hotspur to activity, and he hastened to the spot with all the men that he could collect. Conway being one of Edward's fortified and chartered English towns, the inhabitants were presumably loyal to the King. But Hotspur brought five hundred archers and men-at-arms and great engines, including almost certainly some of the primitive cannon of the period, to bear on the castle. William ap Tudor and his forty men laughed at their efforts till Hotspur, despairing of success by arms, went on to Carnarvon, leaving his whole force behind, to try the effect of starvation on the garrison.

At Carnarvon Henry Percy held his sessions as Justice of North Wales, openly proclaiming a pardon in the name of his master the Prince to all who would come in and give up their arms. From here, too, he sent word in a letter, still extant, that the commons of Carnarvon and Merioneth had come before him, thanking the King and Prince for their clemency and offering to pay the same dues as they had paid King Richard. He also declared that the northern districts, with the exception of the forces at Conway, were rapidly coming back to their allegiance. How sanguine and premature Hotspur was in this declaration will soon be clear enough.

In the meantime much damage had been done to Conway town by both besiegers and besieged. The latter seem to have overestimated the resources they found within the castle, for by the end of April they were making overtures for terms. William ap Tudor offered on behalf of his followers to surrender the place if a full and unconditional pardon should be granted to all inside. Hotspur was inclined to accept this proposal, but the council at Chester and the King himself, getting word of his intention, objected, and with justice, to such leniency. So the negotiations drag on. The King in a letter to his son remarks that, as the castle fell by the carelessness of Henry Percy's people, that same "dear and faithful cousin" ought to see that it was retaken without concessions to those holding it, and, moreover, pay all the expenses out of his own pocket. In any case he urges that, if he himself is to pay the wages and maintenance of the besieging force, and supply their imposing siege train, he would like to see something more substantial for the outlay than a full and free pardon to the rebels who had caused it. It was the beginning of July before an agreement was finally arrived at, to the effect that if nine of the garrison, not

 F. Frith & Co.

INTERIOR CONWAY CASTLE.

specified, were handed over to justice, the rest should be granted both their lives and a free pardon. The selection of the nine inside the castle was made on a strange method, if method it can be called. For the leaders, having made an arbitrary and privy choice of the victims, had them seized and bound suddenly in the night. They were then handed over to Percy's troops, who slaughtered them after the usual brutal fashion of the time.

A second letter of Henry Percy's to the council demonstrates conclusively how seriously he had been at fault in his previous estimate. This time he writes from Denbigh under date of May 17th, pressing for the payment of arrears in view of the desperate state of North Wales, and further declaring that if he did not receive some money shortly he must resign his position to others and leave the country by the end of the month. But Hotspur rose superior to his threats; for at the end of May, at his own risk and expense, he made an expedition against a force of Glyndwr's people that were in arms around Dolgelly. He was accompanied by the Earl of Arundel and Sir Hugh Browe, a gentleman of Cheshire. An action was fought of an indecisive nature at the foot of Cader Idris, after which Percy returned to Denbigh. Finding here no answer to his urgent appeal for support, he threw up all his Welsh appointments in disgust and left the country for the more congenial and familiar neighbourhood of the Scottish border. For he held office here also, being joined with his father in the wardenship of the Eastern Marches of Scotland.

Hotspur was even now, at this early stage and with some apparent cause, in no very good humour with the King. It is certain, too, that Glyndwr at this time had some special liking for the Percys, though they were his open enemies, and it is almost beyond question that they had a personal interview at some place and date unknown during the summer.

Leaving North Wales in a seething and turbulent state, with local partisans heading bands of insurgents (if men who resist an usurper can be called insurgents) in various parts of the country, we must turn to Owen and the South. Crossing the Dovey, Glyndwr had sought the mountain range that divides Cardigan from what is now Radnorshire (then known as the district of Melenydd), and raised his standard upon the rounded summit of Plinlimmon. It was a fine position, lying midway between North and South Wales, within sight of the sea and at the same time within striking distance of the fertile districts of the Centre and the South. Behind him lay the populous seaboard strip of Ceredigion created at Edward's conquest into the county of Cardigan. Before him lay Radnor, and Carmarthen, and the fat lordships of Brycheiniog, to be welded later into the modern county of Brecon. Along the Cardiganshire coast in Owen's rear a string of castles frowned out upon the Irish Sea, held, since it was a royal county, by the constables of the King, who were sometimes of English, sometimes of Welsh, nationality. Inland, as far as the Herefordshire border, was a confused net-work of lordships, held for the most part direct from the King on feudal tenure by English or Anglo-

Welsh nobles, and each dominated by one or more grim castles of prodigious strength, against which the feeble engines and guns of those days hurled their missiles with small effect. Some of these were royal or quasi-royal property and looked to the Crown for their defence. The majority, however, had to be maintained and held by owners against the King's enemies, subject to confiscation in case of any deficiency in zeal or precaution. Ordinarily impregnable though the walls were, the garrisons, as we shall see, were mostly small, and they were incapable of making much impression upon the surrounding country when once it became openly hostile and armed.

South Wales had as yet shown no great disposition to move. Some riots and bloodshed at Abergavenny had been almost the sum total of its patriotic activity. Now, however, that the Dragon Standard was actually floating on Plinlimmon and the already renowned Owen, with a band of chosen followers, was calling the South to arms, there was no lack of response. The bards had been busy preparing the way on the south as well as on the north of the Dovey. In the words of Pennant:

"They animated the nation by recalling to mind the great exploits of their ancestors, their struggles for liberty, their successful contests with the Saxon and Norman race for upwards of eight centuries. They rehearsed the cruelty of their antagonists, and did not forget the savage policy of the first Edward to their proscribed brethren. They brought before their countrymen the remembrance of ancient prophecies. They showed the hero Glyndwr to be descended from the ancient race of our Princes, and pronounced that in him was to be expected the completion of our oracular Merlin. The band of minstrels now struck up. The harp, the 'crwth,' and the pipe filled up the measure of enthusiasm which the other had begun to inspire. They rushed to battle, fearless of the event, like their great ancestry, moved by the Druids' songs, and scorned death which conferred immortality in reward of their valour."

Glyndwr now fell with heavy hand upon this southern country, crossing the headwaters of the Severn and the Wye, and pressing hard upon the Marches of Carmarthen. The common people rose on every side and joined the forces that acted either under his leadership or in his name. Those who did not join him, as was certainly the case with a majority of the upper class at this early period, had to find refuge in the castles or to fly to safer regions, leaving their property at the mercy of the insurgents. But a battle was fought at the opening of this campaign on the summit of Mynydd Hyddgant, a hill in the Plinlimmon group, that did more, perhaps, to rouse enthusiasm for Glyndwr than even the strains of the bards or his own desolating marches.

The Flemings in Wales at that time were not confined to Western Pembroke, but had still strong colonies below Carmarthen, in the Glamorgan promontory of Gower, and some footing in South Cardiganshire. Whether they had actually felt the hand of Glyndwr upon their borders, or whether they deemed it better to take the initiative, they at any rate collected a force of some fifteen hundred men, and marching northward to the Cardigan mountains, surprised the Welsh leader as he was encamped on the summit of Mynydd Hyddgant, with a body of less than five hundred men around him. The Flemish strategy was creditable, seeing that it was carried out by slow-witted and slow-footed lowlanders against nimble mountaineers and so astute a chieftain. Owen found himself surrounded by a force thrice the number of his own, and either death or capture seemed inevitable. As the latter meant the former, he was not long in choosing his course, and putting himself at the head of his warriors he attacked the Flemings with such fury that he and most of his band escaped, leaving two hundred of their enemies dead upon the mountain slope. This personal feat of arms was worth five thousand men to Owen. It was all that was wanted to fill the measure of his prestige and decide every wavering Welshman in his favour.

For this whole summer Glyndwr was fighting and ravaging throughout South and Mid-Wales. The lands of the English as well as of those Welshmen who would not join him were ruthlessly harried. Stock was carried off, homesteads were burned, even castles here and there were taken, when ill-provisioned and undermanned. New Radnor under Sir John Grendor was stormed and the sixty defenders hung upon the ramparts by way of encouragement to others to yield. The noble abbey of Cwmhir too, whose ruins still slowly crumble in a remote Radnorshire valley, felt Glyndwr's pitiless hand, being utterly destroyed. His animosity to the Church was intelligible, though for his method of showing it nothing indeed can be said. The Welsh Church, though its personnel was largely native, was, with the exception of the Franciscan order, mostly hostile to Glyndwr and upon the side of the English Government. Bards and priests, moreover, were irreconcilable enemies. The latter had in some sort usurped the position the former had once held, and now the patron and the hero of the bards, who were once more lifting up their heads, was not likely to be acceptable to the clergy. This, however, would be a poor excuse for an iconoclasm that would set a Welsh torch to noble foundations built and endowed for the most part with Welsh money.

Glyndwr in the meantime swept down the Severn valley, burning on his way the small town of Montgomery, and coming only to a halt where the border borough of Welshpool lay nestling between the high hills through which the Severn rushes out into the fat plains of Shropshire.

The great Red Castle of Powys, then called "Pole," overlooked in those days, as it does in these, the town it sheltered. The famous Shropshire family of Charlton were then, and for generations afterwards, its lords and owners. From its walls Glyndwr and his forces were now driven back by Edward Charlton with his garrison and the levies of the neighbourhood, which remained throughout the war staunch to its lord and the King. The repulse of Owen, however, was not accomplished without much hard fighting and the destruction of all the suburbs of the town.

But these sallies from castles and walled towns could do little more than protect their inmates. Mid- and South Wales literally bristled with feudal castles containing garrisons of, for the most part, less than a hundred men. These scattered handfuls were unable to leave their posts and act in unison, and when the abandonment of North Wales by Hotspur gave further confidence to those who had risen, or would like to rise, for Glyndwr, the greater part of South Wales fell into line with the Centre and the North. From the border to the sea Owen was now, so far as the open country was concerned, irresistible. Nor was it only within the bounds of Wales that men who were unfriendly to Glyndwr had cause to tremble. The rapid progress of his arms had already spread terror along the border, and created something like a panic even in England. The idea of a Welsh invasion spread to comparatively remote parts, and urgent letters carried by hard-riding messengers went hurrying to the King from beleaguered Marchers and scared abbots, beseeching him to come in person to their rescue.

All this happened in August. As early as the preceding June, when Conway was in Welsh hands, the King had meditated a second invasion in person, and had issued summonses to the sheriffs of fourteen counties to meet him at Worcester, but the approaching surrender of Conway and the optimistic reports from Wales that met him as he came west turned him from his purpose. There was no optimism now; all was panic and the King was really coming. The Prince of Wales in the meantime was ordered forward with the levies of the four border counties, while the forces of twenty-two of the western, southern, and midland shires were hurriedly collected by a proclamation sent out upon the 18th of September.

One reads with constant and unabated surprise of the celerity with which these great levies gathered from all parts of the country to the appointed tryst, fully equipped and ready for a campaign. One's amazement, however, is sensibly modified as the narrative proceeds and discovers them after a week or two of marching in an enemy's country reduced to their last crust, upon the verge of disaster and starvation, and leaving in their retiring tracks as many victims as might have fallen in quite a sharp engagement.

By the opening of October the King and Prince Henry had entered Wales with a large army. The proclamation of September the 18th, calling out the forces of England, had stated that the greater part of the able-bodied men of Wales had gone over to Owen. Now, however, as this great host pushed its way to Bangor, as had happened before, and would happen again, not a Welshman was to be seen. On every side were the sparse grain-fields long stripped of their produce, the barns empty, the abundant pastures bare of the small black cattle and mountain sheep with which in times of peace and safety they were so liberally sprinkled. On the 8th of October the army was at Bangor, on the 9th at Carnarvon, whose tremendous and impregnable fortress John Bolde defended for the King with about a hundred men. Still seeing no sign of an enemy, they swept in aimless fashion round the western edges of the Snowdon mountains (for the route through them, which was even then a recognised one, would have been too dangerous), arriving in an incredibly short space of time in Cardiganshire, where the King called a halt at the great and historic abbey of Ystradfflur or Strata Florida.

The weather for a wonder favoured the English, and we might be excused for giving our imagination play for a moment and painting in fancy the gorgeous sight that the chivalry of half England, unsoiled by time or tempests or war, with its glinting steel, its gay colours, its flaunting pennons, shining in the October sun, must have displayed as it wound in a long, thin train through those familiar and matchless scenes. The great Cistercian house of Ystradfflur had shared with Conway in olden days the honour of both making and preserving the records of the Principality. Around the building was a cemetery shaded by forty wide-spreading and venerable yew trees. Beneath their shade lay the bones of eleven Welsh Princes of the twelfth and thirteenth centuries and perhaps those of the greatest Welsh poet of the age, Dafydd ab Gwilim. Henry cared for none of these things. He allowed the abbey to be gutted and plundered, not sparing even the sacred vessels. He turned the monks out on to the highway, under the plea that two or three of them had favoured Owen, and filled up the measure of desecration by stabling his horses at the high altar.

Meanwhile, Owen and his nimble troops began to

show themselves in Cardiganshire, harrying the flanks and rear and outposts of the royal army, cutting off supplies, and causing much discomfort and considerable loss, including the whole camp equipage of the Prince of Wales.

Henry did his best to bring Owen to action, but the Welsh chieftain was much too wary to waste his strength on a doubtful achievement which hunger would of a certainty accomplish for him within a few days. An eminent gentleman of the country, one Llewelyn ab Griffith Vychan of Cayo, comes upon the scene at this point and at the expense of his head relieves the tedium of this brief and ineffectual campaign with a dramatic incident. His position, we are told, was so considerable that he consumed in his house no less than sixteen casks of wine a year; but his patriotism rose superior to his rank and comforts. He offered to guide the royal troops to a spot where they might hope to capture Owen, but instead of doing this he deliberately misled them, to their great cost, and openly declared that he had two sons serving with Glyndwr, and that his own sympathies were with them and their heroic leader. He then bared his neck to the inevitable axe of the executioner, and proved himself thereby to be a hero, whose name, one is glad to think, has been rescued from oblivion.

The King, having attended to the mangling and quartering of this gallant old patriot, crossed the Montgomery hills with his army and hurried down the Severn valley, carrying with him, according to Adam of Usk, a thousand Welsh children as captives. Beyond this capture, he had achieved nothing save some further harrying of a land already sufficiently harried, and the pillaging of an historic and loyal monastery.

Arriving at Shrewsbury before the end of October he disbanded his army, leaving behind him a Wales rather encouraged in its rebellious ways than otherwise, Glyndwr's reputation in no whit diminished, and his own and his Marchers' castles as hardly pressed and in as sore a plight as when he set out, with so much pomp and circumstance, less than a month before. It must have been merely to save appearances that he issued a pardon to the "Commons of Cardigan," with leave to buy back the lands that had been nominally confiscated. He was also good enough to say that on consideration he would allow them to retain their own language, which it seems he had tabooed; this, too, at a time when the life of no Englishman in Cardigan was safe a bowshot away from the Norman castles, when the Welsh of the country were practically masters of the situation and Glyndwr virtually their Prince.

Still Henry meant well. Since he was their King, his manifest duty was to reconquer their country for the Crown, and this was practically the task that lay before him. But then again this is precisely what he did not seem for a long time yet to realise. He was a good soldier, while for his energy and bodily activity one loses oneself in admiration. But he persistently underrated the Welsh position and gave his mind and his energies to other dangers and other interests which were far less pressing. And when he did bend his whole mind to the subjection of Glyndwr, his efforts were ill-directed, and the conditions seemed to be of a kind with which he not only could not grapple but which his very soul abhorred. It remained, as will be seen, for the gallant son, whose frivolity is popularly supposed to have been the bane of his father's life, by diligence as well as valour, to succeed where the other had ignominiously failed.

Lord Rutland was now appointed to the thorny office of Governor of North Wales, while the Earl of Worcester, a Percy and uncle to Hotspur, was left to face Glyndwr in the southern portion of the Principality. The winter of 1401–2 was at hand, a season when Owen and his Welshmen could fight, but English armies most certainly could not campaign. The castles in the Southern Marches were put in fighting trim, revictualled and reinforced. The chief of those in the interior that Glyndwr had now to face were Lampeter, Cardigan and Builth, Llandovery and Carmarthen, while upon the border the massive and high-perched towers of Montgomery and Powys looked down over the still smoking villages by the Severn's bank, and girded themselves to stem if need be any repetition of such disaster. Owen seemed to think that his presence in the North after so long an absence would be salutary; so, passing into Carnarvonshire, he appeared before its stubborn capital.

But John Bolde had been reinforced with men and money, and, joined by the burghers of the town, he beat off Glyndwr's attack and slew three hundred of his men. This was early in November. All North Wales but the castles and the walled towns around them, where such existed, was still friendly to Owen. The chief castles away from the English border, Criccieth, Harlech, Carnarvon, Conway, Snowdon (Dolbadarn), Rhuddlan, and Beaumaris, complete the list of those in royal keeping and may be readily reckoned up, unlike those of South Wales, whose name was legion; while Denbigh and Ruthin were the only Marcher strongholds, apart from those which were in immediate touch with Salop and Cheshire. Now it so happened that, before most of the events narrated in this chapter had taken place, before, indeed, Hotspur had retired in such seeming petulance from North Wales during the preceding summer, he had contrived a meeting with Glyndwr. The scene of the interview is not known; that it occurred, however, is not merely noted by the chroniclers, but Glyndwr's attitude in connection with it is referred to in the State papers. A council called in November, while Owen was making his attempt on Carnarvon, has upon its minutes, "To know the king's will about treaty with Glyndwr to return to his allegiance seeing his good intentions relating thereto." In the interview with Percy, Owen is said to have declared that he was willing to submit, provided that his life should be spared and his property guaranteed to him. Later in the year, as a well-known original letter of the period affirms, "Jankyn Tyby of the North Countre bringeth letteres owt of the North Countre to Owen as thei demed from Hen[r] son Percy."

In answer Owen expressed his affection for the Earl of Northumberland and the confidence he felt in him. The King was then informed of the proceedings, and with his consent a messenger was sent from Earl Percy to Mortimer, whose sister, as Hotspur's wife, was his daughter-in-law. Through the medium of Mortimer, soon to become so closely allied to Glyndwr, the latter is reported to have declared his willingness for peace, protesting that he was not to blame for the havoc wrought in Wales, and that he had been deprived of his patrimony, meaning no doubt the northern slice of Glyndyfrdwy which Grey, after being defeated at law, had annexed by force, with connivance of the King's council. He added that he would readily meet the Earl of Northumberland on the English border, as was required of him, but that he feared outside treachery to his person, as a man who had made such a host of enemies may well have done. He also declared that, if he came to Shropshire, the Commons would raise a clamour and say that he came to destroy all those who spoke English. That Hotspur had seen Glyndwr earlier in the summer is distinctly stated by Hardyng, who was Hotspur's own page. The fact that Percy did not take the opportunity to treacherously seize the Welsh chieftain was afterwards made one of the grievances urged by the King when he had other really serious ones against his old comrade. It may well, however, be suspected that some of these mysterious overtures in which the Percys and Mortimer figured so prominently contained the germs of the alliance that followed

 Miss Walker.

OLD BRIDGE AT LLANSANTFFRAID, GLYNDYFRDWY.

later between Glyndwr and the two great English houses.

No such suspicions, however, were as yet in the air, and Glyndwr retired, with his captains and his bards, into winter quarters at Glyndyfrdwy. Here, through the short days and long nights, the sounds of song and revelry sounded in the ancient Welsh fashion above the tumbling breakers of the Dee. The very accessibility of the spot to the strong border castles showed the reality at this time of Owen's power. The great pile of Chirk was not a dozen miles off, Dinas Brân was within easy sight, and the Arundels, who held them both, were no less mighty than the Greys who lay amid the ashes of Ruthin across the ridges to the north. But the whole country towards England, to Wrexham upon the one hand and to Oswestry on the other, and even to Ellesmere and that detached fragment of Flint known then as "Maelor Saesnag," was in open or secret sympathy with what had now become a national movement. More men of note, too, and property were with Owen this winter. The rising in its origin had been markedly democratic. The labour agitations that during the century just completed had stirred England, had not left Wales untouched. There, too, the times had changed for the lower orders. The Norman heel pressed more heavily upon them than it did upon their native masters, who were often on friendly terms and connected by marriage with the conquerors' families, while the very fact that Norman feudal customs had grown so general made it harder for the poor. The

Welsh gentry as a class had hitherto fought somewhat shy of the Dragon Standard. Many, especially from South Wales, had fled to England. Now, however, everyone outside the immediate shelter of the castles had to declare himself for Owen or the King. And at this moment there was not much choice,—for those, at any rate, who set any store by their safety.

To make matters worse for Henry, the Scots had again declared war in November, and in December Glyndwr made a dash for the great stronghold of Harlech. This was only saved to the King, for the time being, by the timely despatch of four hundred archers and one hundred men-at-arms from the Prince of Wales's headquarters at Chester. Owen, however, achieved this winter what must have been, to himself at any rate, a more satisfactory success than even the taking of Harlech, and this was the capture of his old enemy, Reginald, Lord Grey of Ruthin.

It was on the last day of January, according to Adam of Usk, that Glyndwr crossed the wild hills dividing his own territory from that of Grey, and, dropping down into the Vale of Clwyd, appeared before Ruthin. There are several versions of this notable encounter. All point to the fact that Owen exercised some strategy in drawing his enemy, with the comparatively small force at his command, out of his stronghold, and then fell on him with overpowering numbers.

An old tale recounts that the Welsh leader drove a number of stakes into the ground in a wooded place and caused his men to hang their helmets on them to represent a small force, while the men themselves lurked in ambush upon either side; and that he caused the shoes of his horses to be reversed to make Grey think that he had retreated. The fight took place, according to one tradition, close to Ruthin; another declares that Brynsaithmarchog ("the hill of the seven knights"), half way to Corwen, was the scene of it. But this is of little moment to other than local antiquaries. Grey's force was surrounded and cut to pieces; that haughty baron himself was taken prisoner, and carried off at once, with a view to making so notable a captive secure against all attempt at rescue, to the Snowdon mountains. The tables were indeed turned on the greedy and tyrannical Lord Marcher who had been the primary cause of all this trouble that had fallen upon Wales and England. Glyndwr would not have been human had he not then drained to the last drop the cup of a revenge so sweet, and Grey was immured in the castle of Dolbadarn, whose lonely tower, still standing between the Llanberis lakes and at the foot of Snowdon, is so familiar to the modern tourist. His treatment as a prisoner, amid the snows of those cold mountains, was not indulgent, if his friends in England are to be believed. But such a captive was too valuable to make experiments upon in the matter of torture or starvation. Owen regarded him as worth something more than his weight in gold, and gold was of infinite value to his cause. So he proceeded to assess Grey's ransom at the formidable sum of ten thousand marks, no easy amount for even the greater barons of that time to realise.

The King was greatly distressed when he heard of

his favourite's fate and pictured him as chained to the wall in some noisome dungeon in the heart of those dreary mountains, at the thought of which he shuddered. Rescue was impossible, for the very frontiers of Wales defied him, while the heart of Snowdonia, the natural fortress of the Welsh nation, was at that time almost as far beyond the reach of his arm as Greenland; moreover he had the Scots just now upon his hands.

Grey's captivity lasted nearly a year. Greatly concerned in the matter though the King was, it was not till the following October that he appointed a commission to treat with Glyndwr for his favourite's ransom. This commission consisted of Sir William de Roos, Sir Richard de Grey, Sir William de Willoughby, Sir William de Zouche, Sir Hugh Hals, and six other less distinguished people. Glyndwr agreed to release his prisoner in consideration of ten thousand marks, six thousand to be paid within a month, and hostages, in the person of his eldest son and others, to be delivered to him as guaranty for the remaining four thousand. The Bishop of London and others were then ordered to sell the manor of Hertleigh in Kent, and Grey was to be excused for six years from the burdensome tax then laid on absentee Irish landowners amounting to one-third of their rentals. These payments left him, we are told, a poor man for life. His Ruthin property had been destroyed by Glyndwr himself, and the latter's triumph was complete when the Lord Marcher had to make a humiliating agreement not to bear arms against him for the rest of his life. Hardyng, the rhyming chronicler, does not omit this notable incident:

> "Soone after was the same Lord Grey in feelde
> Fightyng taken and holden prisoner,
> By Owayne, so that him in prison helde,
> Tyll his ransome was made and finance
> Ten thousand marke, and fully payed were dear
> For whiche he was *so poor than all his lyfe*
> *That no power he had to werr ne strife.*"

An unfounded, as well as quite improbable, tradition has found its way into many accounts, which represents Owen as compelling Grey to marry one of his daughters.

While these stirring events were taking place, Glyndwr's thoughts and his correspondence were busy travelling oversea. He was sending letters both to the King of Scotland and the native chieftains of Ireland, soliciting their aid. At this time, too, a certain knight of Cardiganshire named David ap Tevan Goy, who for twenty years had been fighting against the Saracens, with various Eastern Christians, was sent on Owen's behalf by the King of France to the King of Scotland. He was captured, however, by English sailors and imprisoned in the Tower of London.

Glyndwr's own messengers were equally unfortunate, for letters he sent to Robert of Scotland and the Irish chieftains were seized in Ireland and their bearers beheaded. Adam of Usk has fortunately left us a copy of them. Glyndwr had as yet no chancellor or secretary at his side that we know of.

And, indeed, being a man of the world and a well-educated one, it may safely be assumed that he wrote these letters himself. We have so little from his own hand; his personality is in some respects so vague and shadowy; his deeds and their results comprise such a vast deal more of the material from which the man himself has to be judged than is usually the case, that one feels disinclined to omit the smallest detail which brings him, as an individual, more distinctly to the mind. I shall therefore insert the whole text of the captured letters. The first is to the King of Scotland, the second to the lords of Ireland.

"Most high and Mighty and redoubted Lord and Cousin, I commend me to your most High and Royal Majesty, humbly as it beseemeth me with all honour and reverence. Most redoubted Lord and Sovereign Cousin, please it you and your most high Majesty to know that Brutus, your most noble ancestor and mine, which was the first crowned King who dwelt in this realm of England, which of old times was called Great Britain. The which Brutus begat three sons; to wit, Albanact, Locrine, and Camber, from which same Albanact you are descended in direct line. And the issue of the same Camber reigned loyally down to Cadwalladar, who was the last crowned King of the people, and from whom I, your simple Cousin am descended in direct line; and after whose decease, I and my ancestors and all my said people have been and still are, under the tyranny and bondage of mine and your mortal enemies, the Saxons; whereof you most redoubted Lord and very Sovereign Cousin, have good knowledge. And from this tyranny and bondage the prophecy saith that I shall be delivered by the help and succour of your Royal Majesty. But most redoubted Lord and Sovereign Cousin, I make a grievous plaint to your Royal Majesty, and most Sovereign Cousinship, that it faileth me much in soldiers, therefore most redoubted Lord and very Sovereign Cousin, I humbly beseech you kneeling upon my knees, that it may please your Royal Majesty to send me a certain number of soldiers, who may aid me and withstand, with God's help, mine and your enemies, having regard most redoubted Lord and very Sovereign Cousin to the chastisement of this mischief and of all the many past mischiefs which I and my ancestors of Wales have suffered at the hands of mine and your mortal enemies. And be it understood, most redoubted Lord and very Sovereign Cousin that I shall not fail all the days of my life to be bounden to do your service and to repay you. And in that I cannot send unto you all my business in writing, I send these present bearers fully informed in all things, to whom be pleased to give faith and belief in what they shall say to you by word of mouth. From my Court, most redoubted Lord and very Sovereign Cousin, may the Almighty Lord have you in his keeping."

The letter to the Irish lords runs thus:

"Health and fulness of love most dread Lord and most trusty Cousin. Be it known unto you that a great discord or war hath arisen between us and our and your deadly enemies, the Saxons; which war we have manfully waged now for nearly two years past, and henceforth mean and hope to wage and carry out to a good and effectual end, by the grace of God our Saviour, and by your help and countenance. But seeing that it is commonly reported by the prophecy, that before we can have the upper hand in this behalf, you and yours, our well beloved Cousins in Ireland must stretch forth thereto a helping hand, therefore most dread Lord and trusty Cousin, with heart and soul we pray you that of your horse and foot soldiers, for the succour of us and our people who now this long while are oppressed by our enemies and yours, as well as to oppose the treacherous and deceitful will of those same enemies, you despatch to us as many as you shall be able with convenience and honour, saving in all things your honourable State, as quickly as may seem good to you. Delay not to do this by the love we bear you and as we put our trust in you, although we be unknown to you, seeing that, most dread Lord and Cousin, so long as we shall be able to manfully wage this war in our borders, as doubtless is dear to you, you and all the other Chiefs of your land of Ireland will in the meantime have welcome peace and calm repose. And because, my Lord Cousin, the bearers of these presents shall make things known to you more fully by word of mouth, if it please you, you shall give credence to them in all things which they shall say to you on our behalf, and you may trustfully confide to them whatsoever you will, dread Lord and Cousin, that we your poor cousin shall do. Dread Lord and Cousin, may the Almighty preserve your reverence and Lordship in long life and good fortune.

"Written in North Wales on the twenty-ninth day of November [1401]."

CHAPTER V

THE KING AND HOTSPUR

1402

AS if the world of Britain were not already sufficiently excited, the spring of 1402 opened with tremendous portents. In the month of February a comet with its fiery streaming tail, "a terror to the world," broke across the heavens and set all Europe trembling. The bards of Wales rose with one voice to the occasion, headed by Iolo Goch, who recalled the fiery star that heralded the birth of Arthur, and even that other one which guided the Magi to our Saviour's cradle.

The fiery shapes, too, that "lit the front of heaven" at Owen's birth were recalled again with a fresh outburst of enthusiasm, and the tail of this particular comet, which Adam of Usk saw by day as well as by night, while travelling towards Rome, curled up at times, in the eyes of credulous Welsh patriots, into a dragon's shape, the badge of Welsh nationality. Englishmen beheld it pointing at one time towards Wales, at another towards Scotland, and read in these mysterious changes portents for the coming year. Thunder-storms of terrific violence swept over the country. At Danbury, says Holinshed, while the people were in church, lightning struck the roof and destroyed the chancel, and while the storm was at its height the devil entered the sacred building, dressed as a Franciscan friar (one of Owen's well-wishers, it will be remembered), and leaped three times over the altar from right to left; then, turning black in the face, he rushed down the aisle, actually passing between a man's legs, and leaving an over-powering smell of sulphur in his track. The man's legs were black ever after, so that there was no doubt about the nature of the visitant! Other weird things happened in various parts of the country, which do not concern our story, except to show how strained were men's imaginations in a year which after all proved fruitful enough of events.

Whatever faith Owen may have had in his own magical art, he at any rate did not waste time just now in incantations or in interpreting the prophecy, but swept down the Vale of Clwyd, making on his way a final clearance of Grey's desolated property. With much significance, read by the light of his future relations with the Mortimers and Percys, he spared the lordship of Denbigh, though its owners were still his open enemies. Descending the Vale, however, he fell upon Saint Asaph with merciless hand, destroying the cathedral, the bishop's palace, and the canon's house. Trevor was at this time the bishop,—the same, it will be remembered, who warned Henry and his council against exasperating Owen and the Welsh; he had from the first gone over to the new King, had prominently assisted at the deposition of Richard, and had since held many conspicuous offices. He was now a ruined man, an enforced exile from his diocese, and he must have derived but poor consolation from reminding his English friends of the accuracy of his prophecy. He came of the great border House of Trevor, and, among other things, built the first stone bridge in Wales, which may yet be seen stemming with five massive arches the turbulent torrents of the Dee at Llangollen. In the meantime he was a pensioner on the King, but he will appear later in a character of quite another sort. An entry of £66, paid to him at this time in lieu of his losses, appears on the Pell Rolls.

No danger just now threatened from the English border nor, on the other hand, did any help come to Glyndwr from Ireland or the North. There was indeed something of a lull in Wales throughout this spring, unless perhaps for those unfortunate Welshmen who held back from Glyndwr's cause and yet ventured to remain in the country. They, at any rate, had not much peace.

To this date is assigned the well-known story of Glyndwr and his cousin Howel Sele, that gruesome tragedy which has invested the romantic heights of Nannau with a ceaseless interest to generations of tourists, and many more generations of Welshmen, and has seized the fancy of the romancist and the poet. Now Nannau, where Vaughans have lived for many centuries, enjoys the distinction of being the most elevated country-seat in Wales, being some eight hundred feet above Dolgelly, which lies at the base of the beautiful grounds that cover the isolated hill on whose summit the present mansion stands. It is famous also, even in a region pre-eminent for its physical charms, for the surpassing beauty of its outlook, which people from every part of Britain come annually in thousands to enjoy. To the south the great mass of Cader Idris rises immediately above, with infinite grandeur. To the west the Barmouth estuary gleams seaward through a vista of wood and mountain. To the north the valley of the rushing Mawddach opens deep into the hills, while to the eastward, where the twin peaks of the Arans fill the sky, spread those miles of foliage through which the crystal streams of the Wnion come burrowing and tumbling seawards. Nature showed even a wilder aspect to Glyndwr and the then lord of Nannau as they took their memorable walk together upon these same heights five centuries ago.

At that time there stood in the meadows beneath, near the confluence of the Wnion and the Mawddach, the noble abbey of Cymmer, whose remains are still a conspicuous object in the landscape. Howel Sele was by no means an admirer or follower of his cousin Owen, and if latterly he had not dared openly to oppose him, he had at least held back; his relationship to the chief alone saving him, no doubt, from the punishment meted out to others who were less prudent, or less faint-hearted. The worthy abbot of Cymmer, however, for some motive of his own, or perhaps in a genuine spirit of Christianity, endeavoured to promote a better understanding be-

Copyright C. H. Young.

LOOKING UP THE MAWDDACH FROM NANNAU.

tween the relatives, and so far succeeded that Owen consented to come and visit Howel in peaceful fashion, bringing with him only a few attendants.

The meeting took place and an amicable understanding seemed assured. During the course of the day the two men, so runs the tale, went for a stroll in the park, Howel, at any rate, carrying his bow. He was celebrated for his prowess as a marksman, and Owen, catching sight of a buck through the trees, suggested that his cousin should give him an exhibition of his skill. Howel, falling in apparently with the proposal, bent his bow, and having feigned for a moment to take aim at the deer swung suddenly round and discharged the arrow full at Owen's breast. The latter, either from singular forethought or by great good luck, happened to have a shirt of mail beneath his tunic, and the shaft fell harmlessly to the ground. The fate of Howel was swift and terrible. Accounts differ somewhat, but they all agree in the essential fact that neither his wife and family nor his friends ever set eyes upon the lord of Nannau again. It is supposed that the two men and their attendants forthwith engaged in deadly combat, Glyndwr proving the victor, and consigning his cousin to some terrible fate that was only guessed at long afterwards. In any case, he at once burnt the old house at Nannau to the ground, and its remains, Pennant tells us, were yet there in his day, —a hundred years ago. For more than a generation no man knew what had become of the ill-fated Howel, but forty years afterwards, near the spot where he was last seen, a skeleton corresponding to the proportions of the missing man was found inside a hollow oak tree, and it is said that there were those still living who could and did explain how the vanquished Howel had been immured there dead or alive by Glyndwr. The old oak lived on till the year 1813, and collapsed beneath its weight of years on a still July night, a few hours after it had been sketched by the celebrated antiquary, Sir Richard Colt Hoare, who tells us it then measured twenty-seven feet in girth. It had been an object of pious horror for all time to the natives of the district, and was known as the "hollow oak of demons," and dread sounds were heard issuing from its vast trunk by all who were hardy enough to venture near it after nightfall. Sir Walter Scott, who once visited Nannau, remembered the weird story and the haunted oak when he was writing *Marmion:*

> "All nations have their omens drear,
> Their legends wild of love or fear;
> To Cambria look—the peasant see
> Bethink him of Glyndowerdy,
> And shun the spirit's Blasted Tree."

But while Glyndwr was having things pretty much his own way in Wales throughout the spring of 1402, King Henry was in truth in great anxiety. To add to his cares and trouble he was much concerned with endeavours to secure a husband for his daughter Blanche, and a wife for himself in the person of Joanna of Brittany. For the lavish expenditure inseparable from these royal alliances he had to squeeze his people, and they were in no condition

OLD LODGE AT NANNAU, NEAR THE SITE OF THE "OAK OF DEMONS."

to be squeezed, to say nothing of the fact that his captains and soldiers and garrisons in Wales were in a state of pecuniary starvation, and here and there in actual want of food. All this awakened much discontent and there were serious riots in many places. A plot of which the friars, chiefly represented by Glyndwr's friends the Franciscans, were the leaders, was discovered and crushed with much hanging and quartering. Even Henry's loyal subjects of London turned mutinous and their juries refused to convict the priests. The aid, however, of a packed jury in Islington was invoked, who excused themselves for some manifestly outrageous decisions with the naïve but unanswerable plea that if they did not hang the prisoners they would be hanged themselves. The report was still sedulously bruited abroad that Richard was alive, and, if anything, the idea gained ground; while, to complete the distress of the King, the Scots were waging open war upon him in the North, and proving perhaps better allies to Glyndwr than if they had responded to that warrior's appeals and landed in scattered bands upon the coast of Wales. The Percys, however, the King's "faithful cousins," confronted the Scots and were a host in themselves. He despatched his daughter Blanche and her hardly extracted dower to Germany, and a terrible example was made of the friars. Glyndwr and the condition of Wales one can hardly suppose he underestimated, but he permitted himself, at any rate, to shut his eyes to it.

Henry's dream, since mounting the throne, had been an Eastern crusade. So far, however, his own unruly subjects and neighbours had allowed him but little breathing time, and he had been splashed with the mud of almost every county in England and Wales; but now he had gone to Berkhampstead, his favourite palace, to rest and dream of that long-cherished scheme of Eastern adventure.

> "So shaken as we are, so wan with care,
> Find we a time for frighted peace to pant,
> And breathe short-winded accents of new broils
> To be commenced in strands afar remote.
> No more the thirsty entrance of this soil
> Shall daub her lips with her own children's blood;
> No more shall trenching war channel her fields,
> Nor bruise her flowerets with the armed hoofs
> Of hostile paces."

But the month of June was not yet out, when all at once there came upon the King at Berkhampstead "a post from Wales laden with heavy news," which shattered all dreams of Palestine and turned his unwilling thoughts once more to the stormy hills whence came this urgent message.

Late in May, Glyndwr had again left North Wales and with a large force made his way through the present counties of Montgomery and Radnor, and fallen on the as yet unravaged border of Hereford. Now it so happened that among the districts which here suffered the most were those belonging to the young Earl of March, the rightful heir to the throne, and on that account kept secure under lock and key by Henry. This child, for he was nothing more, was descended from Lionel, Duke of Clarence, third son of Edward the Third. His title to the throne stood next to that of Richard, who had himself officially named him as his heir. Henry, sensible of his dangerous claim, kept the boy and his brother under his own charge, leaving their estates in Denbigh and the South Wales Marches to be administered by their uncle, Edmund Mortimer, who was still a young man and not without renown as a soldier. Mortimer and other Lord Marchers had been notified in good time to raise the forces of the border counties and march out to meet the Welsh.

They met upon the border in a narrow valley at Pilleth near Knighton, and the result was wholly disastrous to the English. The Welsh on this occasion were led by Rhys Gethin, one of Owen's most formidable captains, and they utterly overthrew Mortimer's army, driving it down the narrow valley of the Lugg below Pilleth hill where escape was difficult, and slaying eleven hundred men, among whom were great numbers of knights and gentlemen. Mortimer himself was captured, and it was said, with how much truth does not appear evident, that many of Mortimer's troops, who were his tenants, and Welshmen, turned their arms against their own side and made a bloody day still bloodier. The story of the outrages of the Welsh women upon the bodies of the slain is a familiar topic of dispute and not a very savoury one.* In regard to Owen's

* Some thirty years ago the farmers of the district drove their ploughs into the old sod which from time immemorial had covered the long, steep slope of Pilleth hill, or Bryn Glâs. In turning it up they came upon masses of human bones all collected in one spot,

new captive, Mortimer, as the uncle and representative of the rightful heir to the throne, he was of much more actual importance than Grey of Ruthin. But the Welsh chieftain had no personal grudge against the handsome and gallant young soldier who had fallen into his hands by the ordinary fortune of war. Indeed, as we know, he had a kindly feeling for the Percys and the Mortimers; so much so that some of the King's most ardent friends, as well as Henry himself, strongly hinted that Sir Edmund was no unwilling prisoner, and that it was not wholly the chances of war which had placed him in Owen's hands. Mortimer's relations with Glyndwr later on might lend plausibility to such suggestions; but it is difficult to suppose that had the former wished earlier for an alliance with Owen, he would have chosen such an unnecessarily bloody and risky manner of effecting it. Moreover Henry had reason to misrepresent Mortimer's sentiments, for the question of the hour was his ransom. There can, I think, be little doubt that Mortimer was at first as unwilling a prisoner as Grey. He and Owen may have soon developed a personal liking for each other, but that is of little importance. Mortimer at any rate seems to have been sent to Snowdon, or possibly to Owen's small prison at Llansantffraid in Glyndyfrdwy, which totters even now in extreme decay upon the banks of the Dee; and ransom no doubt was regarded as

which indicated without a doubt the burying-place of the battle of 1402. The space was withdrawn from cultivation and a grove of trees was planted on it, which have now grown to a large size and form a prominent object in the valley.

the ordinary outcome of the affair by all parties, except the King. For it soon became evident that Henry, not unwilling to see a possible rival in durance vile and safe out of the way, was going to oppose all overtures for his ransom.

Hotspur, Mortimer's brother-in-law, waxed hot and angry, as of late he had been apt to do with the King, but he was far away in the North looking after the Scottish invaders. He now wrote to Henry that it was a strange thing, seeing the great concern he had showed for Grey of Ruthin, that he should act thus towards a subject who was of even greater consequence, and moreover his (Percy's) brother-in-law. Getting no satisfaction, according to Leland, who quotes from an old chronicle, the fiery Hotspur went southward himself to Henry and demanded in no gentle terms the right to ransom his wife's brother. To this demand the King replied that he would not strengthen those who were his enemies by paying money to them. Hotspur retorted warmly "that the King owed it to those who had risked their lives upon his account, to come to their aid when in peril." The King rejoined angrily, "You are a traitor; you would succour the enemies of myself and my kingdom." "I am no traitor," said Percy, "but faithful and speak in good faith." The King then drew his sword; whereupon Hotspur, exclaiming, "Not here, but on the field of battle," left the royal presence, as it happened, for ever.

This famous interview is practically endorsed by the rhymer Hardyng, Hotspur's personal attendant:

"Sir Henry sawe no grace for Mortimer,
His wife's brother; he went away unkende
To Berwyk so, and after came no nere,
Afore thei met at Shrowesbury in fere
Wher then thei fought for cause of his extent.
He purposed had Mortimer his coronement."

Hardyng in the preceding verse gives two other reasons for the defection of the Percys, and though our story has not yet reached that notable crisis, the lines may perhaps be quoted here:

"The King hym blamed for he toke not Owen,
When he came to him on his assurance,
And he answered then to the King again,
He might not so kepe his affiaunce,
To shame himself, with such a variaunce
The King blamed him for his prisoner,
Th' Erle Douglas, for cause he was not there."

This distinct statement from such an authority that Hotspur had met Glyndwr, referring of course to the previous year in Wales, should be conclusive, though it is not creditable to Henry's honour that he should throw in Hotspur's face the fact of his having failed to act treacherously towards the Welshman. The reference to the Earl of Douglas will become plain shortly.

The victory of Pilleth had caused great enthusiasm among the Welsh, and made a particularly marked impression upon the southern and south-eastern districts, where the Norman baronial houses were strong, and where even the Welsh "gentiles" had by no means as yet given an eager welcome to

Owen's dragon standard with its accompaniment of flaming torches and pitiless spears. Hundreds of hitherto half-hearted Welshmen now joined Glyndwr, who, flushed with victory and strong in its prestige, turned fiercely upon Glamorgan and went plundering, burning, and ravaging his way through that fair county, taking little reck of the score or two of Norman castles so strong in defence but at this time so powerless for offence. He fell on Cardiff and destroyed the whole town, saving only the street where stood a religious house of his friends, or at any rate Henry's enemies, the Franciscans. Turning eastward he then sacked and burnt the bishop's palace at Llandaff, stormed Abergavenny Castle, and destroyed the town.

Leaving his friends to hold the country he had so effectually roused, we next find him in the North, investing the three castles of Carnarvon, Harlech, and Criccieth, and reminding those who in his absence may have faltered in their allegiance that such an attitude was a costly one. Rhys and William ap Tudor from the small stone manor-house in Anglesey that gave a dynasty to Britain are with him again, though the latter, it will be remembered, had sought and gained at Conway the pardon of the King. Robert ap Meredydd of Cefn-y-fan and Gesail-Gyferch near Criccieth, was another trusty henchman of Glyndwr. But Robert's brother Ievan ap Meredydd stood for the King, and was one of the few men in West Carnarvonshire who did so. He was now in Carnarvon Castle, joint governor with John Bolde, and his brother was outside with Owen,

—a little bit of family detail for which, though of no great importance, one is thankful amid the bloody and fiery chaos in which such a vast amount of personality lies forgotten and ingulfed.

It was not long after this that Ievan died in Carnarvon, but so completely occupied was the surrounding country by Owen's forces and sympathisers, that they had to bring his body round by sea to his old home and bury it secretly in his own parish church of Penmorfa, where his dust still lies. His brother Robert, though he held by Glyndwr throughout most of his long struggle, eventually received the royal pardon, and succeeded to the estates. But even his attachment to the Welsh chieftain had not in any way atoned for his brother's opposition, or averted the inevitable fate which overtook the property of all Glyndwr's opponents. Both Cefn-y-fan and Gesail-Gyferch were burnt this year to ashes. At the former the conflagration was so prodigious, says an old local legend, that the ruins smoked and the coals glowed for two whole years afterwards. Gesail-Gyferch was rebuilt by Robert and may be seen to-day, much as he made it, between the villages of Penmorfa and Dolbenmaen. Its owner, when the war was over, married, and had a host of children, from whom innumerable Welsh families are proud to trace their descent. If this gossip about the sons of Meredydd and about Howel Sele may seem too parenthetical, it serves in some sort to illustrate the severance of families and the relentless vengeance which Glyndwr himself executed upon all who opposed him.

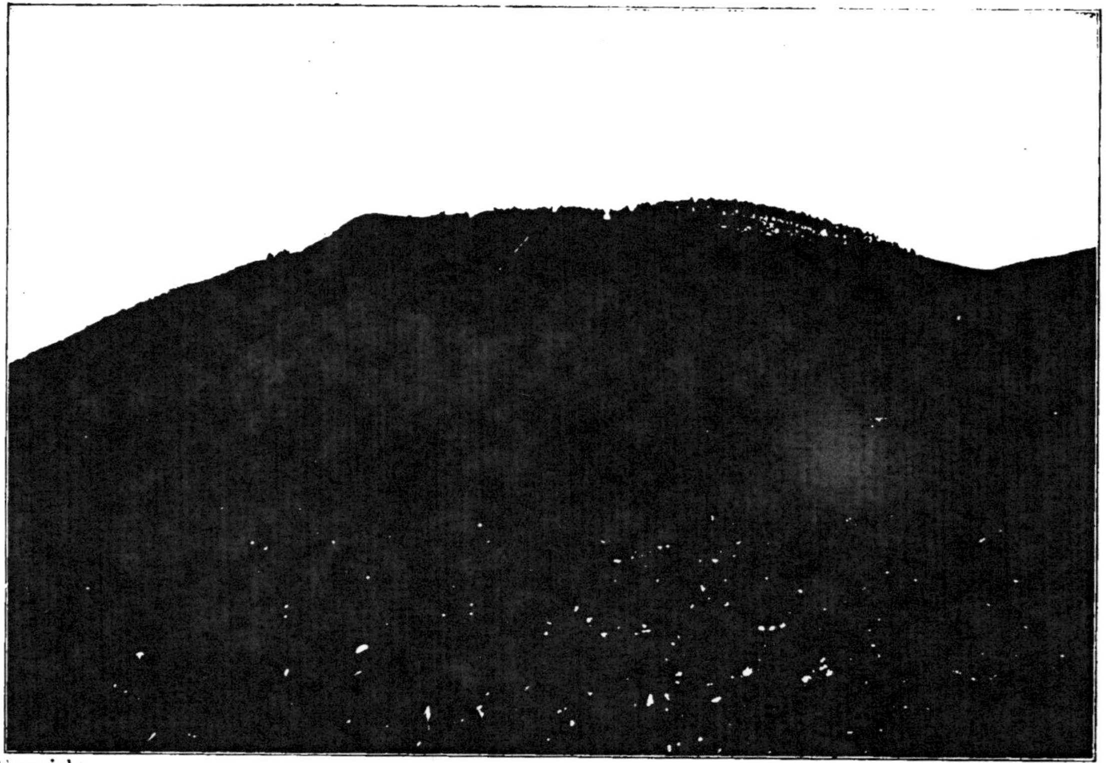

 R. St. John Boddington.

PILLETH HILL, RADNORSHIRE.

In the meantime, while Glyndwr was besieging the castles upon the Carnarvon and Merioneth coast, his great opponent Henry was being sorely pressed. The battle of Pilleth and Mortimer's captivity had raised a storm among those who had been the King's friends, and worse things seemed in the air. Prince Thomas, his second son, who was acting as viceroy in Ireland, was reduced by want of money to sore straits, while forty thousand Scotsmen, with numerous French allies in their train, were far outnumbering any forces the Percys unaided could bring against them. But with all this the King was burning to crush Owen and chastise the Welsh, and it was from no want of will or vigour that he had for so many weeks to nurse his wrath. Richard, Earl de Grey, had been left in charge of the South Wales Marches, while the Earl of Arundel was doing his best to keep order north of the Severn. On July 23rd the King was at Lilleshall, in Shropshire. Provisions, arms, and men were pouring into Welshpool, Ludlow, and Montgomery, Hereford, Shrewsbury, and Chester. Money was scarcer than ever, and had to be borrowed in every direction from private individuals. Henry himself was riding restlessly from Shropshire to Lincoln, from Lincoln to Nottingham, and again from Nottingham to his favourite post of observation at Lichfield.

At last all was ready; the reduction of Wales was for once the paramount object of the King's intentions. Three great armies were to assemble on August the 27th at Chester, Shrewsbury, and Hereford under the commands of the Prince of Wales, the

King himself, and the Earl of Warwick respectively. After much delay this mighty host, numbering in all by a general consensus of authorities one hundred thousand men, prepared to set itself in motion.

It was the first week of September when it crossed the border. The troops carried with them fifteen days' provisions, a precaution much exceeding the ordinary commissariat limitations of those times, but prompted by the bitter memories of three futile and painful campaigns, and more than ever necessary owing to the devastated condition of Wales. With such an army, led by the King himself, England might well think that the Welsh troubles were at an end.

Owen's character as a magician had been firmly established this long time in Wales. His power of eluding the King's armies, to say nothing of his occasional victories, and still more of the way in which the elements had seemed to fight for him, had given him even throughout England something of a reputation for necromancy. The practical mind of Henry himself had been disturbed by the strange rumours that had reached him, coupled with his own experiences of that implacable and irrepressible foe who claimed the power of "calling spirits from the vasty deep," and of being outside "the roll of common men."

If the English had hitherto only half believed that Owen was a wizard, they were in less than a week convinced that he was the very devil himself, against whom twice their hundred thousand men would be of slight avail. Never within man's memory had there been such a September in the Welsh mountains. The very heavens themselves seemed to descend in sheets of water upon the heads of these magnificent and well-equipped arrays. Dee, Usk, and Wye, with their boisterous tributaries that crossed the English line of march, roared bank-high, and buried all trace of the fords beneath volumes of brown tumbling water, while bridges, homesteads, and such flocks as the Welsh had not driven westward for safety were carried downwards to the sea. In these days of rapid travel it seems incredible that so overwhelming and, for the times, well-found a host, could be beaten in less than a fortnight without striking a blow. It is an object-lesson in medieval warfare worth taking to heart and remembering. Night after night the soldiers lay in the open, drenched to the skin, and half starved on account of the havoc wrought upon their provisions by the weather. The thunder roared, we are told, with fearful voice and the lightning flashed against inky skies, above the heads of that shivering, superstitious host, at the will, it seemed to them, of the magic wand of the accursed Glyndwr. Numbers died from exposure. The royal tent was blown flat, and Henry himself only escaped severe injury by being at the moment in full armour.

The King, Hardyng tells us,

> "Had never but tempest foule and raine
> As long as he was ay in Wales grounde ;
> Rockes and mystes, winds and stormes, certaine
> All men trowed witches it made that stounde."

How far the English armies penetrated on this

memorable occasion we do not know; but we do know that by the 22nd of September, just a fortnight after they had first crossed the border, there was not an Englishman in Wales outside the castles, while the King himself, a day or two later, was actually back at Berkhampstead, striving, in the domestic seclusion of his own palace, to forget the unspeakable miseries of his humiliating failure. Where Owen distributed his forces through this tempestuous September, there is no evidence; except that, following the inevitable tactics of his race before great invasions, he certainly retired with his forces into the mountains. It was not even necessary on this occasion to fall upon the retreating enemy. But when one reads of the Welsh retiring to the mountains, the natural tendency to think of them huddling among rocks and caves must be resisted. The Welsh mountains, even the loftiest, in those days were very thickly sprinkled with oak forests, and in the innumerable valleys and foot-hills there was splendid pasture for large herds of stock. There must have been plenty of dwellings, too, among these uplands, and the Welsh were adepts at raising temporary shelters of stone thatched with heather.

Owen now might well be excused if he really began to think himself chosen of the gods. At any rate he was justified in the proud boast that Shakespeare at this time puts into his mouth:

> "Three times hath Henry Bolingbroke made head
> Against my power. Thrice from the banks of Wye
> And sandy-bottomed Severn have I sent
> Him bootless home, and weather-beaten back."

Shakespeare is accurate enough so far, but he is sadly astray when he makes the news of Mortimer's capture and the defeat of Pilleth reach Henry upon the same day as the victory of Percy over the Scots at Homildon. The former was fought in the previous June, whereas the latter took place while Henry was in the very throes of his struggle with the Welsh elements and Owen's art magic. In fact the news of the crushing defeat of the Scots reached him at the moment of his arrival at home, after his disastrous campaign, and might well have afforded him much consolation, unless perchance the contrast between his own luckless campaign and that of Hotspur tempered his joy and galled his pride.

This same battle of Homildon, or Humbledon, near Wooler, exercised considerable influence upon the affairs of Owen. I have already remarked that forty thousand Scots, having with them many French knights and gentlemen, were across the border. They were commanded by Earl Douglas, who had most of the chivalry and nobility of Scotland at his back. There was no particular excuse for the invasion; it was a marauding expedition, pure and simple, on an immense scale, and it swept through Northumberland and Durham almost unopposed, for the forces of Percy were too inadequate for even his venturous spirit to offer battle.

Laden with the spoils of two counties the Scots turned their faces homeward entirely satisfied with their luck. Unfortunately for them, they elected to divide their forces, ten thousand men, including the commander and all the choice spirits of the army, taking a separate route. As these latter approached the Scottish border they found their path barred by Hotspur, who had slipped round them, with a slightly superior force. They would have been glad enough to get home with their booty, but Percy gave them no option; they had nothing for it but to fight.

The result of the battle was disastrous to the Scots. The English archers broke every effort they made to get to close quarters, and finally routed them with scarcely any assistance from the men-at-arms. An immense number were slain; five hundred were drowned in the Tweed; eighty noblemen and knights, the flower of their chivalry, including the Earl of Douglas himself, were captured. A goodly haul for Percy in the shape of ransom! But it was these very prisoners and this very question of ransom that filled Hotspur's cup of bitterness against the King and brought about his league with Glyndwr. The congratulations which went speeding northward from Henry to his "dear cousin" were somewhat damped by instructions that the Scottish prisoners were on no account to be set at liberty or ransomed, but were in fact to be handed over to himself—contrary to all custom and privilege. Large sums were already owing to Percy for his outlay in North Wales on the King's behalf, and he was sullen, as we know, at the King's neglect of his brother-in-law Mortimer, still lying unransomed in Owen's hands. He was now enraged, and his rage bore fruit a few months later on the bloody field of Shrewsbury. Nor did Henry see the face of one of his prisoners till they appeared in arms against him, as the price of their liberty, upon that fateful day.

The close of this year was marked by no events of note; marriage bells were in the air, for the King was espousing Joanna of Brittany, and Mortimer, now embittered against Henry, allied himself with Glyndwr's fortunes and married his fourth daughter, Jane.

Mortimer's alliance was indeed of immense value to Glyndwr. He was not only the guardian and natural protector of the rightful heir to the throne, his nephew, but he was a possibly acceptable candidate himself, in the event of a fresh shuffling of the cards. He had moreover large possessions and castles in the South Wales Marches, and in the Vale of Clwyd, whose occupants would now be irrevocably committed to the Welsh cause.

The monk of Evesham tells us that the marriage was celebrated with the greatest solemnity about the end of November, though where the ceremony took place we do not know. A fortnight afterwards Mortimer wrote to his Radnor tenants this letter in French, which has been fortunately preserved and is now in the British Museum:

"Very dear and well-beloved, I greet you much and make known to you that Oweyn Glyndwr has raised a quarrel of which the object is, if King Richard be alive, to restore him to his crown; and if not that, my honoured nephew, who is the right heir to the said crown, shall be King of England, and that the said Oweyn will assert his right in Wales. And I, seeing and considering that the said quarrel is good and reasonable, have consented to join in it, and to aid and maintain it, and by the grace of God to a good end, Amen. I ardently hope, and from my heart, that you will support and enable me to bring this struggle of mine to a successful issue. I have moreover to inform you that the lordships of Melenyth, Werthresson, Rayadr, the Commote of Udor, Arwystly, Keveilloc, and Kereynon are lately come into our possession. Wherefore I moreover entreat you that you will forbear making inroad into my said lands, or doing any damage to my said tenantry, and that you furnish them with provisions at a certain reasonable price, as you would wish that I should treat you; and upon this very point be pleased to send me an answer. Very dear and well-beloved, God give you grace to prosper in your beginnings, and to arrive at a happy time. Written at Melenyth the 13th day of December.

"EDMUND MORTIMER.

"To my very dear and well-beloved John Greyndor, Howell Vaughan, and all the gentles and commons of Radnor, and Prestremde." *

This note was no doubt chiefly aimed at Sir John Greyndor, or Grindor, who guarded the King's interests and commanded several castles at various times. It was the last incident of moment in the year 1402.

* Presteign.

CHAPTER VI

THE BATTLE OF SHREWSBURY

1403

THE opening of the year 1403 was a time full of promise for Owen's cause. The western castles by whose capture he set such store were hard pressed. Llandovery in the Vale of Towy had been reduced; Llandeilo Fawr, close by, burnt. The noble castle of Dynevor, which had been the royal seat of the Princes of South Wales, was in difficulties, and a descent on the southern shores of England by the French was once more looked for. The Scots, too, had again plucked up their courage, and threatened to give trouble. King Henry was begging or demanding loans from all sorts and conditions of men, that he might be enabled to hold his own against the Welsh, the Scots, and the French. His affairs in truth were anything but prosperous. The Prince of Wales, however, was at his post at Shrewsbury, though pressing for men and money. He informs his father that Glyndwr is preparing to invade England, and Henry communicates the disquieting news to his council, though this is somewhat later, since in May the Prince is writing urgent letters for relief. In these he declares that his soldiers will remain no longer with him unless they are paid, and that Glyndwr is levying all the power of North and South Wales to destroy the Marches and the adjoining counties of England. The Prince goes on to say: "If our men are withdrawn from us we must retire to England and be disgraced forever. At present we have very great expenses, and we have raised the largest sum in our power to meet them from our little stock of jewels." This, it may perhaps be again remarked, is the London roué and trifler of popular fancy!

"Our two castles of Harlech and Lampadarn are besieged and we must relieve and victual them within ten days, and besides that protect the March around us with one-third of our forces. And now since we have fully shown the state of these districts, please to take such measures as shall seem best to you for the safety of these same parts. And be well assured we have fully shown to you the peril of whatever may happen here if remedy be not sent in time."

Reinforcements of some kind must have reached the ardent young soldier very soon. For within a week or two he exercised a most signal piece of vengeance against Glyndwr and apparently without opposition. This was no less than the complete destruction of Sycherth and Glyndyfrdwy, while Owen was busy upon the Merioneth coast. As all we know of this interesting affair is from the Prince's own pen, I cannot do better than quote in full the letter by which he communicated the news to his

Copyright H. H. Hughes.

SYCHERTH, FROM THE NORTH.

father and his council. The original is preserved in the British Museum, and is in the French language. It is dated May 15th, no year unfortunately being affixed. Some difference of opinion as to the latter detail exists, but this year (1403), the latest of those in dispute, seems to me the likeliest.

"Very dear and entirely well beloved, we greet you much from our whole heart, thanking you, very dearly for the attention you have paid to everything needful that concerned us during our absence, and we pray of you very earnestly the continuance of your good and kind disposition; as our trust is in you. By way of news that have here occurred, if you wish to hear of them, we have among other matters been lately informed that Owen de Glyndowrdy has assembled his forces, and those of other rebels adhering to him in great number; purposing to commit inroads, and in case of any resistance being made to him by the English, to come to battle with them, for so he vaunted to his people. Wherefore we took our forces and marched to a place of the said Oweyn well built, which was his principal mansion, called Saghern [Sycherth], where we thought we should have found him, if he had an inclination to fight in the manner he had said, but on our arrival there, we found nobody; and therefore caused the whole place to be burnt, and several other houses near it belonging to his tenants. We thence marched straight to his other place of Glyndowerdy to seek for him there and we caused a fine lodge in his park to be destroyed by fire, and laid waste all the country around. We there halted for the night and certain of our people sallied forth into the country, and took a gentleman of the neighbourhood who was one of the said Oweyn's chief captains. This person offered five hundred pounds for his ransom to preserve his life, and to be allowed two weeks for the purpose of raising that sum of money ; but the offer was not accepted and he received death, as did several of his companions, who were taken the same day. We then proceeded to the Commote of Edeyrnion in Merionethshire, and there laid waste a fine and populous country ; thence we went to Powys, and there being a want of provender in Wales for horses, we made our people carry oats with them and pursued our march ; and in order to give you full intelligence of this march of ours and of everything that has occurred here, we send to you our well beloved esquire, John de Waterton, to whom you will be pleased to give entire faith, and credence in what he shall report to you touching the events above mentioned. And may our Lord have you always in his holy keeping. Given under our Seal at Shrewsbury the 15th day of May."

If, as I think, 1403 is the right year to which we should assign this letter, it may seem strange that Glyndwr should have left his estates to their fate. On the other hand, Sycherth, or Saghern as the Prince calls it, actually touched Offa's Dyke and the English border, while Glyndyfrdwy, as I have before noted, was within sight of Dinas Brân, the grim outpost of English power. Glyndwr's attention had been largely devoted to South Wales and was now bent on securing those great castles on the Merioneth and Carnarvon coast, which with their sea connections threatened him perpetually in his rear. Above all, his aspirations had now soared to such a height and the stake he was playing for was so great it is not likely that the loss of a couple of manor-houses and a few other buildings was of much import to him. If he won his cause, they were of no moment at all. If, on the other hand, he lost it, all was over; they would certainly be no longer his. A want of local knowledge has led many historians astray in the matter of these manors of Glyndwr's, and they have repeated each other's mistakes, ignoring the Cynllaeth property, and only transferring the name of its much larger house to the banks of the Dee. Even Pennant falls into the error, and is probably responsible for that of many of his successors.

This is the more curious in view of Prince Henry's letter, distinctly stating that he first destroyed Owen's principal mansion at that point and naturally so, as it would be the first in his path on the direct route from Shrewsbury, following the valleys of the Vyrnwy and the Tanat, and then up the Cynllaeth brook, where Sycherth lies. Prince Henry's failure to spell the name of Owen's residence intelligibly is of no moment whatever, and is almost lucid compared to some of the Norman attempts to render Welsh names into English.

Sir Henry Ellis and others who, though realising that Owen had two separate properties, are not familiar with the district, fall back on Leland, who alludes to Rhaggat, the present seat of the Lloyds, as having been "a place of Glyndwr's," and explain Prince Henry's "Sagherne" in that manner. Rhaggat, beyond a doubt, whatever dwelling may then have stood there, was the property of Glyndwr, seeing that it was on his Glyndyfrdwy estate and less than two miles up the Dee from his Glyndyfrdwy house. But the Prince would have had to pass by the latter to reach Rhaggat, reversing the stated order of his operations, whereas his short campaign as described by himself took the objects of his attack, Sycharth, Glyndyfrdwy, and the Vale of Edeyrnion in due order. These are matters, it is true, rather of local than of general interest. Still as the locality is one which great numbers of strangers visit for its beauty, I may perhaps be pardoned for entering somewhat minutely into these details.

While the Prince was thus doing his best upon a small scale near the border, and sore distressed for money to pay his men, the castles of Harlech, Criccieth, Conway, Carnarvon, and Rhuddlan were hard pressed. Being in the royal counties, they were held and manned at the royal charge and were feeling to the full the pinch of poverty. Owen, entirely satisfied with the prospect of their speedy reduction, moved south about the time that the Prince was wasting his property on the Cynllaeth and the Dee. We hear of him in piteous letters for aid, sent by Jankyn Havard, the Constable of Dynevor Castle, on the Towy, to his brother—Constable of Brecon, who was in but little better plight. In this correspondence the writer declares that Glyndwr dominates the whole neighbouring country with 8240 spears at his back; that Rhys Gethin, the victor of Pilleth, is with him, also Henry Don, Rhys Ddu, and Rhys ap Griffith ap Llewelyn, the son of that gallant gentleman of Carmarthenshire who made such a cheerful sacrifice of his head, it will be remembered, two years

HAY.

before, when King Henry was at Strata Florida, trying in vain to come to blows with Owen.

"There is great peril for me" continues the panic-stricken Constable, "for they [Glyndwr's soldiers] have made a vow that they will all have us ded therein; wherefor I pray thee that thou wilt not boggle us, but send to us warning within a short time whether we schule have any help or no." The garrison, he reports, are fainting, in victuals and men, and they would all be glad enough to steal away to Brecon, where the castle is in a better state for holding out. "Jenkin ap Llewelyn, William Gwyn, Thomas ap David, and moni other gentils be in person with Owen." He tells also of the capture of Carmarthen just effected by Glyndwr,—both town and castles,—with a loss of fifty men to the defenders. A second letter, written early in July, a few days only after the first one and from the same frightened commandant, describes Glyndwr as still halting in his mind as to whether or no he should burn Carmarthen. It goes on to relate how Owen and most of his army moved forward to the great castle of Kidwelly, which stood upon the seacoast near the mouth of the Towy, some ten miles distant.

But in the meantime the Anglo-Flemings from Western Pembroke and Gower, of all districts in Wales the most hostile to a Cymric revival, were coming up again in strong force, under their lord and governor, Thomas Earl Carew. Glyndwr halted on July 9th at St. Clear's and opened negotiations with Carew, influenced probably by the view that Western Pembroke with its sturdy Teutonic stock, and line of impregnable castles, would prove more difficult to conquer and to hold than the effort was worth. While pourparlers were proceeding, he sent forward seven hundred men, to discover if it were possible to get to the rear of the Anglo-Flemish force, but they were cut off to a man and killed. This was the most serious loss the Welsh had yet sustained. Carew, however, did not follow up his advantage, and Glyndwr, who, we are told, had much booty stored in what was left of Carmarthen, made his headquarters there for several days.

It is impossible to follow Owen step by step through the hurly-burly of ruin, fire, and slaughter which he created during this summer in South Wales. It would be wearisome work, even if we could track his steps from castle to castle, and from town to town with accuracy. But there is ample enough evidence of his handiwork and of the terror he spread, in the panic-stricken correspondence that came out of the Marches from all sorts of people during these months, and which anyone may read to-day. We hear from time to time of his lieutenants, of Rhys Gethin, the Tudors, and many others, but no name in the minds of men ever seems to approach that of the dread chief, who was the life and organiser of every movement. Whether Owen is present in person at a siege or a battle or not, it is always with his enemies, "Owen's men," and "Owen's intentions," "Owen's magic, ambition, and wickedness"; and at the terror of his name nervous people and monks were trembling far into the midland counties. An invasion of England was thoroughly expected at various times during 1403, and such a visit from a warrior who could call at will the lightning and the tempest to his aid, and whose track was marked by a desolation, so it was rumoured, more pitiless than even medieval ethics approved of, was a terrible eventuality. In the eastern counties men were informed for certain that he was soon to be at Northampton, while the monks of St. Albans hung a supplication upon the chancel wall to the Almighty God to spare them from Glyndwr.

John Faireford, Receiver of Brecon, writes urgently to the authorities of the county of Hereford, telling them how all the gentry of Carmarthen had now risen treasonably against the King, and how his friend, the Constable of Dynevor, was in vain appealing to him for help; how Owain Glyndwr with his false troops was at Llandover, the men of that castle being assured to him, and the Welsh soldiers all lying around the castle at their ease; and again how Glyndwr was on his march to that very town of Brecon for the destruction of the same, "which God avert." Faireford begs them to rally all the counties round and to prepare them at once for resisting these same rebels with all haste possible for the avoiding of greater peril. "And you will know," writes he, "that all the Welsh nation, being taken a little by surprise, is adhering to this evil purpose of rebellion, and if any expedition of cavalry can be made be pleased to do that first in these Lordships of Brecon and Cantref Sellys."

Within a few days a letter from the same hand is forwarded to the King himself.

"My most noble and dread Lord, I have received at Brecon certain letters addressed to me by John Skidmore, the which enclosed within this letter, I present unto your high person by the bearer of these, that it may please your gracious lordship to consider the mischief and perils comprised in them, and to ordain thereupon speedy remedy for the destruction and resistance of the rebels in those parts of South Wales, who are treacherously raised against you and your Majesty, so that your castles and towns and the faithful men in them be not thus ruined and destroyed for lack of aid and succour. And besides, may it please your lordship to know that the rebels of this your lordship of Brecon, together with their adherents, are lying near the town of Brecon doing all the mischief they can to its town and neighbourhood, and they purpose, all of them together, to burn all pertaining to the English in these same parts if they be not resisted in haste. The whole of the Welsh nation are by all these said parties conformed in this rebellion, and with good will consent together as only appears from day to day. May it please your royal Majesty to ordain a final destruction of all the false nation aforesaid, or otherwise all your faithful ones in these parts are in great peril."

The sheriff of Hereford had been warned by the King to proceed against Brecon with the forces of his county, and relieve the siege. This he reports later, that he has done with some success; slaying 240 of the Welsh, though with what loss to himself he refrains from mentioning. This diversion seems in no way to have relieved the general situation; for after describing the fight at Brecon he goes on to state that "these same rebels purpose again to come in haste with a great multitude to take the town (which God avert) and to approach to the Marches and counties adjoining to the destruction of them, which force we have no power to resist without your most earnest aid and succour, and this greatly displeases us by reason of the grievous costs and labours which it will be needful for us to sustain. In reference to which matters, our most dread and sovereign Lord, may it please you to ordain speedy remedy, which cannot be as we deem without your gracious arrival in these parts for no other hope remains."

This appeal is signed "your humble lieges the Sheriffs, Knights, Esquires, and Commons of your County of Hereford." Hugh de Waterton follows in the same alarmist strain:

"For the honour of God and the preservation of your estate and honour may it please your Highness to have this in your remembrance and soon to cause to commit to such an array of sufficient persons, knights, and esquires, as shall be willing to give their whole diligence and trouble for the protection of your honour in the preservation of your faithful lieges and the punishment of your rebels, or otherwise the only thing that can be said, is, it is likely you will find all in confusion which God avert."

Then follows William de Beauchamp writing to the same purpose in a long, rambling letter to the King. Lastly Richard Kingeston, Archdeacon of Hereford and Dean of Windsor and general administrator for the King on the Southern Marches, within the same period of panic, appeals direct to his Majesty.

In one of these missives he says:

"From day to day letters are arriving from Wales by which you may learn that the whole country is lost unless you go there as quick as possible. Be pleased to set forth with all your power and march by night as well as by day, for the salvation of those parts. It will be a great disgrace as well as damage to lose in the beginning of your reign a country which your ancestors gained and retained so long; for people speak very unfavourably; . . ."

This is signed "Your lowly creature, Richard Kingeston," with a postscript added, "And for God's love, my liege Lord, think on yourself."

The second letter, written somewhat later, contains the following:

"There are come into our country more than four hundred of the rebels of Owen and they have captured and robbed within your county of Hereford many men and beasts in great number as Miles Walter the bearer of these presents will more fully tell you by mouth than I can write to you at present, to whom may it please you to give your faith and credence in that on which he shall inform you for the preservation of your said county and of all the country around."

The said Miles Walter, moreover, is

"the most valiant man at arms in Herefordshire or the Marches as he has served his Majesty well and lost all that he hath. He begs for a hundred lances and six hundred archers at once until your most gracious arrival for the salvation of us all; for, my most dread

Lord, you will find for certain that if you do not come in your own person to await your rebels in Wales you will not find a single gentleman that will stop in your said county [Hereford], and leave naught that you do not come, for no man that may counsel you to the contrary. This day the Welshmen suppose that and trust that you will not come there and therefore for God's love make them false men. . . . For salvation of your shire and Marches trust you naught to any lieutenant.

"Written at Hereford in very great haste.

"Your humble creature and
continual orator."

I have somewhat tried the reader's patience, perhaps, with such a multiplication of extracts all sounding the same note; but in dealing with scenes so scanty of all record save the bare detail of siege and slaughter, it seems to me that human voices, full of the fears and alarms of the moment, coming to us out of this almost forgotten period, have more than ordinary value. Glyndwr, too, at this moment steps out of his armour and gives us one of those brief glimpses of the man within, which one so eagerly grasps at. To what extent he was himself imbued with the superstition that surged around him and so conspicuously centred upon his own name, must always be a matter of curiosity. That he was very far from a sceptic, however, he gives us conclusive proof; for while lying at Carmarthen after settling matters with Carew, he was seized with a desire to consult a soothsayer; and acting upon this he sent for a certain Welshman out of Gower, whose reputation for forecasting future events, and "skill in interpreting the Brut," was great. Hopkyn ap Thomas was the name of this prophet of Gower, and when Owen demanded what the future had in store for himself and his cause, the local wise man showed himself at any rate no sycophant, though a false prophet, as it so turned out. For he boldly informed the Welsh leader that within a short time he would be taken prisoner under a black banner between Carmarthen and Gower.

But all this earlier period of the summer, while Glyndwr was marching this way and that throughout South Wales, now repelling the Flemings on the west, now ravaging the English border on the east, matters in England closely connected with his own fortunes were quickly ripening for one of the most critical events of this period of English history. The Prince of Wales, after his brief raid on Sycherth and Glyndyfrdwy, had remained inactive at Shrewsbury, unable from lack of means to move the levies of the four border counties, who remained in whole or part, and somewhat discontented, beneath his banner. The Pell Rolls show a note for July 17th, of the sum of £8108 for the wages of four barons, 20 knights, 476 esquires, and 2500 archers. The King, who had been by no means deaf to the frantic appeals which had come pouring in upon him from Wales, had fully intended to act upon them in person. He was always as ready, however, to answer a summons from the North as he was reluctant to face the truth in the West. Wales had been virtually wrested from him by Glyndwr, and he had ample warning that the latter was even preparing for an invasion of England, where there existed a growing faction, wearied by his ceaseless demands for money, which produced so little glory and so much disgrace.

But once again he turned from scenes that for a long time had been a standing reproach, both to himself and England, and started for the North. Even if he had been only bent on assisting the Percys in stemming a threatened invasion of the Scots, one might well suppose that the virtual loss of what was a considerable portion of his dominions near home, together with an equally imminent invasion from that quarter, would demand his first attention. But there is not even this much to be said. The King cherished aspirations to be another Edward the First; he had already achieved a precarious footing in Scotland and made grants of conquered territory across the border to English subjects, always providing, of course, they could maintain themselves there. One has the strange picture of an otherwise sensible and long-headed monarch accepting perennial defeat and defiance in Wales, while straining after the annexation of distant territories that were as warlike as they were poor. The Percys had in fact for the past few months been playing at war with the Scots, and deceiving Henry, while laying plans for a deep game in quite another part of Britain. The King, stern and at times even cruel towards the world in general, was astonishingly complacent and trustful towards that arch-plotter, the Earl of Northumberland, who in defiance of his master, though in strict accord with equity, had kept his hold upon the Scottish prisoners of Homildon;

answering the King's letters of remonstrance in light and even bantering vein. But now all trace of ill-feeling would seem to have vanished, as Henry and his forces, on July 10th, rest for a day or two at Higham Ferrers, on their way to the assistance of the Percys; not to stem an invasion of the Scots, but to further the King's preposterous and ill-timed designs upon their territory. But this mad project was nipped in the bud at the Northamptonshire town in a manner that may well have taken Henry's breath away and brought him to his senses.

He has just informed his council that he has received news from Wales telling him of the gallant bearing of his beloved son, and orders £1000 to be paid to his war chest. He then proceeds to tell them that he is on his way to succour his dear and loyal cousins, the Earl of Northumberland and his son Henry, in the conflict which they have honourably undertaken for him, and as soon as that campaign shall have ended, with the aid of God he will hasten to Wales. The next day he heard that his "beloved and loyal cousins" were in open revolt against him, and, instead of fighting the Scots, were hastening southwards with all their Homildon prisoners as allies and an ever gathering force to join Glyndwr.

What was the exact nature of this alliance, whose proclamation fell upon the King like a thunderclap, can only be a matter of conjecture. There are whispers, as we know, of messages and messengers passing between Glyndwr and Mortimer on the one hand and the Percys on the other, this long time. That they intended to act in unison there is, of

Copyright J. Bartlett.

BATTLE-FIELD CHURCH, NEAR SHREWSBURY.

course, no doubt. Shakespeare has anticipated by some years and used with notable effect the famous "Tripartite Alliance," which was signed by Glyndwr, Mortimer, and the Earl of Northumberland at the Dean of Bangor's house at Aberdaron on a later occasion. One regrets that in this particular he is not accurate, for the dramatic effect, which as a poet he had no reason to resist, is much more telling before the field of Shrewsbury than it can be at any subsequent time.

The well-known scene, where Glyndwr, Mortimer, and Hotspur stand before an outspread map of England, and divide its territory between them, is probably to thousands of Englishmen their only distinct vision of the Welsh chieftain as an historical character. But though this formal indenture, as we shall see, was entered into much later, there is no doubt that some very similar intention existed even now in the minds of the allies. Glyndwr's reward was obvious. As to the throne of England, Richard's ghost was to be resuscitated for the purpose of creating enthusiasm in certain credulous quarters and among the mob; but the young Earl of March was the real and natural candidate for the throne. Edmund Mortimer, however, stood very near to his young nephew. He was Hotspur's brother-in-law, and who could tell what might happen? He had the sympathy of the Welsh, not only because his property lay in their country, but because he could boast the blood of Llewelyn ap Iorwerth, to say nothing of his intimate connection with the Welsh hero himself. The Earl of Northumberland may have had some understanding with regard to northern territory, such as he bargained for in later years, but of this we know nothing. It was an ill-managed affair in any case, and it is probable that the conditions in case of victory were loosely defined.

The King had reached Lichfield when the astounding news burst upon him that he was betrayed, and that he had not only to fight Glyndwr and the Scotch, but to wrestle with the most powerful of his subjects for his crown. Glyndwr was, of course, in the secret, but plans had miscarried, or messengers had gone astray. Without wearying the reader with proofs and dates, it will be sufficient to recall the fact that on July 12th Owen was negotiating with Carew, and for the next few days his hands and head were busily at work before the castle of Dynevor. He had at that time no thought of leaving South Wales, and this was within four or five days of the great fight at Shrewsbury, nearly a hundred miles off, which poets and romancists have painted him, of all people, as cynically regarding from the safe vantage-point of a distant oak tree!

Henry, prompt in an emergency and every inch a soldier when outside Wales, lost not a moment. He had with him but a moderate force, mostly his loyal Londoners. The Prince of Wales was near Shrewsbury with his recent reinforcements, and quickly summoned. Urgent orders were sent out to the sheriffs of the home counties, and on Friday, July 20th, in the incredibly short space of five days, the King and Prince entered Shrewsbury with an army of nearer thirty than twenty thousand men. They were just in time, for that same evening Hotspur (for his father had been detained in Northumberland by illness) with a force usually estimated at about 15,000, arrived at the city gates, only to find to his surprise the royal standard floating from the castle tower, and the King already in possession. It was then late in the afternoon and Hotspur led his army to Berwick, a hamlet three miles to the north-west of Shrewsbury. Though his father was not present, his uncle, Thomas Percy, Earl of Worcester, had lately joined him, having stolen away from the side of Prince Henry, whose chief adviser he had lately been. The Scottish Earl Douglas, who had been his prisoner at Homildon, was now his ally, having, together with his comrades in misfortune, purchased liberty in this doubtless congenial fashion. Percy had left Northumberland with 160 followers. His force had now grown, as I have already remarked, to something like 15,000 men.

The County Palatine of Chester, always turbulent and still faithful to Richard's memory, was most strongly represented in his ranks, and its archers were among the best in England.* Numbers, too, of Glyndwr's supporters from Flint and the Powys lordships joined his standard, and Richard's badge

* It had been made a military Palatinate by William the Conqueror, with the special object of coercing North Wales. Having lapsed to the Crown in Richard's time, that King had leaned greatly in his difficulties on its warlike and independent population. The latter with its military efficiency had developed a corresponding arrogance and local pride, and Richard had been the last object of its provincial devotion.

of the White Hart was prominent on their shields and tunics. But Hotspur had assuredly reckoned on meeting Glyndwr, and now where was he? He had certainly never counted on being stopped by the King with a superior force upon the borders of Wales. He had now no choice but to fight, and even Hotspur's fiery spirit must have drooped for a moment when he counted the odds.

The morning of the 21st broke and there was still no Glyndwr and no alternative but battle; so, marching his troops to Heytely or Bull field, a short three miles to the north of Shrewsbury on the Wem road, he drew them up in order of battle, near the place where the church that was raised above their graves now stands.

Hotspur for the moment was depressed. He had just discovered that the hamlet where he had spent the night was called Berwick, and a soothsayer in the North had foretold that he should "fall at Berwick," meaning, of course, the famous town upon the Tweed. The coincidence affected Percy and showed that if Glyndwr was superstitious so also was he; for, turning pale, he said: "I perceive my plough is now drawing to its last furrow." But the most lion-hearted soldier in England soon shook off such craven fears and proceeded to address his men in a speech which Holinshed has preserved for us: a spirited and manly appeal which we must not linger over here. The King was curiously slow in moving out against his foes, and even when, after noontide, he had drawn up his formidable army in their front, he gave his faithless friends yet one more chance, sending the Abbot of Shrewsbury to offer them good terms even at this eleventh hour, and it was certainly not fear that prompted the overture. Hotspur was touched and inclined to listen, but his hot-headed or mistrustful uncle of Worcester overruled him, even going himself to the King's army and using language that made conciliation impossible. It must have been well into the afternoon when the King threw his mace into the air as a signal for the bloodiest battle to open that since the Norman conquest had dyed the soil of England.

With such a wealth of description from various authors, more or less contemporary, it is not easy to pick out in brief the most salient features of this sanguinary fight. It will be sufficient to say that the shooting of Percy's Cheshire archers was so terrific at the opening of the battle that the royal army was thrown into confusion and only saved from rout by the valour and presence of mind of the King, who rallied his shaken troops and bore upon the smaller forces of his enemy with irresistible pressure; that the desperate charges of Hotspur and Lord Douglas, cleaving lanes through their enemy as they sought the King's person, were the leading personal features of a fight where all were brave. The valour of the young Prince Henry, too, seeing how prominent a figure he is in our story, must be recorded, and how, though badly wounded by an arrow in the face, he resisted every effort to drag him from the field and still sought the spot where the fight was fiercest and the dead thickest. The courage and coolness of the King, too, whose crown and kingdom were at stake, shone brightly in the deadly mêlée, where his standard was overthrown, its bearer slain, and the Constable of England, Lord Stafford, killed at his feet. Hotspur, who had fought like a lion with a score of knightly opponents, fell at length, pierced by a missile from some unknown hand; and before sunset his army was in full flight. The slaughter was tremendous, and lasted far into the dark hours; for it is curiously significant that as an early moon rose over that bloody field, its face was quickly hidden by an eclipse that may well have excited the already strained imaginations of so superstitious an age. About four thousand men lay dead upon the field, among them two hundred knights and gentlemen of Cheshire alone, who had followed Percy. The Earl of Worcester and Lord Douglas were both captured, the former receiving a traitor's death. The corpse of the gallant Hotspur, after being buried by a kinsman, was dug up again and placed standing upright between two millstones in Shrewsbury market-place, that all men might know that the fierce Northumberland whelp, the friend of Glyndwr, was dead. His quarters were then sent, after the manner of the time, to decorate the walls of the chief English cities, the honour of exhibiting his head over the gates being reserved for York.

Under Henry's patronage.

The more illustrious dead were buried in the graveyards of Shrewsbury. The rest were, for the most part, huddled into great pits adjoining the spot where the old church, that was raised under Henry's patronage as a shrine wherein masses might be said for their souls, still lifts its grey tower amid the quiet Shropshire fields.*

And all this time Glyndwr, in far Carmarthen, was in total ignorance of what a chance he had missed, and what a calamity had occurred. If Hotspur had been better served in his communications, or fate in this respect had been kinder, and Glyndwr with 10,000 men had stood by the Percys' side, how differently might the course of English history have run! It is fortunate for England, beyond a doubt, that Hotspur fell at Shrewsbury and that Glyndwr was not there, but from the point of view of his after reputation, one cannot resist the feeling that a great triumph upon the open plains of Shropshire, in an historic fight, would have set that seal upon Glyndwr's renown which some perhaps may think is wanting. Reckless deeds of daring and aggression are more picturesque attributes for a popular hero. But Glyndwr's fame lies chiefly in the patience of his strategy, his self-command, his influence over his people, his tireless energy, his strength of will, and dogged persistence. He had to do a vast deal with small means: to unite a country honeycombed with

* Battle-field Church, which now serves a small parish, is probably the only instance in England of a church erected over the burial-pits of a battle for the purpose of saying masses for the victims of a great slaughter, and that now does duty as a parish church. The fabric has had periods of dilapidation and been much restored, but a good part of the walls is original. There was a college originally attached to it, but all trace of this has disappeared. My first visit to the battle-field was in company with the Rev. Dymock Fletcher, well known as a Shropshire antiquary, who has published an interesting pamphlet on this subject.

alien interests, to fight enemies at home and beyond the mountain borders of his small fatherland, and to struggle with a nation that within man's memory had laid France prostrate at its feet. Private adventures and risky experiments he could not afford. A great deal of statecraft fell to his share. His efforts for Welsh independence could not ultimately succeed without allies, and while he was stimulating the irregular military resources of the Principality, and making things safe there with no gentle hand, his mind was of necessity much occupied with the men and events that might aid him in the three kingdoms and across the seas. His individual prowess would depend almost wholly on tradition and the odes of his laureate, Iolo Goch, if it were not for his feat against the Flemings when surrounded by them on the Plinlimmon Mountains:

> "Surrounded by the numerous foe,
> Well didst thou deal the unequal blow,
> How terrible thy ashen spear,
> Which shook the bravest heart with fear.
> More horrid than the lightning's glance,
> Flashed the red meteors from thy lance,
> The harbinger of death."

But Glyndwr's renown, with all its blemishes, rests on something more than sword-cuts and lance-thrusts. He had been three years in the field, and for two of them paramount in Wales. Now, however, with the rout and slaughter of Shrewsbury, and the immense increase of strength it gave to Henry, a crushing blow had surely been struck at the Welsh chieftain and his cause. Numbers of Owen's people in Flint and the adjoining lordships, cowed by the slaughter of half the gentry of sympathetic Cheshire, and their own losses, came in for the pardon that was freely offered. The King had a large army, too, on the Welsh border, and the moment would seem a singularly propitious one for bringing all Wales to his feet, while the effect of his tremendous victory was yet simmering in men's minds. But Henry was too furious with the Percys for cool deliberation. The old Earl had not been absent from the field of Shrewsbury from disinclination, but from illness; and he was now in the North stirring up revolt upon all sides. But the ever active King, speeding northward, checkmated him at York in such a way that there was no option for the recusant nobleman but to throw himself at his injured prince's feet and crave forgiveness. It is to Henry's credit that he pardoned his ancient friend. Perhaps he thought the blood of two Percys was sufficient for one occasion; so the old Earl rode out of York by the King's side, under the festering head of his gallant son, on whom he had been mean enough to throw the onus of his own faithlessness, and was placed for a time out of mischief at Coventry.

By the time, however, that Henry came south again the battle of Shrewsbury, so far as Wales was concerned, might never have been fought. Glyndwr's confidence in the South was so great that he had himself gone north to steady the men of Flint and the borders in their temporary panic. His mission seems to have been so effective that by the time the King was back it was the town of Chester and the neighbouring castles that were the victims of a panic. An edict issued by Prince Henry, who lay recovering from his wound at Shrewsbury, ordered the expulsion of every Welshman from the border towns, the penalty for return being death. Strenuous efforts were again made to stop all trade between England and Wales, but it was useless; a continuous traffic in arms and provisions went steadily on, the goods being exchanged for cattle and booty of all kinds in which Owen's mountain strongholds now abounded. On the Welsh side of Chester, hedges and ditches were hastily formed as a protection against invasion, and watchers were kept stationed night and day along the shores of the Dee estuary.

It was the 8th of September when Henry arrived from the north and prepared at Worcester for his long-deferred expedition against Glyndwr. He first issued formal orders to the Marcher barons to keep their castles in readiness against assault and in good repair!—a superfluous warning one would have thought, and not devoid of irony, when addressed to men who for a year or two had just managed to maintain a precarious existence against the waters of rebellion that surged all round them. Henry was at his very wits' end for money, and all those in his interest were feeling the pinch of poverty. It so happened that at this juncture the Archbishop of Canterbury was attending the Court at Worcester, and the sight of his magnificent retinue aroused dangerous thoughts in the minds of the barons around the King, who had spent so much blood and treasure in his service and were now sorely pinched for want of means. The same ideas occurred to Henry, if indeed they were not suggested to him, and in no uncertain voice he called upon the Church for pecuniary aid against Glyndwr. The Archbishop took in the situation and sniffed spoliation in the air. At the bare idea of such intentions he grew desperate, and with amazing courage bearded the King himself, swearing that the first man who laid a finger on church property should find his life no longer worth living and his soul for ever damned. The King was forced to soothe the excited cleric, who in later and calmer moments came to the conclusion that it would be perhaps prudent for the Church to offer some pecuniary assistance to the Crown. This was ultimately done, and the sum contributed was about enough to pay the expenses of one of the forty or fifty castles that were gradually falling into Owen's hands.

In the meantime, Glyndwr had invaded Herefordshire, penetrating as far as Leominster, and had compelled that county to make special terms with him and pay heavily for them too. The King, however, had now everything in train for a general advance through South Wales. What he did there and what he left undone must be reserved for another chapter.

CHAPTER VII

OWEN AND THE FRENCH

1403–1404

KING Henry's fourth expedition against Glyndwr, in spite of all the talk, the preparations, the hard-wrung money grants, the prayers and supplications for aid, will make but scant demands upon our space. He spent some days at Hereford, issuing orders for stores to be forwarded to the hard-pressed castles of South Wales from the port of Bristol, though it is obvious that only some of them could be relieved by sea. The names of a few of these may interest Welshmen. They were Llandovery, Crickhoell, Tretower, Abergavenny, Caerleon, Goodrich, Ewyas, Harold, Usk, Caerphilly, Ewyas, Lacy, Paines, Brampton Bryan, Lyonshall, Dorston, Manorbier, Stapleton, Kidwelly, Lampeter, Brecon, Cardiff, Newport, Milford, Haverford-west, Pembroke, and Tenby.

The King left Hereford about the 15th of September and he was seated a few days later among the ruins of Carmarthen, the very centre of the recent wars and devastations. Glyndwr and his people were, of course, nowhere to be seen, nor did the King show any disposition to hunt for them. He remained about two days at Carmarthen, and contented himself with issuing all kinds of orders, proclamations, pardons, and confiscations, which were for the most so much waste paper. Leaving behind him the Earl of Somerset with an inefficient garrison and no money to pay them, he then faced about, and made the best of his way back again, arriving at Hereford within four days. When one recalls Edward the First, who considered nearly three years of personal residence none too short a time in which to establish order in Wales, which was at that time by no means so wholly hostile as now, the feebleness of Henry's Welsh policy strikes one with singular force. Had he been his cousin Richard or an Edward the Second, a man sluggish in war and a slave to luxury, the explanation would be simple enough; but though his Court was extravagant, almost culpably so, the King himself was an energetic, serious-minded soldier, and a man of affairs rather than of pleasure. One might well have supposed, after the decisive victory at Shrewsbury, and the firm grip on the throne which the destruction of his domestic enemies gave to the King, that Glyndwr's hour had at last come.

It is almost wearisome to tell the same old tale of "scuttle," the same trumpeting forth of orders to captains and governors of castles and Marcher barons to do, with scant men and means, what their master had so conspicuously flinched from with the power of England, such as he had made it, at his command. It is needless to say that the King's homeward tracks through Wales were obliterated, when his back was turned, like those upon sand, before the returning tide of Owen and his Welshmen, who had swept through Glamorgan and were pressing Cardiff, even while Henry was still travelling homewards. He had hardly reached London before he received piteous letters from the chiefs of the garrison that had been left at Carmarthen, begging him to send the Duke of York there with strong reinforcements or they were lost men, and protesting that in no case could they stay there a day longer than the stipulated month, for their men would not stand by them.

Glyndwr had received some sort of consolation from the French for the blow struck at his English allies on the plains of Shrewsbury. Their corsairs had been harrying the shores of England throughout the summer. Plymouth, Salcombe, and other places had been raided, while flotillas were even now hovering round the coast of Wales, in the interests of Owen. Herefordshire, which had received the long-looked-for King with such unbounded joy in September, and hailed him as its deliverer, was, in October, in as bad a plight as ever, for Glyndwr's men had again poured over the borders. And though the King with his thousands had come and gone like a dream, the people of Hereford and Gloucester were now glad enough to welcome the Duke of York with nine hundred spearmen and archers. The Courtenays with a force of Devonshire men had been ordered across the Severn sea to relieve Cardiff, but this they failed in doing, as now not only that fortress, but Caerphilly, Newport, Caerleon, and Usk fell into Owen's hands.

The number of men that Glyndwr had with him at various times is difficult to estimate. Now and then contemporary writers quote the figures. In South Wales lately it will be remembered he had nearly ten thousand. In Carmarthen at another time the number from an equally credible source is estimated at thirty thousand. His spearmen were better than his archers. The Welsh archers, till the Union and the wars with France, had used short bows made generally of twisted twigs and formidable only at a close range. Archery, however, in its highly developed state must have become familiar by this time, through the co-operation of the Welsh in the French wars. The Welsh spears were exceptionally long, and the men of Merioneth had a special reputation for making efficient use of them. They were all, however, eminently light troops, though equipped with steel caps, breastplates, and often with greaves. "In the first attack," says Giraldus Cambrensis, "the Welsh are more than men, in the second less than women," and he knew them well. But their want of staunchness under repulse, he takes care to tell us, was temporary. They were a people well-nigh impossible to conquer, he declares, from the rapidity with which they recovered from defeat and the tenacity with which they returned, not always immediately, but sooner or later, to the attack, refusing to acknowledge ultimate defeat, and desperately attached to liberty. Glyndwr had practically no cavalry. Horses were very widely in use, perhaps ponies still more so, amid the mediæval Welsh, and their gentry and nobility went mounted to war from the earliest times. But it is likely that in Wales itself, at any rate, all ranks did their actual fighting on foot.

Of the disposition of Glyndwr's forces and their personnel beyond a few of his captains we know little. It seems almost certain that the men of the South for the most part fought in the south, and those of the North in the north. If he had a nucleus of soldiers that followed him in his rapid movements from one end of the Principality to the other it was a comparatively small one. In every district he had trusted leaders who looked after his interests, and on his appearance, or at his summons, rallied their followers to battle, and upon their own account made the lives of the beleaguered Saxons in their midst intolerable. By this time, however, and indeed before it, every man who was not a professed subject of the descendant of Llewelyn and of Madoc ap Griffith, had fled Wales, except those who were swelling the population of the ill-victualled and closely beleaguered castles. Glyndwr had before him many a doughty Anglo-Norman warrior, under walls well-nigh impervious to anything but starvation, whose crumbling shells on many a Welsh headland and hilltop still wake memories of the past and stir our fancy.

Lord Audley was at Llandovery, Sir Henry Scrope at Langhame, John Pauncefote held Crickhowl, and James Berkeley, Tretower. At Abergavenny was a

Beauchamp, at Goodrich a Neville. The splendid pile of Caerphilly, whose ruins are the largest in Britain, was in the charge of a Châtelaine, Lady Despenser. The noble castle of Manorbier, where Giraldus was born, in that of Sir John Cornwall, while the Earl of Warwick was at Paines, and a Charlton, of course, at Welshpool.

About the same time, some French companies were landing in Carmarthen to add further to the woes of Henry in Wales; and for the comfort of Glyndwr. The King himself was entering London, and to show how little the people of one end of the country sometimes realised what was actually happening at the other, the citizens, who were always his particular friends, gave him quite an enthusiastic reception. It should, however, be remembered that the Londoners had been in great force at Shrewsbury, and the triumphs of that bloody fight were still ringing in men's ears.

It was not till two years after this that the great French effort was made on Owen's behalf, of which we shall hear in due course, but even now a few hundred Bretons, as already related, had found their way to Wales. They flinched from the great Pembroke castles and, adventuring upon their own account, crept round the coast of Lleyn and made an attempt upon Carnarvon. A very short stay before that matchless pile of Norman defensive art sufficed upon this occasion for the invaders, though soon afterwards they landed and joined Glyndwr in its investment. The island of Anglesey in the meantime, cut off from the rest of Wales by the castles and "English towns" of Conway and Carnarvon, and its own almost equally formidable stronghold of Beaumaris, had for the moment given in to English reinforcements from Chester, and accepted the freely offered pardon of the Prince of Wales. It is a singular fact that, while so many of Glyndwr's soldiers, headed by the Tudors, came from Anglesey and near the close of his wars 2000 of its inhabitants were actually in arms, no battle or even skirmish took place there, so far as we know, during the whole period of these operations.

But Carnarvon, now at this date, January, 1404, was as a matter of fact in a lamentable condition as regards defenders. The garrison had declined to less than thirty men, and there are letters in Sir Henry Ellis's collection showing the desperate state to which this and other castles were reduced. It seems at the first sight incredible that such a handful of men could hold so great a fortress against serious attacks. The walls and defences of Carnarvon Castle are to-day much what they were in the times of Glyndwr. It is perhaps almost necessary to walk upon its giddy parapets, to climb its lofty towers, in order to grasp the hopelessly defiant front such a fortress must have shown to those below it before the time of effective artillery: the deep moat upon the town side, the waters of the harbour a hundred feet below the frowning battlements upon the other, the huge gateway from which the portcullis grinned and the upraised drawbridge swung. Twenty-eight men only were inside when Owen with a force of his own people and the French threw themselves against it.

Copyright F. Frith & Co.

CARNARVON CASTLE.

The besiegers had engines, "scowes," and scaling ladders, but the handful of defenders were sufficient, for the time being at any rate, to hurry from point to point, and frustrate all attempts to surmount the lofty walls, though these attempts, no doubt, were made at many points simultaneously. The Constable John Bolde was away, but one Parry, his deputy, was in command. It was urgent that a message should be sent to Chester, acquainting Venables, the governor, of their desperate situation. Not a man, as may well be believed, could be spared, so a woman was despatched to take the news by word of mouth, for few dared in those days to carry letters.

Harlech was in an equally bad plight, its defenders being reduced to twenty-six, but it was as impregnable as Carnarvon, and much smaller. The garrison had been so mistrustful of their governor's fidelity that they had locked him up. During January their numbers were reduced to sixteen, but they still held manfully out against the Welsh under Howel Vychan. They eventually succeeded in sending word across the bay to Criccieth, and to Conway also, of their condition. Conway had been urgently petitioning the King and assuring him that 400 more men would suffice to hold the castles till the spring, but that then "when the rebels can lie out which they cannot now do" a far greater number would be required; but the King either could not or would not understand. Harlech, grim and grey on its incomparable rocky perch, required fewer defenders even than the rest. The sea then swept over the half-mile strip of land, the "Morfa Harlech," that now lies dry beneath it, and lapped the base of the lofty rock on whose summit the great Edward's remotest castle still stands defiant of the ages.*

Henry had issued orders that these seagirt castles should be looked to by his navy. But Henry's admirals seem to have had as little liking for Welsh seas as the King himself had for Welsh mountains, though happily some Bristol sailors appear to have done their best to supply the deficiency. Glyndwr, however, was determined to have Harlech without loss of further time. Coming there from Carnarvon he parleyed with the garrison, and offered terms which all but seven accepted. What became of this uncompromising minority it would be hard to say, but at any rate Owen entered into possession and there is good reason to suppose that he planted his family here and made his headquarters upon the historic rock where Bran the Blessed and a long line of less shadowy Welsh chieftains had dwelt, ages before the rearing of these Norman towers.

Later on we hear of his summoning a parliament to Harlech, but during this year the first of these legislative assemblies that he called together met at Machynlleth, as being unquestionably a more convenient rendezvous for Welshmen in general. Hither came "four persons of sufficient consequence" out of each "Cantref" (the old unit of division in Wales), to take counsel for future action and to gather around

* That ships could reach the gate at the foot of the rock of Harlech is undoubted. What course the water took or how much of the Morfa was actually under water is a matter of uncertainty.

MACHYNLLETH.

the throne, upon which they had now seated a crowned Prince of their own race. One of the Welsh gentlemen, however, who attended this historic parliament, came with very different intentions, and this was David ap Llewelyn ap Howel, otherwise known as Davy Gam, or "squint-eyed Davy," a landowner near Brecon and the scion of a family distinguished both then and for long afterwards, his great-grandfather having fought at Crecy and Poitiers. He himself was a short, long-armed man with red hair and a cast in his eye. In youth he had been compelled to fly from Brecon for killing a neighbour, and indeed he seemed to have enjoyed all his life a somewhat sinister reputation for recklessness and daring. Flying to England he was received into the household of John of Gaunt, where he grew up side by side with Henry of Bolingbroke and was entirely devoted to his service. Henry, when he came into power, had restored Gam to his property and position in Brecon, and moreover bestowed upon him Crown appointments in South Wales. Glyndwr had a brother-in-law named Gam, which has given rise to some confusion, but Davy was at any rate no relation to the Welsh chieftain, though, both having been in Henry's household, it is probable they knew each other well.

Gam had hitherto and naturally been a staunch King's man; he now, however, feigned conversion and attended the parliament at Machynlleth, not to do homage to Owen, but to kill him. The almost certain death to which he exposed himself in case of success prompts one to something like admiration for so single-minded and fearless an avenger. But his intentions were by some means discovered and his rash project nipped in the bud. He was seized and doomed to the cruel fate which the nature of his crime made inevitable. Old friends and relatives, however, were in strength at Machynlleth and successfully interceded for his life. Perhaps Glyndwr was induced to this act of clemency by the reflection that imprisonment for an indefinite period, as practised by himself and others at that time, was a worse punishment than torture and death to a man of spirit. Whether the captive lay in the dungeons of Dolbadarn under Snowdon, at Harlech, or in the still surviving prison house (Cachardy Owen) at Llansantffraid-Glyndyfrdwy, we do not hear. He probably tasted the sweets of all of them and must indeed have spent a miserable time in those later years when Owen was himself at bay in the mountains and more or less of a fugitive.

But Davy was freed eventually, though only just before the final disappearance of Glyndwr, and lived to fight at the King's side at Agincourt together with his son-in-law Roger Vychan, where both fell gloriously on that memorable day. He is said to have been knighted on the field while dying and to be moreover the original of Shakespeare's Fluellin, and to have made the memorable reply to Henry V. when returning from a survey of the vast French hosts just before the battle: "There are enough to kill, enough to take prisoners, and enough to run away."

When next Glynwdr went campaigning through

Brecon he took the opportunity of burning his would-be murderer's mansion of Cyrnwigen. A well-known tradition relates how, while the flames were leaping high around the devoted homestead, Owen addressed David Gam's bailiff who was gazing disconsolately at the scene, in an *englyn*, which by some means has found its way down to posterity and is well known in Wales. Seeing that it is the only instance we have of so great a patron of bards breaking out himself into verse, I venture to print it here. There have been various translations; this is one of them:

> "Canst thou a little red man descry,
> Looking around for his dwelling fair?
> Tell him it under the bank doth lie,
> And its brow the mark of a coal doth bear."

No special effort was made this spring from England to break Glyndwr's power or to relieve the castles. While some of Owen's captains were hovering on the Marches, the chief himself, having dismissed his parliament, moved with his principal councillors to Dolgelly. Tradition still points out the house at Machynlleth where gathered the first and almost the only approach to a parliament that ever met in Wales. It stands nearly opposite the gates of Plâs Machynlleth, an unnoticeable portion of the street in fact, a long low building now in part adapted to the needs of a private residence, and having nothing suggestive about it but the thickness of its walls. The chief outcome of this conference at Dolgelly of "sufficient persons" from all over

Wales, was a much more formal and serious overture to the French King than the letters of 1402. Glyndwr had now fully donned the mantle of royalty and wrote to the King of France as a brother and an equal, proposing to make an offensive and defensive alliance with him.

The ambassadors chosen for the conduct of this important business were Griffith Yonge, doctor of laws, Owen's Chancellor, and his own brother-in-law, John Hanmer. The instrument is in Latin, "Dated at Dolgelly on the 10th day of May 1404 and in the fourth year of our principality," and begins: "Owen by the grace of God, Prince of Wales," etc. The two Welsh plenipotentiaries crossed the sea without misadventure and were received in a most friendly manner at Paris by the French King. His representative, the Count de la Marche, signed the treaty upon July 14th, together with Hanmer and Yonge, at the house of Ferdinand de Corby, Chancellor of France, several bishops and other notabilities being present. By this intrument Glyndwr and the French King entered into a solemn league and covenant to assist each other against all the attacks of Henry of Lancaster (Charles had never yet recognised him as King) and his allies. The Welshmen signed the document on behalf of "our illustrious and most dread Lord, Owen, Prince of Wales." The treaty was ratified on the 12th of January following at Llanbadarn near Aberystwith. The seal which Glyndwr now used in all his transactions represents the hero himself, with a biforked beard, seated on a chair, holding a sceptre in his right hand and a

Copyright C. H. Young.

OWEN'S COUNCIL HOUSE, DOLGELLY.

globe in his left, and has recently been adopted as the corporate arms of Machynlleth. Nor should it be overlooked that Owen sent a list of all the chief harbours and roads of Wales to Charles, while the latter in return loaded the Welsh ambassadors with presents for their master, including a gilded helmet, a cuirass, and sword, as an earnest of his promised help.

About the same time as the departure of Owen's mission to France, he wrote another letter, which is extant. It is not of much importance, except as an illustration of the confidence he felt at this time in his ultimate success. It is addressed to "our dear and entirely well beloved Henry Don," urging his co-operation, and concluding with the remark: "Their sway is ending and victory coming to us, as from the first, none could doubt God had so ordered."

Among other signs of Glyndwr's increased importance this year, was the coming over to his cause of that Tudor Trevor, Bishop of St. Asaph, who it will be remembered had warned the King and his council against despising Owen's peaceful appeal for justice against Grey of Ruthin, and urgently protested against those ill-fated and misplaced sneers at the "barfoots."

It was Trevor's cathedral at St. Asaph, of course, and its precincts, which Glyndwr had so ruthlessly burned in 1402. The Bishop had since then been not only supported by grants from the English exchequer, but had well earned them by much serious official work in the King's service. Whether his Welsh blood warmed at the prospects of a revived Cambrian independence or whether ambition was the keynote of his actions, no one may know. At any rate it was not want or neglect at the hands of the King that drove him back into the arms of Owen. The latter gave him a cordial welcome, and it must be said for Trevor that through good and ill he proved faithful to his new master's cause. Militant clerics were common enough in those times. Trevor, with the martial instincts of the great border race from which he sprang, and whose history is written deep for centuries beside the Ceiriog and the Dee, had been in the thick of the fight at Shrewsbury beneath the King's banner. He now followed Glyndwr both in the council and in the field, dying eventually in Paris, a fugitive and an exile, in the year 1410.

All through this spring Owen's followers on the borders were making life upon the English side intolerable. Bonfires were laid ready for the match on every hill. The thirty towers and castles that guarded Shropshire were helpless to stem the tide. The county was again laid waste to the very walls of Shrewsbury and many of the population fled to other parts of England for a livelihood. Archdeacon Kingston at Hereford once again takes up his pen and paints a lamentable picture:

"The Welsh rebels in great numbers have entered Archenfield [a division of the county] and there they have burnt houses, killed the inhabitants, taken prisoners and ravaged the country to the great dishonour of our King and the unsupportable damage of the country.

We have often advertised the King that such mischief would befall us, we have also now certain information that within the next eight days the rebels are resolved to make an attack in the March of Wales to its utter ruin, if speedy succour be not sent. True it is indeed that we have no power to shelter us except that of Lord Richard of York and his men, which is far too little to defend us; we implore you to consider this very perilous and pitiable case and to pray our Sovereign Lord that he will come in his Royal person or send some person with sufficient power to rescue us from the invasion of the said rebels. Otherwise we shall be utterly destroyed, which God forbid; whoever comes will as we are led to believe have to engage in battle, or will have a very severe struggle with the rebels. And for God's sake remember that honourable and valiant man, the Lord Abergavenny [William Beauchamp], who is on the very point of destruction if he be not rescued. Written in haste at Hereford, June 10th."

A fortnight later the dread of Owen's advance was emphasised by Prince Henry himself, who was still, in conjunction with the Duke of York, in charge of the Welsh wars.

"Most dread and sovereign Lord and Father, at your high command in your other gracious letters, I have removed with my small household to the city of Worcester, and may it please your Royal Highness to know that the Welsh have made a descent on Herefordshire, burning and destroying the county with very great force, and with a supply of provisions for fifteen days." The Prince goes on to say that the Welsh are assembled with all their power, and to save the county of Hereford he has sent for all sorts of considerable persons (mentioned by name) to meet him at Worcester. In conjunction with these he tells the King he will "do to the utmost of his little power," and then comes the inevitable want of money and the impossibility of maintaining troops in the field or meeting the expenses of the garrisons. Another letter from the same hand a few days afterwards warned the King still more urgently of the pressing danger and declared how impossible it was to keep his troops upon the frontier without pay or provisions.

There is no evidence that these strong representations brought any satisfaction to the anxious writers. The sieges of those castles not yet taken Owen continued to prosecute with vigour, while his captains continued to desolate the border counties. Glyndwr was much too skilful a strategist to undertake a serious expedition into England. The cause of Richard and Mortimer, which would have been his only war-cry, had been shattered, so far as England was concerned, at Shrewsbury. All Glyndwr wanted was Wales, and at present he virtually possessed it. He felt confident now, moreover, of substantial assistance from the French King, and when that arrived he might perhaps take the initiative seriously against Henry on behalf of his son-in-law's family. Nor is there any doubt but that he was greatly indebted for the extraordinary position he had achieved to the chronic impecuniosity of his enemy, and perhaps indeed to his own reputation for magic art. Who can say?

One brief and spirited campaign, however, distinguished this summer, or more probably the late spring of 1404, for the actual date is uncertain. It was undertaken by a strong force which Beauchamp, Earl of Warwick, led right through the present county of Montgomery. Glyndwr threw himself across the Earl's path at Mynydd-cwm-du ("the black mountain hollow"): a fierce battle ensued, in which the Welsh were defeated and were so closely pressed that Owen's banner was captured and he himself very nearly taken. Warwick does not seem to have followed up his advantage; on the contrary, Glyndwr, rallying his men, followed the Earl back to the Herefordshire border whither the usual lack of provender had sent him, and there turned the tables on his enemy, beating him badly in a pitched battle at Craig-y-dorth. The scene of this second encounter is on the road between Chepstow and Monmouth, near Trelog common.

Early in August, 1404, the Shropshire Marches were so sorely pressed, and the English defences so worn out, that the council were compelled to listen to the urgent appeals of the Salopians and grant the people of that county leave to make terms with Owen on their own account and pay him exemption money. The same privilege had also to be extended to Edward de Charleton, Lord of Powys, who from his "Castle de la Pole" (Welshpool) made a truce with the Welsh. It is worthy of note that the people of Welshpool, though practically all of Welsh blood, stood by their lord and resisted Owen throughout the whole of the struggle. For this reason Charleton gave them a fresh charter immensely enlarging the boundaries of the borough, which to this day occupies the unique position of extending over something like twenty thousand acres.

Towards the end of August, King Henry was forced once more to turn his attention to Wales. The scandal and the danger were growing grievous. So he held a council at Tutbury, the minutes of which are significant. Eight bishops, eighteen abbots and priors, nineteen great lords and barons, and ninety-six representatives of counties, we are told, attended it. The news was here confirmed that the French had equipped sixty vessels in the port of Harfleur and were about to fill them with soldiers and proceed to Owen's assistance. It was decided, however, that since the King was not at present able to raise an army sufficiently imposing for his high estate, he should remain at Tutbury till the meeting of Parliament in October. As campaigning against Owen even in the summer season had sufficient horrors for the King, the logic of deferring the expedition till November can only be explained by sheer lack of money. At least one would have supposed so if Henry had not burked the whole question, turned his back once more on his lost and desolated province, and hastened to the North.

Prince John, the King's second son, was now joined with Prince Henry in the titular Governorship of the South Wales Marches, and the royal brothers were voted two thousand five hundred archers and men-at-arms. How many of these they got is another story, of which we have no certain knowledge. For a fortnight it was all they could do to hold their own as they pushed slowly through to the relief of Coity Castle (now Oldcastle Bridgend), which was being bravely defended by Sir Alexander Berkrolles.

With the exception of the chronic pressure on the still resisting castles, this autumn and winter was comparatively quiet in Wales, for the excellent reason that Owen had it all his own way. Aberystwith had fallen soon after Harlech; and those of my readers who are familiar with the wave-washed situation of the ruins of the later Norman castle which still mark the site of the ancient palace of Cadwallader, may well wonder why a spot so accessible from a score of English seaports should have been abandoned to its fate. The tower and monastery of Llanbadarn, too, hard by, became a favourite resting-place of Owen's at this time, and it was here he ratified this winter his treaty with the King of France. But as his family and that of Mortimer would appear to have made Harlech their headquarters, and as later on he summoned his second parliament to that historic spot, it is more than likely that the late autumn and winter months saw the old castle the gathering-point of the bards, and the rallying-place of Owen's faithful captains—a court, in fact, and one more adequately housed by far than that other one at the mansion on the Dee, since reduced to a heap of ashes. As one wanders to-day amid the grim walls of Harlech and presses the soft turf that centuries of sun and showers and sea mists have spread over what was once the floor of its great banqueting hall, the scenes that it must have witnessed in this winter of 1404 are well calculated to stir the fancy and captivate the imagination. Death and battle have been in ancient times busy enough around the rock of Harlech and upon the green slopes of the Ardudwy Mountains that from high above its grey towers look out upon the sea. From the days of Brân the Blessed, the first Christian Prince, whose fortress, Twr Bronwen, men say, stood upon this matchless site, till those of the fighting Maelgwyn, King of Gwynedd, when the coasts of Wales were strewn with the victims of plague and battle, it was a notable spot. From Colwyn ap Tangno, the fountainhead of half the pedigrees in North-west Wales, till forty years after Glyndwr's time, when, in the Wars of the Roses, David ap Sinion made that celebrated defence against Lord Herbert which inspired the writing of the stirring and immortal march, Harlech was a focus of strife, the delight of the bard, the glory of the minstrel. Of all Welsh castles, save the fragment of Dinas Brân,—and that is indeed saying much,—it is the most proudly placed; and the great medieval fortress, still in its exterior so perfect, is well worthy of its site. Amid a pile of mountains to the north Snowdon lifts its shapely peak; far westward into the shining sea stretches the long arm of West Carnarvon, throwing up here and there its shadowy outstanding peaks till it fades into the dim horizon behind which Ireland lies. As the eye travels southward, the lofty headlands of Merioneth give way to the fainter capes of Cardigan, and upon the verge of

HARLECH.

sight in clear weather the wild coast of Pembroke, its rugged outline softened by distance, lies low between sea and sky.

Those to whom such things appeal will see much that is appropriate in the gathering of Glyndwr, his bards, his warriors, his priests, his counsellors, at Harlech during this winter which perhaps marked the high-tide of his renown. His wife, "the best of wives," with the fair Katherine, wife of Mortimer, was here, and a crowd of dames, we may be well assured, whose manors were not at that time, with their husbands in the field, the safest of abodes for lonely females. Owen's three married daughters were not here, for the Scudamores, Monningtons, and Crofts, whose names they bore, being Herefordshire men, were all upon the other side. Edmund Mortimer, of course, was present, and it is strange how a soldier of such repute and of so vigorous a stock should have sunk his individuality so absolutely in that of his masterful father-in-law. Glyndwr's two elder sons, now grown to man's estate, Griffith and Meredith, and his own younger brother, Tudor, who was soon to fall, with his brother-in-law, John Hanmer, just returned from his French mission, complete the family group that we may be fairly justified in picturing at Harlech, assembled round the person of their now crowned Prince. Rhys Gethin, the victor of Pilleth and the terror of the South Wales Marches, was probably there, and the two Tudors of Penmynydd, whom from first to last several thousand men had followed across the Menai from the still unmolested fields of Anglesey. Yonge the Chancellor, too, fresh from France, Llewelyn Bifort, whom, with the consent of the Avignon Pope, Owen had nominated to the wasted estate and the burnt cathedral of Bangor, and Bishop Trevor of St. Asaph, most eminent of them all, were at Harlech beyond a doubt. Robert ap Jevan of Ystymcegid in Eivioneth was most probably there, with Rhys Dwy, "a great master among them," who was executed in London eight years later, and last, but by no means least, Owen's faithful laureate, Griffith Llwyd, or "Iolo Goch," who, among all the bards that had tuned their voices and their harps to Owen's praise and been stirred to ecstasy by his successes, stood first and chief.

Glyndwr had in truth no cause to complain of his chief bard, who was a veteran in song when war came to stimulate him to patriotic frenzy, and the stirring tones in which he sang of his Prince's deeds were echoed by every native harp in Wales.

"Immortal fame shall be thy meed,
Due to every glorious deed,
Which latest annals shall record,
Beloved and victorious Lord,
Grace, wisdom, valour, all are thine,
Owain Glyndowerdy divine,
Meet emblem of a two-edged sword,
Dreaded in war, in peace adored.

"Loud fame has told thy gallant deeds,
In every word a Saxon bleeds,
Terror and flight together came,

Obedient to thy mighty name;
Death in the van with ample stride
Hew'd thee a passage deep and wide,
Stubborn as steel thy nervous chest
With more than mortal strength possessed."

Though a metrical translation may be unsatisfactory enough to the Celtic scholar, this rendering will not be without interest to English readers as giving the sense, at any rate, of words addressed to Glyndwr by the man nearest to his person. The fourteenth century was the halcyon period of Welsh song; Dafydd ap Gwylim, the greatest of all Welsh love-poets, was still alive in Glyndwr's youth, while Gutyn Owen was almost a contemporary. Welsh poetry had attuned itself, since the Edwardian conquest had brought comparative peace in Wales, to gentler and more literary themes. The joys of agriculture and country life, the happiness of the peasant, the song of birds, the murmur of streams, and, above all, the gentler passions of human nature had supplanted to a great extent the fiercer notes of martial eulogies, the pæans of victory, and the plaintive wails over long-past but unforgotten defeats. It is strange, too, that this flow of song should have signalised a century when the profession of a wandering minstrel was in Wales for the first time ostracised by law.

But the old martial minstrelsy was not dead. The yearning of the soldier and the man of ancient race to emulate the deeds or the supposed deeds of his predecessors, and to be the subject after death of bardic eulogy in hall or castle, was still strong. It helped many a warrior to meet with cheerfulness a bloody death, or with the memory of heroic deeds performed to sink with resignation at the hands of disease or old age into the cold grave.

CHAPTER VIII

WELSH REVERSES

1405

GLYNDWR was now, by the lowest estimate, in his forty-sixth year. For that period, when manhood began early, and old age, if it came at all, came quickly, he certainly carried his years with remarkable lightness. Who can say, however, with what feelings he surveyed his handiwork? From end to end, with almost the sole exception of Anglesey and Carnarvonshire and western Pembroke, Wales lay desolate and bleeding. Owen's hands were red, not only with the blood of Saxons, but with that of old friends and even kinsmen. Red ravage had marked his steps, and there were few parts of the country that he had not at some time or other crossed and recrossed in his desolating marches. Carnarvonshire and western Merioneth and the Plinlimmon Mountains were full of booty, stock, and valuables brought from Norman-Welsh lordships and from beyond the English border. The admirers of Glyndwr would fain believe, and there is something to be said for the theory, that passion and revenge had no part in the havoc which the Welsh hero spread throughout his native land, but that it was due to a deliberate scheme of campaign by which the country was to be made not only too hot, but too bare, to hold the Saxon.

It would be waste of words to speculate on motives that can never be divulged and schemes that have left no witnesses. We have at any rate to face tradition, which counts for much. And this places Glyndwr in the eyes of most Welshmen, with all his ravagings and burnings, on a pedestal above the greatest and most patriotic of their older Princes—above Llewelyn ap Iorwerth, above the last Llewelyn, the son of Gryffydd, above Owen Gwynedd. The cool-headed student may be much less enthusiastic. But he will also call to mind the ethics of war in those days, and then perhaps remember that even in modern conflicts, whose memories stand out with conspicuous glory, there has been no very great improvement on the methods of Glyndwr. The Carolinian who preferred King George to Washington and Congress—and King George after all was at least no usurper—suffered neither more nor less than the Welshmen of Glamorgan or Carmarthen or Merioneth who from prudence or inclination preferred Bolingbroke to Glyndwr. Wars of this type have ever been ferocious. The Anglo-Americans of the eighteenth century were a civilised and peaceful people; Glyndwr lived at a time when war was a trade, ravage its handmaid, and human life of but small account.

It is quite possible to overestimate the effect upon a country in those days of even the most merciless treatment. The torch was not the instrument of irreparable loss that it would have been if applied with equal freedom only a hundred and fifty years later. Outside the feudal castles and the great ecclesiastical foundations, there were few permanent structures of much value either in England or Wales. It was late in the century with which we are dealing before the manor-house and grange of the yeoman or country gentleman became buildings of the style with which careless fancy is apt to associate their names. It is salutary sometimes to leave the ordinary paths of history and refresh one's mind with the domestic realities of olden days as they are shown to us by writers who have given their attention to such humble but helpful details. The ordinary English manor-house of Glyndwr's time was a plain wooden building,* with an escape-hole in the thatched roof for the smoke, a floor covered with rushes, and filthy from lack of change, with bare boards laid on rude supports doing duty as tables. A little tapestry sometimes relieved the crudeness of the bare interior where such a crowd of human beings often gathered together. Here and there an important person built for himself a compromise between a manor and a castle, Glyndwr himself being an instance to the point. The average manor-houses

* Mr. Denton, in his *England of the Fifteenth Century*, allows no more than four, and usually only three rooms, to an average manor-house: one for eating in, with a second, and perhaps a third, for sleeping; a fire in the centre of the first.

of Wales, the abodes of the native gentry, were certainly no more, probably less, luxurious, and not often—though some were even then—built of stone. As for the peasantry, their dwellings in either the England or Wales of that time were mere huts of mud, wood, or wattle, and were often, no doubt, not worth the trouble of destroying.

The Welsh of those days, unlike the English, did not group themselves in villages. Each man not an actual servant, whether he were gentleman or small yeoman, lived apart upon his property or holding. If we eliminate the present towns, the country must have been in most parts almost as thickly populated as it is now. A valuable survival, known as the *Record of Carnarvon*, a sort of local doomsday book, dating from the thirteenth century, may be seen to-day, and it gives very detailed information as to the persons, manors, and freeholds of that country, and some idea of how well peopled for the times was even the wildest part of wild Wales. Prince Henry, it will be remembered, speaks of the Vale of Edeyrnion as a fine and populous country. Giraldus Cambrensis, in his graphic account of his tour with Archbishop Baldwin in the twelfth century, gives the same impression. Still the destruction of such buildings as the mass of its people lived in, even if they were destroyed, was of no vital consequence. The loss of a year's crop was not irreparable, particularly in a country where sheep and cattle, which could often be driven away, were the chief assets of rural life. Glyndwr, to be sure, did what few other makers of war, even in Wales, had done, for he destroyed some of the chief ecclesiastical buildings. He burnt, moreover, several of the small towns and dismantled many castles. "Deflower'd by Glindor" is a remark frequently in the mouth of old Leland as he went on his immortal survey not much more than a hundred years later.

The term "rebel," as applied to Glyndwr and those Welshmen who followed him, is more convenient than logical. However bad a king Richard may have been, the Welsh had never wavered in their allegiance to him. However excellent a monarch Henry might have made if he had been given the chance, he was at least an usurper, and a breaker of his word. London and parts of England had welcomed him to the throne. The Percys and innumerable other Englishmen who then and at various other times conspired against him were rebels beyond a doubt. But the Welsh had never even been consulted in the *coup d'état* by which he seized the crown. They had never recognised him as king nor sworn allegiance. To them he was simply an usurper and the almost certain assassin of their late King. If Richard were alive, then Henry could not be their lawful sovereign. If, on the other hand, he had been done to death, which either directly or indirectly he surely had been, then the boy Earl of March, as all the world knew, should be on the throne. Henry of Monmouth, too, being the son of an usurper, could not possibly be Prince of Wales. The place was vacant, and the opportunity for electing one of their own race and blood was too good to be missed. Whatever historians may choose to call

Glyndwr, he was logically no rebel in a period when allegiance was almost wholly a personal matter. His enemies, whom he hunted out of Wales or pent up in their castles, were, on the other hand, from his point of view, rebels and traitors in recognising the authority and protection of an usurper. The Welsh people owed no allegiance to the English, but to the King of England and Wales, to whom for the protection of the isle of Britain, as the old tradition still ran, they paid a sum of £60,000 a year. In their eyes, as in those of many persons in England and of most in Europe, Henry was Henry of Lancaster, not King of England. The Welsh tribute, it is hardly necessary to say, had dwindled, since the rising of Glyndwr, to insignificant proportions, while the war expenses it entailed, together with this loss of income, was one of the chief causes of that impecuniosity which prevented Henry from ever really showing of what stuff as a ruler he was made.

The chief incident of the early part of the year 1405 was a nearly successful plot to carry off from the King's keeping the young Earl of March, the rightful heir to the crown, and his brother. Being nephews of Sir Edmund Mortimer, the attempt to bring them to Glyndwr's headquarters in Wales and to the protection of their uncle was a natural one. The King, who was spending Christmas at Eltham, had left the boys behind him at Windsor, under the charge of Hugh de Waterton, Constable of the Castle. Their domestic guardian was the widow of the Lord Despencer and sister of the Duke of York, who at this time, it will be remembered, was in joint charge with Prince Henry of Welsh affairs. The Despencers had been Norman-Welsh barons for some generations, their interests at this time lying for the most part in what is now Monmouthshire, and though ostensibly hostile, they had old ties of blood and propinquity with the house of Mortimer. This Christmas witnessed one of the many plots against the King's life, but with these we have nothing to do, except in so far that the moment was regarded as being a favourable one for making an effort to get hold of the two royal boys. How unstable were Henry's friends for the most part may be gathered from the fact that the Duke of York, his trusted representative in Wales, was himself privy to the scheme.

To Lady Despencer was entrusted the chief part in this dangerous work. As sister to the Duke of York, she was in the King's eyes above all suspicion. When the latter had left Windsor for Eltham she caused a locksmith secretly to make false keys, and by means of these, with the connivance of some servants, she contrived to get her two wards safely out of the castle precincts, taking with her at the same time her own son. Horses and attendants were ready in waiting, and the whole party pushed for the West with all the expedition of which they were capable. They had passed through Berkshire before the King heard the news of their escape. When it reached him, however, no time was lost. Sending out swift messengers upon the track of the fugitives he himself at once hastened to Windsor. The pursuers were just in time and overtook the illustrious fugitives in Gloucestershire within a day's ride of the security which Mortimer and Glyndwr's people were waiting to afford them in Wales. A lively brush, not without slaughter on both sides, signalised the meeting, but the lady and the boys were captured and conveyed back to London. Lady Despencer then revealed the plot to murder the King, denouncing her brother, the Duke of York, as a leading conspirator. This was not a sisterly action, and the Duke loudly denied all knowledge of such dastardly intentions. At this the lady, whose private reputation was not all that it should have been, waxed indignant and clamorously demanded a champion to maintain her declaration with lance and sword. Whereupon a gentleman named William Maidstone flung down his glove to the Duke in the very presence of the King. The challenge was accepted, but, the Duke being apparently of corpulent build and the challenger both at a physical advantage and of no distinction, the romantic combat never took place. Perhaps the King wished to get the Duke into his hands without loss of time, for he seized him and sent him to the Tower instead of into the lists. He was soon, however, as an illustration of how forgiving Henry could at times be, pardoned and reinstated to the full in all his honours. His sister, however, whose tenants were nearly all supporters of Glyndwr, was stripped of her property. But they, too, were eventually restored, and their feudal superior, who made no little stir in her time, lies buried amid the ruins of the old abbey at Reading. The unfortunate locksmith who had made the keys had both his hands chopped off.

CAERPHILLY CASTLE.

The castles of Caerleon, Caerphilly, Newport, and Usk had fallen, and in the manuscripts collected by Iolo Morganwg (Edward Williams), who flourished in the last century, an apparently contemporaneous though anonymous writer, has somewhat to say about Glyndwr in Morganwg or Glamorgan. He tells how Owen came to Cardiff, "destroyed it and won the castle," demolishing at the same time the castles of Penllan, Llandochau, Flemington, Dunraven of the Butlers, Tal-y-fan, Llanblethian, Llangeinor, Malefant, and Penmark, and burning many villages the men of which would not join him. "The country people collected round him with one accord and demolished houses and castles innumerable, laid waste and quite fenceless the lands, and gave them in common to all." The manuscript goes on to say how Glyndwr "took away from the rich and powerful and distributed the plunder among the weak and poor." Many of the higher orders of chieftains had to fly to England under the protection and support of the King. A bloody battle took place at Bryn Owen (Stallingdown) near Cowbridge, between Glyndwr and the King's men. The latter were put to flight after eighteen hours' hard fighting, "during which the blood was up to the horses' fetlocks at Pant-y-wenol, that separates both ends of the mountain." Here beyond a doubt was a fulfilment of one of the dread portents that attended Owen's birth, when the horses, it will be remembered, in his father's stable were found standing with the blood running over their feet. There is no date to this anonymous but evidently sincere and suggestive narrative, or rather the date assigned to the event is evidently an error. The matters here spoken of belong to 1403, or 1404, in all probability, though they can only be inserted parenthetically as one of those scraps of local Welsh testimony from the period itself that have an interest of their own.

The year 1405 opened with reports that the renowned Rhys Gethin was to cross the English border with a large force. Prince Henry, now eighteen years of age, with an experience of war under difficulties and of carking cares of state such as has fallen to the lot of few men so young, prepared to make ready for him. Short of men and money, the young soldier had long begun to show of what mettle he was made and to give evidence of the ability that was eventually to do more to arrest the resistance of Glyndwr than all the combined efforts of Lord Marchers and their royal master.

Rumour on this occasion proved true, for Rhys, passing through Glamorgan with eight thousand men and skirting Abergavenny, attacked the border town of Grosmont, in the valley of the Monnow, and burnt it to the ground. Grosmont had hitherto been a flourishing place, but it never recovered from the blow then dealt it. In Camden's time the remains of streets and causeways could be traced beneath the turf of the surrounding fields in evidence of its vanished glories. To-day it is a picturesque and peaceful village crowning a high ridge, from which a glorious prospect can be enjoyed of the vale of the Monnow with the sparkling river hurrying downwards between lofty hills to meet the Wye. A simple street, and that a short one, is all that remains, while an old town hall speaks eloquently of its departed importance. A cruciform church of great age with an octagonal tower and spire springing from the centre lends force to the tradition of Grosmont's former glories. Above all, the walls of the Norman castle, whence issued Prince Henry's gallant band, still stand hard by the village, their reddish stonework half hidden amid a mass of ivy and the foliage of embowering trees; the moat half full of the leaves of many autumns, the ramparts green with the turf of ages; a quiet enough spot now but for the song of birds and the tumble of the river upon its rocks three hundred feet below. It was here that Glyndwr's forces met with their first serious disaster upon the border, for the Prince, together with Gilbert Talbot and Sir Edward Newport, sallying out of the castle, attacked Rhys Gethin and inflicted upon the Welsh a severe and bloody defeat, completely routing them with a loss of eight hundred men left dead upon the field. It is especially stated in some accounts that no quarter was given, and only one prisoner taken alive and spared for ransom, of whom Prince Henry, in a letter to his father which is worth transcribing, speaks as "a great chieftain."

"My most redoubted and most Sovereign Lord and father, I sincerely pray that God will graciously show His miraculous aid towards you in all places, praised be He in all His works, for on Wednesday the eleventh of this present month of March, your rebels of the parts of Glamorgan, Morgannok, Usk, Netherwent, and Overwent, assembled to the number of eight thousand men, according to their own account, and they went on the same Wednesday, in the morning, and burnt a part of your town of Grossmont within your Lordship of Monmouth and Jennoia [*sic*]. Presently went out my well beloved cousin the Lord Talbot and the small body of my household, and with them joined your faithful and valiant knights William Newport and John Greindor, the which formed but a small power in the whole; but true it is indeed that victory is not in the multitude of people, and this was well proved there, but in the power of God, and there by the aid of the blessed Trinity, your people gained the field, and vanquished all the said rebels, and slew of them by fair account in field, by the time of their return from the pursuit, some say eight hundred, others a thousand, being questioned upon pain of death; nevertheless whether it were one or the other I will not contend, and to inform you fully of all that has been done, I send you a person worthy of credit therein, my faithful servant the bearer of this letter, who was at the engagement and performed his duty well, as he has always done. And such amends has God ordained you for the burning of your houses in your aforesaid town, and of prisoners were none taken except one, a great chief among them, whom I would have sent to you but he cannot yet ride at ease.

"Written at Hereford the said Wednesday at night.

"Your most humble and obedient son,

"Henry."

Glyndwr, as soon as he heard of the disaster on the Monnow, pushed up fresh forces under his brother Tudor to meet the fugitives from Grosmont, with a view to wipe out, if possible, that crushing defeat. What strength they got, if any, from Rhys Gethin's scattered army there is no evidence, but in less than a week they encountered the Prince himself advancing into Wales with a considerable force, and at Mynydd-y-Pwll-Melyn, in Brecon, received a defeat more calamitous than even that of Grosmont. Fifteen hundred of the Welsh were killed or taken prisoners. Among the slain was Owen's brother Tudor himself; and so like the chief was he in face and form that for some time there was much rejoicing, and the news was bruited about that the dreaded Glyndwr was in truth dead. The spirits of the English were sadly damped when the absence of a wart under the left eye, a distinguishing mark of Glyndwr, proclaimed that their joy was premature, and that it was the dead face of his younger brother on which they were gazing. Among the prisoners, however, was his son Gryffydd, who was sent by the Prince to London and confined in the Tower, statements of money allowed for his maintenance there appearing from time to time on the Rolls. Gryffydd's (Griffin he is there called) fellow-prisoner is Owen ap Gryffydd, the son probably of the valiant Cardiganshire gentleman whom Henry quartered in 1402. A year later the young King of Scotland, whose life was safer there, no doubt, than in his own country, was the companion of Glyndwr's son. The Iolo manuscript before mentioned tells us:

"In 1405 a bloody battle attended with great slaughter that in severity was scarcely ever exceeded in Wales took place on Pwll Melin; Gryffyth ap Owen and his men were taken and many of them imprisoned, but many were put to death when captured, whereupon all Glamorgan turned Saxon except a small number who followed their lord to North Wales."

These two severe defeats were a great blow to Owen's prestige. They caused numbers of his adherents in South Wales to fall away and to seek that pardon which the King, to do him justice, was at all times very free in extending to Welshmen. Indeed, it would almost seem as if he himself secretly recognised the fact that they had much justice on their side and were rebels rather in name than in actual fact.

About the time of the second of these two victories over the Welsh, the King, encouraged no doubt by such successes, began making great preparations for a personal expedition against Glyndwr. His activity in other parts, for the North was always simmering, had been prodigious. He now arrived at Hereford early in May, full of determination to support in person the zeal so lately aroused in his hard-worked constables and lieutenants, and once and for all to suppress the accursed magician who for five years had so entirely got the better of him.

But Glyndwr previous to these defeats had sent emissaries to the North. Three of his immediate councillors were in Northumberland in secret conclave with its crafty and ill-advised Earl. The King, it will be remembered, had not only forgiven Percy but had restored to him all his confiscated estates. That he was prepared again to risk the substance for the shadow (to say nothing of committing an act of ingratitude that even for those days was indecent) is conclusive evidence that his dead son, Hotspur, was not the evil genius his father had with poor spirit represented him to be when craving mercy from the King. Glyndwr, however, had nothing to do with the old Earl's conscience when for the second time he seemed anxious for an alliance. Bishop Trevor, with Bifort, Glyndwr's Bishop of Bangor, and David Daron, Dean of Bangor, were now all in the North intriguing with Northumberland. In the early days of the Welsh rising Glyndwr seemed to have some personal and even sentimental leaning towards the Percys. There was nothing of that, however, in his present attitude, which was purely a business one, seeing that the French, as he thought, and rightly so, were on the point of coming to his assistance, and the North about to rise in arms against Henry. Even the loss of men and of his own prestige, entailed by the defeats of Grosmont and Pwll-Melyn and the falling away of Glamorgan, might be much more than counterbalanced. The first mutterings of the outbreak came from York, but they were loud enough to pull the King up at Hereford and start him at full speed for Yorkshire. Once more his sorely tried servants in Wales had to do as best they could without him, though some compensation in the way of men and supplies was sent to their relief. It is not within my province to follow Henry's operations this summer in the North, but it is necessary to our narrative to state that Percy escaped from York only just in time, having refused the really magnanimous conditions of pardon that the

King sent on to him. He fled to Scotland, taking with him his fellow-conspirator, Earl Bardolph, and Glyndwr's three emissaries, Trevor, Bifort, and David Daron. Another Welshman of Owen's party, however, who has not been hitherto mentioned, Sir John Griffith, was caught at York and executed. Many persons besides Percy were implicated in the plot, Archbishop Scrope for one, whose execution, with many accompanying indignities, sent a thrill of horror throughout Britain and Europe; Judge Gascoine's courageous refusal to sentence the prelate being, of course, one of the familiar incidents of the reign. For the second time the Percy estates were confiscated, while the suppression of the revolt and the punishment of the rebels kept the King lingering for a long time in the North. At the end of July he received the serious news that the French had landed in South Wales, and, hurrying southward, reached Worcester about the 10th of August, to find Glyndwr with some ten thousand Welshmen and nearly half as many French within nine miles of that city.

We must now return to Wales and to the earlier part of the summer, that we may learn how this transformation came about within so short a time. After Glyndwr's two defeats in March, and the subsequent panic among the men of Glamorgan and no doubt also among those of Gwent and parts of Brycheiniog, the chieftain himself with a following of tried and still trusty men went to North Wales. Welsh historians, following one another, paint most dismal pictures of Owen this summer, representing him as a solitary wanderer, travelling incognito about the country, sometimes alone, sometimes with a handful of faithful followers, now lurking in friends' houses, now hiding in mountain caverns, but always dogged by relentless foes. All these things he did in after years with sufficient tenacity to satisfy the most enthusiastic lover of romance. That his condition can have come to such a pass in the summer of 1405 is too manifestly absurd to be worth discussion. He had received, it is true, a blow severe enough to discourage the localities near which it happened, and probably to frighten a good many of his friends in other parts. It is possible, too, some may have sued secretly for pardon. But when we consider that in March all Wales except certain castles was faithful, and that his troops were attacking the English border when repulsed; that in May the King and his lieutenants were only preparing to invade Wales; that no operations of moment were so far as we know executed during the early summer against the Welsh; and finally that in July Glyndwr met the French at Tenby with ten thousand men behind him, it is quite incredible that 1405 can have been the season in which he spent months as an outcast and a wanderer. We may, I think, take it as certain that Glyndwr's star had not yet sensibly declined, and that what he had recently lost might well be considered as more than cancelled by the appearance in Milford Bay of 140 French ships full of soldiers.

While the coming of the French was still an uncertainty, it is probable that there was considerable depression even among Owen's immediate followers. But neither he nor they were cherishing it in caves and solitudes. On the contrary, another parliament, similarly constituted to the former one at Machynlleth, was summoned to Harlech. Of the result of its deliberations we know nothing, but a letter of the period suggests that Glyndwr was not wholly without thought of making terms in case of the non-arrival of the French. At the same time this is not quite in keeping with the stubborn resistance that in after years, when all hope had fled, he maintained with such heroic fortitude. Two of the county representatives, at any rate, who came to Harlech on this occasion were trimmers or worse. David Whitmore and Ievan ap Meredydd were supposed to represent his interests in Flint, but we are told that, before departing for the West, they held private communication with Sir John Stanley, who was in charge of the important castle of Hope for the King. To be brief, they went as spies rather than as supporters, and with the intention of keeping the English informed of what took place. But it was now already summer and while this season was still at its height, the event which Glyndwr was hoping and looking for took place.

The French had made many attempts in the preceding year to reach Wales; a few, as we know, touched the coast, and lent some slight assistance at Carnarvon and elsewhere. Now, however, a more successful effort and upon an infinitely larger scale was made, and 140 ships found their way from Brest to Milford without any mishap save the loss of their horses from lack of fresh water. The number of troops carried by this fleet is variously estimated at from about 3000 to 12,000 men. Madame De Lussan, the French historian of the period, is very definite so far as she goes, for without mentioning the grand total she states that there were among them 800 men-at-arms, 600 crossbows, and 1200 foot-soldiers, all picked troops. But then, again, the French "man-at-arms" of the period included a squire, a page, and three archers, so that the entire French force probably numbered from 4000 to 5000 men. The command was nominally in the hands of Jean de Rieux, Marshal of France, but the Sire de Hugueville was the leading spirit, not only in the inception but also in the conduct of the enterprise. He had actually sold to the Church his large estate of Agencourt near Montdidier, and devoted the proceeds to the adventure which he had so much at heart. There seems at any rate to have been no stint of money in the undertaking, for it is particularly noted what bravery of apparel and fine trappings distinguished this French army when it landed at Milford Haven. The fleet left Brest on July 22nd and arrived early in August in excellent condition, with the exception, as I have said, of the horses, which had all been thrown overboard. Glyndwr in the meantime had heard that the French were on the sea, and, moving down into Pembrokeshire with 10,000 men, he joined forces with them almost immediately upon their landing.

There was no time to be lost and the united armies turned first to Haverford-west, an Anglo-Flemish centre of some importance. The town was soon taken and burnt, but the great Norman castle proved altogether too hard a task even for so large a force. So, falling back, Glyndwr and his French allies marched to Tenby, laying waste the Flemish settlements, though they had to look helplessly on while an English fleet attacked the French ships and destroyed fifteen of them. Thence under Glyndwr's guidance the army moved on to Carmarthen, which surrendered without much resistance. Glamorgan, it will be remembered, had fallen away from its allegiance to the Welsh cause, so Glyndwr took it on his route towards England and gave the backsliders of that unfortunate county some experience of his relentless methods. Passing on thence through Herefordshire in a fashion of which we know nothing but may readily guess, the allied forces entered Worcestershire and arrived within nine miles of the capital of that county just as King Henry reached it.

As early as the beginning of July, when the King first heard of the intended French invasion, he had issued proclamation to the sheriffs of several counties to be in readiness with their forces, and it was these that must now have been his chief support at Worcester. On his way south he had issued another summons to the forces of Herefordshire and the lower counties to muster at the city of Hereford. It was now about the middle of August, and without more delay he marched his army out from Worcester to meet the formidable combination that had penetrated so far into his kingdom.

The spot where Glyndwr and Huguevilie encamped their forces was an old British fort on the summit of Woodbury hill and is still known as Owen's camp. Pennant visited it and made careful notes and observations. It covers, he says, about twenty-seven acres and is surrounded by a single foss. The hill itself is lofty and of an oblong form. One end is connected with the Abberly hills, which, with this one of Woodbury, form a crescent, the hollow between constituting an ideal arena for a battle-ground.

When the King arrived he proceeded to take up his position on the northern ridge, and the two armies lay for eight days, both so admirably placed that each feared to give advantage to the other by moving out and risking so great a stake in the gage of battle. Skirmishing, however, went on daily in the valley below. The brave spirits of either army descended into the arena and performed individual deeds of arms between and in sight of both camps. "They had a fine slope," says Pennant, "to run down, the Welsh having a hollowed way as if formed especially for the purpose."

Some four or five hundred men in all fell during this week of desultory skirmishing, including some French knights of note. One might well have looked, at this crisis, for some decisive and fierce fight like that of Shrewsbury, which should live in history. Never had Glyndwr penetrated so far into Saxon territory; never before had ten thousand Welshmen threatened Worcester as invaders; never since England had become a united country had a hostile French army sat down in its very heart as this one was now doing.

But the King at any rate showed his wisdom in not venturing on a battle. He had ample provisions behind him and was gathering strength. Glyndwr and Hugueville, on the other hand, had wasted the country on their route, and they were running short of food. Yet even if Glyndwr had struck at once and gained a victory, it is quite certain that with his friends in the North already crushed he would not have been able with what was left of his fifteen thousand or so Welsh and French, to affect in any way the fortunes of England by merely capturing Worcester, and would have himself been in imminent danger. Moreover, as the King clung to the top of the hill and had perhaps nearly as many men with him as the enemy, the risk attending an attack would have been still greater. The Franco-Welsh army, too, had a good deal of booty among them, which to most of the individuals composing it was probably a leading item for consideration.

When his enemies struck their camp and commenced their backward march to Wales, the King essayed to follow them, and found it no easy task in a region already twice traversed by a hungry and hostile army. He took some provisions with him, but after eighteen waggon-loads of these had been captured by Glyndwr's hungry soldiers he gave up his barren attempts to harass their rapid march. Hall's account of this campaign does not tally with the account of the invaders, as is perhaps natural, and he probably drew to some extent on his imagination when he described Henry's pursuit in such curiously quaint language:

> "From hills to dales," he writes, "from dales to woodes, from woodes to marshes, and yet he could never have them at an advantage. A worlde it was to see his quotidian removings, his busy and painful wanderings, his troublesome and uncertayne abiding, his continual mocian, his daily peregrenacion in the desert fells and craggy mountains of that barrenne infertile and depopulate country."

But the Franco-Welsh army was soon deep in the heart of Wales, and Henry, having given up the pursuit in much more summary fashion than Hall would have us believe in the face of dates, was concentrating his forces at Hereford. Prince Henry had already done something to harass the march of the Welsh through Monmouth. Sir John Grendor was negotiating with Owen's supporters in the valley of the Usk. Sir John Berkrolles still held the great castle of Coity with the utmost difficulty, and the Bristol captains who had enabled Harlech to hold out so long were now ordered down the Bristol channel with supplies for the still beleaguered garrisons of South Wales.

On September 10th Henry with a large force commenced his fifth invasion of Wales. The reader, wearied no doubt by the chronicle of these futile endeavours, might now well look for some tangible result, some crushing blow. There is nothing, however, but the old, old story to tell. The King entered Glamorgan and succeeded in relieving the single castle of Coity; he then turned tail, and the Welsh at once, as in every case but one, when there was no need for it, sprang upon his back. Besides his spears and arrows Glyndwr once more worked with his magic wand. The heavens descended and the floods came and soaked and buffeted the hapless monarch and his still more wretched and ill-provisioned troops. Every river ran bank-high and every brook was in flood; and the clumsy carts that carried the commissariat were captured by Glyndwr's men or whirled away in the rapids. The old story of 1402 was repeated in the autumn of 1405. The royal army on their return had to cross the valley of the Rhondda, where the national cause, though more than once suppressed, was always vigorous and responded to its famous war-cry, "Cadwgan, whet thy battle-axe." This valley runs from the westward into the Taff at Pontypridd and is now astir with the hum of grimy industry and bright with the flare of forges. It was then a hive of fighting stock-farmers fired with a great enthusiasm for Glyndwr.

"There was a certain Cadwgan," says the old Iolo manuscript already quoted, "who was a leader among the men of the valley and a doughty henchman of Glyndwr, and when it became necessary for him to call the people to battle he used to march up and down the valley whetting his axe. So when Owen came to Glyn Rhondda he would say, 'Cadwgan, whet thy battle-axe,' and the moment he was heard to do so all living persons collected about him in military array and from that day to this the battle shout of Glyn Rhondda has been 'Cadwgan, whet thy battle-axe.'"

By October 1st the King was back at Worcester. It would be of little profit to relate the various orders he gave for resisting and pacifying the Welsh, nor yet to give the names of the various Lord Marchers whom he ordered to proceed upon expeditions with small forces, where he himself had failed with large ones. One is not surprised to find that Owen and his French allies had Wales for the most part to themselves and were unmolested during the winter. The greater part of the French, however, returned home again before Christmas, some seventeen hundred remaining, for whom Glyndwr found comfortable quarters. He seems to have been greatly disappointed at the departure of the others, as well as at the conduct of those who remained. The alliance, indeed, proved unsatisfactory to both parties. The French individually counted on booty as their reward, whereas they found for the most part a plundered and ravaged country. It is possible, too, there may have been some racial friction between the Welsh and their French allies. At any rate the latter, as one of their old chroniclers remarks, did not do much bragging when they got home to Brittany, nor did those who remained in Wales conduct themselves by any means to the satisfaction of Glyndwr, but were altogether too much given up to thoughts of plundering their friends. Upon the whole their motives were too obvious and the prospect of further assistance from them not very cheering.

Western Pembroke in the meantime (Little England beyond Wales), finding itself cut off from all assistance, in spite of the girdle of splendid castles by which it was protected, began to find Glyndwr at last too much for it. The earldom was in abeyance and Sir Francis À' Court was governor of the county and known as Lord of Pembroke. He called together the representatives of the district, who solemnly agreed to pay Glyndwr the sum of £200 for a truce to last until the following May. So Pembroke, having humbled itself and in so doing having humbled England, which had thus failed it in its hour of need, had peace. And Glyndwr, still supreme, but not without some cause for depression, returned to Harlech to take counsel with his friends and prepare for a year that promised to be exceptionally fruitful of good or ill.

MANORBIER CASTLE.

CHAPTER IX

THE TRIPARTITE INDENTURE

1406

DURING the lull of this winter of 1405–6 messengers were going backwards and forwards between Harlech and Scotland.

The chief event of the early part of the new year was the signing of that Tripartite Indenture which I have already spoken of as being so often attributed to the period before the battle of Shrewsbury. Pity, for the sake of dramatic effect, that it was not, and as Shakespeare painted it! Hotspur was then alive and the power of the Percys at its height, while Mortimer had not tarnished the splendour of his house and dimmed such measure of reputation as he himself enjoyed, by sinking his individuality in that of his wife's strenuous father. Glyndwr alone was greater than he had then been, though the zenith of his fortunes had been reached and he was soon to commence that long, hopeless struggle against fate and overwhelming odds that has caused men to forget the ravager in the fortitude of the hero.

Northumberland had outworn, as we have seen,

the King's marvellous forbearance, and was now a fugitive in Scotland with Bardolph, whose estates, like his own, had been confiscated, and whose person, like Northumberland's, was urgently wanted by Henry. The old Earl had lost his nerve and had taken alarm at certain indications on the part of the Scots that they would not object to hand him over to Henry in exchange for the doughty Lord Douglas who had been held in honourable captivity since the battle of Shrewsbury. Fearing this he and Bardolph took ship from the western coast for France. But either by prior agreement with Glyndwr or on their own initiative they rounded the stormy capes of Lleyn and, turning their ships' prows shorewards, landed in the sandy and sequestered cove of Aberdaron.

Aberdaron is to this day the Ultima Thule of Wales. It was then a remote spot indeed, though in times long gone by, when pilgrims crept in thousands from shrine to shrine along the coasts of Lleyn to the great abbey, "The Rome of the Welsh," on Bardsey Island, it had been famous enough. It was not alone its remoteness that recommended this lonely outpost, flung out so far into the Irish Sea, to the two fugitives and irrepressible conspirators. David Daron, Dean of Bangor, a friend of Glyndwr, had been with them in the North as one of his commissioners and seems to have remained longer than his colleagues with Percy. At any rate he was Lord of the Manor of Aberdaron and had a house there to which he welcomed his two English friends. The object of the latter was not merely to fly to France but to stir up its King to renewed efforts against Henry. Glyndwr, too, as we shall see, had been sending messengers to France, and the impending meeting at Aberdaron might be fruitful of great results.

It is an easy run by sea of twenty miles or so from Harlech to the farther capes of Lleyn where the romantic island of Bardsey, sanctified by the bones of its twenty thousand saints, lifts its head to an imposing height above the waves. To Aberdaron, just short of the farthest point of the mainland, then came Glyndwr, bringing with him Mortimer and no doubt others of his court. It was on February 28, 1406, that the meeting took place when the somewhat notable *Indenture of Agreement* was signed by the three contracting parties. The date of this proceeding has been by no means undisputed, but of all moments this particular one seems the most likely and has the sanction of the most recent and exhaustive historians of the period.

The bards had been prolific and reminiscent during this quiet winter, and there seemed special call as well as scope for their songs and forecasts. The ancient prophecies of Merlin that were never allowed to slumber, regarding the future of Britain and the Welsh race, were now heard as loudly as they had been before the battle of Shrewsbury, interpreted in various ways in uncouth and strange metaphor. Henry was the "mouldwharp cursed of God's own mouth." A dragon would come from the north and with him a wolf from the west, whose tails would be tied together. Fearful things would happen upon the banks of the Thames and its channel would be choked with corpses. The rivers of England would run with blood. The "mouldwharp" would then be hunted out of the country by the dragon, the lion, and the wolf, or, in other words, by Glyndwr, Percy, and Mortimer. He would then be drowned and his kingdom divided between his three triumphant foes.

Who framed the Indenture is not known; perhaps Glyndwr himself, since he had been a barrister in his youth and was certainly a ready penman. The chronicler tells us that the contracting parties swore fidelity to each other upon the gospels before putting their names to the articles, and then proceeds to give what purports to be the full text of the latter in Latin, of which the following is a translation.

"This year the Earl of Northumberland made a league and covenant and friendship with Owyn Glyndwr and Edmund Mortimer, son of the late Earl of March, in certain articles of the form and tenor following: In the first place that these Lords, Owyn, the Earl, and Edmund shall henceforth be mutually joined, confederate, united and bound by the bond of a true league and true friendship and sure and good union. Again that every one of these Lords shall will and pursue, and also procure, the honour and welfare of one another; and shall in good faith, hinder any losses and distresses which shall come to his knowledge, by anyone whatsoever intended to be inflicted on either of them. Every one also of them shall act and do with another all and every of those things, which ought to be done by good true and faithful friends to good, true and faithful friends, laying aside all deceit and fraud. Also, if ever any of the said Lords shall know and learn of any loss or damage intended against another by any persons whatsoever, he shall signify it to the others as speedily as possible, and assist them in that particular, that each may take such measures as may seem good against such malicious purposes ; and they shall be anxious to prevent such injuries in good faith; also they shall assist each other to the utmost of their power in the time of necessity. Also if by God's appointment it should appear to the said Lords in process of time that they are the same persons of whom the Prophet speaks, between whom the Government of the Greater Britain ought to be divided and parted, then they and every one of them shall labour to their utmost to bring this effectually to be accomplished. Each of them, also, shall be content with that portion of the kingdom aforesaid, limited as below, without further exaction or superiority ; yea, each of them in such proportion assigned to him shall enjoy liberty. Also between the same Lords it is unanimously covenanted and agreed that the said Owyn and his heirs shall have the whole of Cambria or Wales, by the borders, limits and boundaries underwritten divided from Lœgira, which is commonly called England ; namely from the Severn Sea as the river Severn leads from the sea, going down to the north gate of the city of Worcester ; and from that gate straight to the Ash tree, commonly called in the Cambrian or Welsh language Owen Margion, which grows on the highway from Bridgenorth to Kynvar ; thence by the highway direct, which is usually called the old or ancient way, to the head or source of the river Trent : thence to the head or source of the river Mense ; thence as that river leads to the sea, going down within the borders, limits and boundaries above written. And the aforesaid Earl of Northumberland shall have for himself and his heirs the counties below written, namely, Northumberland, Westmoreland,

Lancashire, York, Lincoln, Nottingham, Derby, Stafford, Leicester, Northampton, Warwick, and Norfolk. And the Lord Edmund shall have all the rest of the whole of England, entirely to him and his heirs. Also should any battle, riot or discord fall out between two of the said Lords (may it never be) then the third of the said Lords, calling to himself good and faithful counsel, shall duly rectify such discord, riot and battle; whose approval or sentence the discordant parties shall be held bound to obey. They shall also be faithful to defend the kingdom against all men; saving the oak on the part of the said Owyn given to the most illustrious Prince Charles by the Grace of God King of the French, in the league and covenant between them made. And that the same be, all and singular, well and faithfully observed, the said Lords Owyn, the Earl, and Edmund, by the holy body of the Lord which they now steadfastly look upon and by the holy gospels of God by them now bodily touched, have sworn to observe the premises all and singular to their utmost, inviolably; and have caused their seals to be mutually affixed thereto."

Little, however, was to come of all this. Earl Percy and Bardolph, after spending some two years partly under Glyndwr's protection and partly in France, found their way back to Scotland and in the spring of 1408 played their last stake. Their fatuous attempt with a small and ill-disciplined force of countrymen to overturn Henry's throne was easily defeated at Bramham Moor in Yorkshire by the sheriff of that county, and their heads and limbs were suspended from the gateways of various English cities as a testimony to the dismal failure which the great house of Percy had made of its persistent efforts to depose the King it had created.

Glyndwr for his part was neither now, nor yet to be at any future time, in a position to help his friends outside Wales. His power had passed its zenith, though its decline is not marked by any special incidents in this year 1406. Much the most interesting event to be noted by the student of his career and period, at this turning-point of his fortunes, is a letter he wrote to the King of France, almost immediately after his return from the rendezvous with Northumberland and Bardolph. His headquarters in the early spring of this year seem to have been at Machynlleth, for the letter in question was written from Pennal, a village about four miles from this ancient outpost of Powys. Before touching, however, on the main object of this memorable communication, it will be well to recall the fact that the remnants of the French invaders of the previous year were just leaving Wales, to the great relief of Owen. But his disappointment at the nature of the help the French King had sent on this occasion by no means discouraged him from looking in the same direction for more effectual support.

It was now the period of the Papal Schism. For nearly thirty years there had been two rival popes, the one at Rome, the other at Avignon, and Catholic Europe was divided into two camps, the countries who adhered to the one spiritual chief professing to regard the followers of the other as heretics unfit to breathe the air of this world and without hope of pardon in the next. The Christian Church was shaken to its foundations and degenerated into an arena of venomous strife. Nor was this only a war of words, beliefs, interdicts, and sacerdotal fulminations, for 200,000 lives are said to have been lost over this squabble for the vicarship of Christ. Pious men deplored the lamentable state to which those who should have been the upholders of religion had reduced it. France, of course, in common with Spain, maintained the cause of her own Pope. England held to the Roman Pontiff, but even apart from the Lollard element, which was now considerable, regarded the wearisome dispute with a large measure of contemptuous indifference. Scotland as a matter of course took the opposite side to England. There was no sentiment about "the island" among the Anglo-Normans who lived north of the Tweed and who had resisted successfully every attempt of their kinsmen on the south of it to include them in their scheme of government. They were all aliens alike so far as those who had power were concerned, and would not have understood, probably, that strange sort of lingering loyalty to the soil that in spite of everything still survived among the remnant of the Britons. Glyndwr, of course, had acted directly against this ancient theory, but mercenary soldiers were now such a feature of military life that the importation of these Frenchmen was perhaps of less significance, more particularly as foreign troops were continually serving in England in the pay of various kings. Now, however, as a bait to the French King and to quicken his interest in his cause, Glyndwr offered to take Wales over to the allegiance of the

Avignon Pope. In this Pennal letter Owen dwells at some length upon the details of the elections of the rival popes which the French King himself had sent over to him, and he excuses himself for following the English lead in the past and adhering to the Roman Pontiff on the score of not having hitherto been properly informed regarding the rights and wrongs of this same election. He recapitulates the promises made to him by the King if he would acknowledge Benedict XIII. and not his rival, Gregory XII.

After holding a council of the "princes of his race," prelates, and other clergy he had decided to acknowledge the Avignon Pope. He begs the King of France, as interested in the well-being of the Church of Wales, to exert his influence with the Pope and prevail upon him to grant certain favours which he proceeds to enumerate:

In the first place, that all ecclesiastical censures pronounced either by the late Clement or Benedict against Wales or himself or his subjects should be cancelled. Furthermore that they should be released from the obligation of all oaths taken to the so-called Urban and Boniface lately deceased and to their supporters. That Benedict should ratify ordinations and appointments to benefices and titles (*ordines collatos titulos*) held or given by prelates, dispensations, and official acts of notaries, "involving jeopardy of souls or hurt to us and our subjects from the time of Gregory XI." Owen urges that Menevia (St. Davids) should be restored to its original condition as a Metropolitan church, which it held from the time of that saint himself, its archbishop and confessor, and under twenty-four archbishops after him, whose names, beginning with Clind and ending with the significantly Anglo-Saxon patronymic of Thompson, are herein set forth. Formerly, the writer goes on to say, St. Davids had under it the suffragan sees of Exeter, Bath, Hereford, Worcester, Leicester (now transferred to Coventry), Lichfield, St. Asaph, Bangor, Llandaff, and should rightly have them still, but the Saxon barbarians subordinated them to Canterbury. In language that in later centuries was to be so often and so vainly repeated, he represents that none but Welsh-speaking clergy should be appointed, from the metropolitan down to the curate. He requests also that all grants of Welsh parish churches to English monasteries or colleges should be annulled and that the rightful patrons should be compelled to present fit and proper persons to ordinaries, that freedom should be granted to himself and his heirs for their chapel, and all the privileges, immunities, and exemptions which it enjoyed under their predecessors. Curiously significant, too, and suggestive, is the point he makes of liberty to found two universities, one for North and one for South Wales. Indeed this is justly regarded as one of many bits of evidence that Owen was not merely a battle-field hero, an avenging patriot, an enemy of tyrants, but that he possessed the art of constructive statesmanship had he been given the opportunity to prove it. The educational zeal that does so much honour to modern Wales is fond of pointing to Glyndwr as the original mover in that matter of a Welsh national university which has so recently been brought to a successful issue. King Henry in this letter is naturally an object of special invective, and Owen prays that Benedict will sanction a crusade in the customary form against the usurper Henry of Lancaster for burning down churches and cathedrals, and for beheading, hanging, and quartering Welsh clergy, including mendicant friars, and for being a schismatic. The writer would appear by this to have unladen his conscience of the burden of the smoking ruins of Bangor and St. Asaph and of many, it is to be feared, less noteworthy edifices. Indeed, we find him earlier in his career excusing himself for these sacrilegious deeds and putting the onus of them on the uncontrollable fury of his followers. But the verdict of posterity has in no way been shaken by these lame apologies. Finally he asks the French King to make interest with Benedict for plenary forgiveness for his sins and those of his heirs, his subjects, and his men of whatsoever nation, provided they are orthodox, for the whole duration of the war with Henry of Lancaster.*

This document, a transcript of which is in the Record Office, is preserved at Paris among the French government archives and has attached to it by a double string an imperfect yellow seal, bearing the inscription, "Owenus Dei Gratia princeps Walliæ."

* This letter, which covers many folio pages, has never been printed. It is in indifferent Latin with the usual abbreviations. In the matter of making and elucidating copies of it at the Record Office, Mr. Hubert Hall gave me some valuable assistance, as also did Mr. C. M. Bull.

It is dated the last day of March in the year of our Lord 1406 and "the sixth of our reign." The original is endorsed with a note in Latin to the effect that the above is the letter in which Owen, Prince of Wales, acknowledged obedience to "our Pope."

This year was not a stirring one in Wales. France, to whom Owen was appealing, was in no condition, or at any rate in no mood, to try a serious fall with England. The policy of pin-pricks, to adapt a modern term to the more strenuous form of annoyance in practice in those times, had been pursued with tolerable consistency since the first year of Henry's reign, and the most Christian King had never yet recognised his rival of England as a brother monarch. Richard the Second's child-Queen and widow, Isabel, had, after much haggling, been restored by Henry to France, but that portion of her dower which, according to her marriage settlement, should have been returned with her, was unobtainable. She was married to the Duke of Orleans's eldest son, aged eleven, the greater portion of her dower being a lien on Henry of England for the unpaid balance of the sum above alluded to, an indifferent security. International combats had been going merrily on in the Channel and piratical descents upon either coast were frequent. But this, of course, was not formal war, though a French invasion of England had been one of the chief nightmares of Henry's stormy reign. Internal troubles in France, however, now began somewhat to relax the strained nature of the relationship with England, and Owen's chances of Gallic help grew fainter. His son Griffith, or Griffin, was a prisoner in Henry's hands; he had been committed to the Tower, and by an irony of fate was under the special charge of one of that powerful family to whom his father's old captive, Reginald Grey of Ruthin, belonged. This gentleman, Lord de Grey of Cedmore, so the Issue Rolls of the reign inform us, was paid the sum of three and fourpence a day for Griffin, son of Owen de Glendowdy, and Owen ap Griffith ap Richard, committed to his custody. Another companion in captivity for part of the time, of this "cub of the wolfe from the west," strange to say, was the boy-king of Scotland, who, like most monarchs of that factious and ill-governed country, was probably happier even under such depressing circumstances than if he were at large in his own country, and his life most certainly was much safer.

The Rolls during all these years show a constant drain on the exchequer for provisions and money and sinews of war for the beleaguered Welsh castles. Here is a contract made with certain Bristol merchants, mentioned by name, for sixty-six pipes of honey, twelve casks of wine, four casks of sour wine, fifty casks of wheat flour, and eighty quarters of salt to be carried in diverse ships by sea for victualling and providing "the King's Kastles of Karnarvon, Hardelagh, Lampadarn, and Cardigarn." Here again are payments to certain "Lords, archers and men-at-arms to go to the rescue of Coity castle in Wales." The rate of pay allowed to the soldiers of that day for Welsh service is all entered in these old records and may be studied by the curious in such matters.

"To Henry, Prince of Wales, wages for 120 men-at-arms and 350 archers at 12d. and 6d. per day for one quarter of a year remaining at the abbey of Stratflur and keeping and defending the same from malice of those rebels who had not submitted themselves to the obedience of the Lord the King and to ride after and give battle to the rebels as well in South as in North Wales £666.13.4." Again, in the same year: "To Henry Prince of Wales, for wages of 300 men-at-arms and 600 archers and canoniers and other artificers for the war who lately besieged the castle of Hardelagh [Harlech]."

From the latter of these extracts, which are quoted merely as types of innumerable entries of a like kind, it will be seen that cannons were used, at any rate in some of these sieges, and it is fairly safe to assume that those used against Glyndwr were the first that had been seen in Wales.

As the year 1406 advanced, the star of Owen began most sensibly to wane. He was still, however, keeping up the forms of regal state along the shores of Cardigan Bay, and we find him formally granting pardon to one of his subjects, John ap Howel, at Llanfair near Harlech. The instrument is signed "per ipsum Principem," and upon its seal is a portrait of Owen bareheaded and bearded, seated on a throne-like chair, holding a globe in his left hand and a sceptre in his right. Among the witnesses to the instrument are Griffith Yonge, Owen's Chancellor, Meredith, his younger son, Rhys ap Tudor, and one or two others. There is much that is hazy and mysterious about the events of this year, but in most parts of Wales one hears little or nothing of any shifting of the situation or any loosening of the grip that Glyndwr's party had upon the country. An armed neutrality of a kind probably existed between the Royalists in those towns and castles that had not fallen and the purely Celtic population in the open country, which had long before 1406 been purged of the hostile and the half-hearted of the native race, and purged as we know by means of a most trenchant and merciless kind.

> "While quarrels' rage did nourish ruinous rack
> And Owen Glendore set bloodie broils abroach,
> Full many a town was spoyled and put to sack
> And clear consumed to countries foul reproach,
> Great castles razed, fair buildings burnt to dust,
> Such revel reigned that men did live by lust."

Old Churchyard, who wrote these lines, lived at any rate much nearer to Glyndwr's time than he did to ours, and reflects, no doubt, the feeling of the border counties and of no small number of Welshmen themselves who were involved in that ruin from which Wales did not recover for a hundred years. In this year 1406, say the Iolo manuscripts, "Wales had been so impoverished that even the means of barely sustaining life could not be obtained but by rewards of the King," referring, doubtless, to the Norman garrisons. "Glamorgan," says the same authority, "turned Saxon again at this time though two years later in 1408 they were excited to commotions by the extreme oppressions of the King's men," and when Owen returned once more to aid them, their chiefs who had forsaken his cause burnt their barns and stack-yards, rather than that their former leader and his people should find comfort from them. They themselves then fled, the chronicler continues, to England or the extremities of Wales, where in the King's sea-washed castles they found refuge from Owen's vengeance and were "supported by the rewards of treason and strategem."

More serious, however, than Glamorgan, bristling as it was with Norman interests and Norman castles and always hard to hold against them, the powerful and populous island of Anglesey in the north and the Vale of the Towy in the south fell away from Glyndwr. Sheer weariness of the strife, coupled perhaps with want of provisions, seems to have been the cause. It was due certainly to no active operations from the English border. Pardons upon good terms were continually held out in the name of Prince Henry and the King throughout the whole struggle to any who would sue for them, always excepting Owen and his chief lieutenants, though even his son, as we have seen, was well treated in London. Anglesey was threatened all the time by the great castles of Conway, Carnarvon, and Beaumaris, which held out steadily for the King. Though there was no fighting in the island it is not unnatural that Glyndwr's supporters from thence, being cut off from their homes, which were liable to attacks by sea even when the castles were impotent, were among the first to give in. The strength of the following which he gathered from beyond the Menai is significant of the ardour of national enthusiasm in this old centre of the Princes of Gwynedd, no less than

2112 names of Anglesey men being submitted at one time in this year for pardon. It is possible that these backsliders did not all go home empty-handed, but that a fair amount of plunder from the sack of Marcher castles and the ravage of Marcher lands found its way back with them. However that may be, a royal commission was opened at Beaumaris on November 10th of this year 1406 for the granting of pardons and the assessment of fines to be paid therefor. There is a list still extant in manuscript of the whole two thousand-and-odd names. It will be sufficient to notice, as a point not without interest, that the six commotes of Anglesey paid £537. 7. 0. in fines upon this account. The goods of those slain in battle were forfeited to the King, to be redeemed at prices ranging from 2s. for a horse to 4d. for a sheep. A few were outlawed, among whom was David Daron, Dean of Bangor, at whose house the Tripartite Convention was signed early in the year, while Bifort, Bishop of Bangor, Owen's agent as he might almost be called, together with the Earl of Northumberland, was naturally excluded from purchasing his pardon. Henceforward we hear little of Anglesey in connection with Owen, though the remaining years of his resistance are so misty in their record of him that it would be futile to attempt a guess at the part its people may or may not have played in the long period of his decline.

The defection of Ystrad Towy, the heart and life of the old South Welsh monarchy and always a great source of strength to Owen, must have been still more disheartening, but it seems likely that the submission of his allies between Carmarthen, Dynevor, and Llandovery was of a temporary nature. Mysterious but undoubtedly well-founded traditions, too, have come down concerning the movements of Glyndwr himself during the latter part of this year. He is pictured to us as wandering about the country, sometimes with a few trusty followers, sometimes alone and in disguise. This brief and temporary withdrawal from publicity does not admit of any confusion with the somewhat similar circumstances in which he passed the closing years of his life. All old writers are agreed as to this hiatus in the midst of Glyndwr's career, even when they differ in the precise date and in the extent of his depression. One speaks of him as a hunted outlaw, which for either the year 1405 or 1406 is of course ridiculous. Another, with much more probability, represents him as going about the country in disguise with a view to discovering the inner sentiments of the people. A cave is shown near the mouth of the Dysanni between Towyn and Llwyngwril, where during this period he is supposed to have been concealed for a time from pursuing enemies by a friendly native. Upon the mighty breast of Moel Hebog, over against Snowdon, another hiding-place is connected with his name and with the same crisis in his fortunes. A quite recently published manuscript * from the Mostyn collection contains a story to the effect that when the abbot of Valle Crucis, near Llangollen, was walking on the Berwyns early one morning he came across Glyndwr wandering alone and in desultory fashion. The

* *A Soldier of Calais.*

abbot, as head of a Cistercian foundation, was presumably unfriendly to the chieftain whose iconoclasms must have horrified even his friends the Franciscans. There is nothing of interest in the actual details of this chance interview. The fact of Glyndwr being alone in such a place is suggestive and welcome merely as a little bit of evidence recently contributed to the strong tradition of his long wanderings. The abbot appears from the narrative to have been anything but glad to see him and told him that he had arisen a hundred years too soon, to which the Welsh leader and Prince made no reply but "turned on his heel and departed in silence."

A much fuller and better-known story, however, of this mysterious period of Glyndwr's career survives in the Iolo manuscripts. Sir Laurence Berkrolles of St. Athan was a famous scion of that Anglo-Norman stock who had carved up Glamorganshire in Henry the First's time. He had inherited the great castle and lordship of Coity from his mother's family, the Turbervilles, whose male line had only just failed after three centuries of such occupation as must have made men of them indeed. Sir Laurence, it need hardly be rémarked, had experienced a stormy time for the past few years, battling for his patrimony with Glyndwr's sleepless legions. There was now a lull, presumably in this year 1406, and Sir Laurence was resting in his castle and rejoicing doubtless in the new sense of security to which Glamorgan had just settled down. Hither one day came a strange gentleman, unarmed and accompanied by a servant, and requested in French a night's lodging of Sir Laurence. The hospitable Marcher readily assented and placed the best that the castle afforded before his guest, to whom he took so great a fancy that he ended in begging him to prolong his stay for a few days. As an inducement he informed the traveller that it was quite possible he might in such case be fortunate enough to see the great Owen Glyndwr, for it was rumoured that he was in that neighbourhood, and he (Sir Laurence) had despatched his tenants and servants and other men in his confidence to hunt for Owen and bring him in, alive or dead, under promise of great reward.

"It would be very well," replied the guest, "to secure that man were any persons able to do so."

Having remained at Sir Laurence's castle four days and three nights the stranger announced his intention of departing. On doing so he held out his hand to his host and thus addressed him:

"Owen Glyndwr, as a sincere friend, having neither hatred, treachery, or deception in his heart, gives his hand to Sir Laurence Berkrolles and thanks him for his kindness and generous reception which he and his friend (in the guise of a servant) have experienced from him at his castle, and desires to assure him on oath, hand in hand, and hand on heart, that it will never enter his mind to avenge the intentions of Sir Laurence towards him, and that he will not, so far as he may, allow such desire to exist in his own knowledge and memory, nor in the minds of any of his relations or adherents." Having spoken thus and with such astonishing coolness disclosed his identity,

Glyndwr and his pseudo-servant went their way. Sir Laurence was struck dumb with amazement, and that not merely in a metaphorical but in a literal sense, for the story goes on to say that he lost the power of speech from that moment! Glyndwr's faithful laureate, Iolo Goch, strengthens the tradition of his master's mysterious disappearance at this time by impassioned verses deploring his absence and calling on him to return to his heartbroken poet:

"I saw with aching heart
The golden dream depart;
His glorious image in my mind,
Was all that Owain left behind.
Wild with despair and woebegone
Thy faithful bard is left alone,
To sigh, to weep, to groan.

"Thy sweet remembrance ever dear,
Thy name still ushered by a tear,
My inward anguish speak;
How could'st thou, cruel Owain, go
And leave the bitter tears to flow
Down Gryffydd's furrowed cheek?"

CHAPTER X

ABERYSTWITH. OWEN'S POWER DECLINES

1407-1408

LITTLE is known of Owen's movements during the first half of the year 1407. Entries here and there upon the Rolls indicate that no improvement so far as the general peace of Wales was concerned had taken place, whatever there may have been in Henry's prospects of ultimately recovering his authority there, prospects which now wore a much brighter look. For though Glyndwr and his captains were still active in the field, there nevertheless runs through all the scant scraps of news we now get of him an unmistakable note of depression on the part of his friends, with proportionate confidence on that of his enemies. Prince Henry was still Lieutenant of the Marches of South Wales, in addition to his hereditary jurisdiction, such as it now was, over the royal counties. A great effort was in contemplation, in view of Owen's failing strength, to put a complete end to the war. Pardons were freely offered to his supporters, and even urged, upon the most lenient terms, and the Marcher Barons, who were inclined at times, when not personally in danger, to forget the conditions on which they held their lands, were sternly forbidden to leave their castles. Things had not been going well in France; Calais had been hard pressed and the great English possessions in the South had been lamentably reduced in extent. Edward the Third is computed to have reigned over six million subjects to the north of the Pyrenees, a population much greater than that of England and Wales combined. Henry had but a fraction left of this kingdom, and that fraction most unsteady in its devotion. He had been several times on the very point of making a personal attempt to repair his failing fortunes beyond the Channel. But his health was beginning even thus early to fail, and his nerves were completely unstrung. He had made up his mind, however, to lead one more expedition against Owen, now that the chances seemed so much more favourable than on former occasions. From even this, however, it will be seen that he ultimately flinched, and it was perhaps well that he did so. His son and the captains round him understood Welsh warfare much better than Henry. The rush of great armies through Wales had failed hopelessly as a means of coercing it, and would fail again. The steady pressure of armed bands upon Owen's front and flanks, and liberal terms to all who deserted him, were the only methods of wearing out the resources of this stubborn patriot, and they were already succeeding. That he was himself pressing hard upon Pembrokeshire, however, just at this time is evident from the orders which were issued for forwarding arms and provisions for the defence of the royal castles in that county, the recipient being Sir Francis À'Court, the King's constable there. Aberystwith castle, however, was to be the chief point of the Prince's attack this autumn, and his father, as I have said, was expected to take part in an expedition that came to be associated with much éclat.

An impression not altogether easy to account for, that the fall of this great castle would prove the final blow to Owen's resistance, got abroad, and there was a great rush of knights and nobles to take part in the ceremony. A picked force of 2400 archers and men-at-arms was told off for the service, and an entry in the Issue Rolls notes the sum of £6825 as being set aside for their pay over the period of six months beginning in June. This was a strong nucleus for an expedition that could be supplemented by the levies of the border counties and the spare strength of the local Marcher barons. Aberystwith Castle occupies a site of much distinction, placed upon a bold promontory projecting into the sea. Its ruins still survive as one of the innumerable witnesses to Cromwell's superfluous vandalism, and afford a favourite lounge to summer visitors at the popular Welsh watering-place. But the first castle built on Norman lines was erected in the twelfth century by Gilbert de Strongbow, the earliest Norman adventurer in this district. A centre for generations of Norman-Welsh strife, dismantled and restored again and again by contentious chieftains, it was finally rebuilt by Edward I.; and what Cromwell and time's destroying hand have left of it dates chiefly from that luminous epoch in Welsh history. Not many of those, perhaps, who loiter amidst its lifeless fragments are aware that in the season of 1407 it was the object of quite a fashionable crusade on the part of the chivalry of England, well supplied with every requisite of siege warfare that the primitive science of the period could provide.

Harlech was at this time the headquarters of Glyndwr's family, including Edmund Mortimer, but to localise Glyndwr himself becomes now more difficult than ever. Since Carmarthen and most of South Wales had forsaken their allegiance, his energies must have been still more severely taxed in keeping up the spirit and directing the movements of his widely scattered bands. We heard of him lately raiding through Pembroke and threatening the Flemish settlements. Merioneth and Carnarvon in the North were still faithful, and we can well believe that the great castles of Aberystwith and Harlech, lying midway between the remnant of his southern followers and those of the North, were in some sort the keys to the situation. Aberystwith, in which Glyndwr had placed a strong garrison under a trusty captain, seemed so, at any rate, to the English. Great guns were sent all the way from Yorkshire to Bristol, to be forwarded thence by sea to the coast of Cardigan, while ample stores of bows and arrows, bowstrings, arblasts, stone-shot, sulphur, and saltpetre were ordered to be held in readiness at Hereford. Woods upon the banks of the Severn were to be cut down and the forest of Dean to be picked over for trees, out of which was to be contrived the siege machinery for the subjugation of hapless Aberystwith. A troop of carpenters were to sail from Bristol for the devoted spot and erect scaffolds and wooden towers upon a scale such as had not been before witnessed at any of the innumerable sieges of this Welsh war. Proclamations calling out the great nobility of western England and the Marches to meet the King and Prince at Hereford were sent out. Owen, as well as Aberystwith and Harlech, was to be crushed, and the King himself, with the flower of his chivalry, was to be there to witness the closing scene. How far off even yet was the final extinction of Owen, no one then could have well imagined.

But a temporary check came to these great preparations. The King, as he had shrunk from crossing the Channel, now shrank from crossing the Welsh border. A pestilence, somewhat more severe than those which were almost chronic in the country in those days, swept over the island and was more virulent in the West than elsewhere. It may have been this that for a time suspended operations. Strange to say, too, the Richard myth was not quite extinct, for during this summer bills were found posted up about London proclaiming that he was "yet alive and in health, and would come again shortly with great magnificence and power to recover his kingdom." But neither pestilence nor the vagaries of the King nor false rumours of the dead Richard were allowed to permanently unsettle the Aberystwith enterprise. Fighting in Wales had by no means been a popular or fashionable pastime, when there was no territory to be won or to be defended. It was poor sport for the heavy-armed sons of Mars of that period, all athirst for glory, this tilting over rough ground at active spearmen who melted away before their cumbrous onslaught only to return and deal out death and wounds at some unexpected moment or in some awkward spot. But now whole clouds of gay cavaliers, besides men scarred and weather-beaten with Welsh warfare, gathered to the crusade against Aberystwith. French wars just now were at a discount, not because the spirit was unwilling, but because the exchequer was weak, so, the supply of fighting knights and squires being for the moment greater than the demand, Prince Henry reaped the benefit of the situation in his march through South Wales.

But the bluest blood and the most brilliant equipment were futile in attack against castles that nature and Edward the First had combined to make invulnerable. The guns and scaffolds and wooden towers were all there, but they were powerless against Aberystwith and the brave Welshmen who, under Owen's lieutenant, Rhys ap Griffith ap Llewelyn, defended it. The King's particular cannon, weighing four and one half tons, was there, which, with another called the Messenger, shook the rock-bound coasts, striking terror, we may well fancy, into the peasants of that remote country and proving more destructive to those behind it than those before, for we are told that it burst during the siege, a common thing with cannons of that day, dealing death to all around. Once an hour, it is usually estimated, was the greatest rapidity with which these cumbrous pieces could be fired with safety, and we may well believe that the moment of explosion must have been a much more anxious one, seeing how often they burst, to their friends beside them than to their foes hidden behind the massive walls of a Norman castle. The Duke of York was there, and the Earl of Warwick, who, two years previously, had defeated Glyndwr in a pitched battle and was eager, no doubt, to meet him again. Sir John Grendor, too, was present, no courtier, but a hero of the Welsh wars, and Sir John Oldcastle, a typical border soldier, who became Lord Cobham and was ultimately hunted down as a Lollard at Welshpool and burned by Henry V.; while Lord Berkeley commanded the fleet and managed the siege train. It was not known at Aberystwith, either by the Welsh or the besiegers, where Owen was. He could not readily trust himself in castles, besieged both by land and sea, and run the risk of being caught like a fox in a trap. He bided his time, on this occasion, as will be seen, and arrived precisely at the right moment. Prince Henry found the castle impregnable to assault, and there was nothing for it but to sit down and reduce it by starvation. The only hope of the garrison lay in Owen's relieving them, and with such an army before them the possibility of this seemed more than doubtful. Provisions soon began to fail, and in the middle of September Rhys ap Griffith made overtures and invited seventeen of the English leaders within the castle to arrange a compromise.

Copyright F. Frith & Co.

ABERYSTWITH CASTLE.

One of these was Richard Courtney of the Powderham family, a scholar of Exeter College, Oxford, and Chancellor of the University. Mass was said by this accomplished person to the assembled Welsh and English leaders, after which they received the sacrament and then proceeded to draw up an agreement which seems a strange one. By it the Welsh undertook to deliver up the castle on November 1st if Glyndwr had not in the meantime appeared and driven off the besiegers. Till that date an armistice was to continue. Those of the garrison who would not accept these terms were to be turned out to take their chance; the rest were to receive a full pardon at the capitulation. The abbot of Ystradfflur, who, though a Cistercian, had taken Owen's side, and three Welsh gentlemen, were given up as hostages.

The Prince and his nobles were doubtless glad enough to get away from so monotonous a task in so remote a spot, though their return to England was hardly a glorious one. No one seems to have expected Owen, and only five hundred soldiers were left in camp at the abbey of Ystradfflur, some fifteen miles off, to insure the proper fulfilment of the agreement when November should come round. Parliament was to meet and did meet at Gloucester in October, and the King himself, so much importance did he attach to Aberystwith, still talked of returning with his son to receive its surrender at the appointed time. But neither the royal progress nor the surrender became matters of fact, for during October Owen slipped unexpectedly into the castle with a fresh force, repudiated, as indeed he had a right to repudiate, the agreement, and branded as traitors to his cause those who had made it, which was hard. The five hundred royal soldiers at Ystradfflur had shrunk in numbers and relaxed in discipline, and had at any rate no mind to encounter Owen, who remained in possession of the west coast and its castles throughout a winter which so far as any further news of him is concerned was an uneventful one. In the meantime the Parliament which sat at Gloucester for six weeks in the autumn was greatly exercised about Welsh affairs. Wales had returned no revenue since Glyndwr first raised his standard, and the sums of money that had been spent in vain endeavours to crush his power had been immense. The feeling was now stronger than ever that taxation for this purpose, one that brought no returns either in glory or plunder, had reached its limit, and that it was high time the nobles whose interests lay in Wales should take upon themselves for the future the heavy burden of Welsh affairs.

One incident occurred at this Parliament which had some significance and was not without humour. The Prince of Wales was publicly thanked for his services before Aberystwith almost upon the very day when, unknown, of course, to him and to those at distant Gloucester, Owen had slipped into the castle about which so much stir was being made, upset the whole arrangement, and turned the costly campaign into an ignominious failure. It is significant, too, that the Prince, after acknowledging the praises of his father and the Parliament, kneeled before the former and "spake some generous words" concerning the Duke of York, whose advice and assistance "had rescued the whole expedition from peril and desolation." This looks as if Owen's people had not allowed the return journey of the Prince and his friends and his even still large force to be the promenade that was expected. It may well indeed have been the ubiquitous Glyndwr himself from whom the sagacity of the Duke delivered them in the wilds of Radnor or Carmarthen. Though Aberystwith and Harlech were safe for this winter, the Prince, with a deliberation perhaps emphasised by chagrin at his failure, made arrangements for a second attempt to be undertaken in the following summer.

The winter of 1407–1408 was the most terrible within living memory. It is small wonder that no echo of siege or battle or feat of arms breaks the silence of the snow-clad and war-torn country. Birds and animals perished by thousands, for a sheet of frozen snow lay upon the land from before Christmas till near the end of March. Yet outside Wales even so cruel a winter could not still all action. For Glyndwr's old ally, Northumberland, selected this, of all times and seasons, for that last reckless bid for power which has been before alluded to, and with Bardolf and Bifort, Owen's Bishop of Bangor, went out across the bitter cold of the Yorkshire moors, the first two of them, at any rate, to death and ruin. Bifort, however, seems to have got away and carried the nominal honours of his bishopric for many years.

The opening of summer in 1408 found Owen still

active and dangerous. No longer so as of old to the peace of England and to Henry's throne,—that crisis had passed away,—but he was still an unsurmountable obstacle to the good government of Wales. We know this rather from the anxiety to subdue him manifested this year by the King's council to the exclusion of all other business, than from any detailed knowledge of his actions. Of these one can guess the general tenor, and the necessary sameness of a guerilla warfare somewhat mitigates the disappointment natural at the lack of actual detail. One gathers from the brief but, from one point of view, significant entries in the public records how entirely demoralised most of the country still remained. Here is an order to prevent supplies being sent to the rebels; there a caution to keep the bonfires in Cheshire or Shropshire ready for the match; there again are notes of persons becoming surety for the good behaviour of repentant Welshmen, or Lord Marchers trying to come again to terms with their rebellious Cymric tenants. Panic-stricken letters, however, came no more from beleaguered castles, nor do the people of Northampton any longer quake in their beds at the name of Glyndwr, though the border counties, and with good cause, feel as yet by no means wholly comfortable.

"In 1408," says the Iolo manuscript, "the men of Glamorgan were excited to commotion by the extra oppression of the King's men; many of the chieftains who had obtained royal favour burnt their stacks and barns lest Owen's men should take them. But these chieftains fled to the extremity of England and Wales, where they were defended in the castles and camps of the King's forces and supported by the rewards of treason and stratagem. Owen could not recover his lands and authority because of the treachery prevalent in Anglesey and Arvon, which the men of Glamorgan called the treason of the men of Arvon."

All this is sadly involved, but one treasures anything that has a genuine ring about it in connection with this shadowy year. Arvon, it may be remarked, is the "cantref" facing the submissive Anglesey, and no doubt the royal castle of Carnarvon was able by this time to exercise an intimidating influence on that portion of the country.

Prince Henry's commission as Lieutenant of both North and South Wales was again renewed; and, gathering his forces at Hereford in June, he again moved on towards the stubborn castle of Aberystwith, making Carmarthen, the old capital of South Wales, his base of operations. Aberystwith this time held out till winter, when it at last fell, the garrison meeting with no harsher treatment than that of ejection without arms or food. Harlech, which Gilbert and John Talbot had by the throat, with a thousand well-armed men and a big siege train, resisted even longer. The Welsh this time were able to utilise the sea, which in those days beat against the foot of the high rock upon which the castle stands, a rock now removed from the shore by half a mile or more of sandy common. Glyndwr, too, was now able to move freely from one beleaguered fortress to another. Both of them held out with singular valour and tenacity, attacking the provision boats which came from Bristol for the besieging armies, and disputing every point that offered an opportunity with sleepless vigilance and tireless energy. Edmund Mortimer died either during the siege or immediately after the surrender, of starvation some writers say, though privation would perhaps be a more appropriate and likely term. Mortimer's wife and three girls, with a son Lionel, together with that "eminent woman of a knightly family," Glyndwr's own consort, fell into the King's hands with the capture of Harlech, and seem to have been taken to London in a body.

There is something pathetic about this wholesale termination of Owen's domestic life, in what for that period would be called his old age. One longs, too, to know something about it. How Margaret Hanmer deported herself under the reflected glories of her lord. Whether indeed she saw much of him, and if so, where; whether she was a stout-hearted patriot and bore the trials and the uncertainties of her dangerous pre-eminence with proud fortitude, or whether she wept over the placid memories of Sycherth and Glyndyfrdwy, and deplored the fortune that had made her a hero's wife and a wanderer. She had three married daughters to give her shelter in Herefordshire. Let us hope that she found her way to one of them, as her husband did years later when the storms of his life were over. As for the Mortimers, that branch of the family was entirely wiped out. The children died, and the gentle Katherine, who had married so near the throne of England, soon followed them and lies somewhere beneath the roar of London traffic in a city churchyard. One account places the capture and removal to London of Glyndwr's family at a later period, but as the interest in this is chiefly a matter of sentiment, the precise date is of no special moment.

The lines were now rapidly tightening round Owen. The English government, by this time fairly free from foreign complications, showed a viligance in Wales which it would have been well for it to have shown in former years, when the danger was much greater. Owen, on his part, relapsed gradually into a mere guerilla leader, though the hardy bands that still rallied round him and scorned to ask for pardon were still so numerous and formidable that it was with difficulty the King could prevent some of the Marcher barons even now from purchasing security against his attacks. Talbot with bodies of royal troops still remained as a garrison in Wales. It is curiously significant, too, and not readily explicable, that in this year 1409 the town of Shrewsbury closed her gates against an English army marching into Wales and refused them provisions. It looks as if even the honest Salopians, tired of keeping guard against the ubiquitous Glyndwr, had thus late, and for the second time in the war, made some sort of terms with him. We find also Charleton, Lord of Powys, about this time granting pardons to those of his tenants who had been "out with Glyndwr," while he was rewarding his more faithful lieges in the borough of Welshpool by an extension of their corporation limits to an area of twenty thousand acres, an unique distinction which that interesting border town enjoys to this day.

Meanwhile it must not be supposed that the royal party treated all Welsh captives with the leniency we have seen at Aberyswith, Harlech, and elsewhere. Rhys Ddu, a noted captain of Glyndwr's, and Philip Scudamore, a scion of that famous Herefordshire family into which the Welsh leader's daughter had married, were taken prisoners while raiding in Shropshire and sent to London and placed in the Tower, where several Welsh nobles had been this long time languishing. Rhys was taken to the Surrey side of the river by the Earl of Arundel, tried, and handed over to the sheriff, who had him dragged upon a hurdle to Tyburn and there executed. His quarters, like those of many Welsh patriots before him, were sent to hang over the gates of four English cities, and his head was affixed to London Bridge. Ten Welsh gentlemen were under lock and key at Windsor Castle. They were now handed over to the Marshal and kept in the Tower till heavy ransoms were forthcoming. But Henry's treatment of his Welsh enemies was upon the whole the reverse of vengeful, and he was wise in his generation. His wholesale pardons to men wearied with years of war in a cause now so utterly hopeless were infinitely more efficacious against that implacable foe who would not himself dream of asking terms. Owen, too, on his part had many prisoners, hidden away in mountain fastnesses, chief of whom was the hapless David Gam, whom my readers will almost have forgotten. Nine of these, we are told by one writer, his followers hung, greatly to their leader's chagrin, since he wanted them for hostages or for exchange.

The Avignon Pope had done Owen little good. A certain religious flavour was introduced into the martial songs of the bards, and Owen's native claims to the leadership of Wales were now supplemented by papal and ecclesiastical blessings from this new and very modern fount of inspiration. But everything ecclesiastical at Bangor was in ashes, the torch, it will be remembered, having been applied by Glyndwr himself. The royal bishop, Young, had years before fled to England and was now enjoying the peaceful retirement of Rochester. Owen's bishop, Bifort, as we have seen, was a wandering soldier. The more vigorous Trevor, who came back to Owen in 1404, was at this time in France, making a last effort, it is supposed, to interest the French King in Glyndwr's waning cause. But death overtook him while still in Paris, and he lies buried in the chapel of the infirmary of the Abbey de St. Victor beneath the following epitaph:

"Hic jacet Reverendus in Christo Pater Johannes Episcopus asaphensis in Wallia qui obiit A.D. 1410 die secundo mensis aprilis cujus anima feliciter requiescat in pace. Amen."

CHAPTER XI

LAST YEARS OF OWEN'S LIFE

1410-1416

OF the last six years of Owen's life, those from 1410 to 1416, there is little to be said. His cause was hopelessly lost and he had quite ceased to be dangerous. Wales was reconquered and lay sick, bleeding, and wasted beneath the calm of returning peace. Thousands, it is to be feared, cursed Glyndwr as they looked upon the havoc which the last decade had wrought. The unsuccessful rebel or patriot, call him what you will, has far more friends among those yet unborn than among his own contemporaries, above all in the actual hour of his failure. Of this failure, too, the Welsh were reminded daily, not only by their wasted country and ruined homesteads but by fierce laws enacted against their race and a renewal on both sides of that hatred which the previous hundred years of peace had greatly softened.

Men born of Welsh parents on both sides were now forbidden to purchase land near any of the Marcher towns. They were not permitted to be

Copyright W. H. Bustin.

MONNINGTON COURT AND CHURCH.

citizens of any borough, nor yet to hold any office, nor carry armour nor any weapon. No Welshman could bind his child to a trade, nor bring him up to letters, while English men who married Welsh women were disfranchised of their liberties. In all suits between Englishmen and Welshmen the judge and jury were to be of the former race, while all "Cym-morthau," or gatherings for mutual assistance in harvest or domestic operations, were strictly forbidden.

These laws were kept on the statute books till the real union of Wales and England in Henry the Eighth's time, but gradually became a dead letter as the memory of the first ten bloody years of the century grew fainter. Glyndwr, however, believed in the justice of his cause, and if he expressed remorse for the methods which he had used to uphold it, we hear nothing of such apologies. That he showed the courage of his convictions in heroic fashion no one can gainsay. That men could be found to stand even yet in such numbers by his side is the most eloquent tribute that could be paid to his personal magnetism. He had lost all his castles, unless indeed, as seems likely, those grim towers of Dolbadarn and Dolwyddelan in the Snowdon mountains were left to him. He became henceforward a mere outlaw, confined entirely to the mountains of Carnarvon and Merioneth, between those fierce and rapid raids which we dimly hear of him still making upon the Northern Marches. His old companions, Rhys and William ap Tudor, who had been with him from the beginning, were in the King's hands, and were about this time executed at Chester with the usual barbarities of the period. The elder was the grandfather of Owen Tudor, and consequently the ancestor of our present King. David Gam was still a prisoner in Owen's hands till 1412, when the King entered into negotiations for his release through the agency of Llewelyn ap Howel, Sir John Tiptoft, and William Boteler. What terms were made we know not; an exchange was in all likelihood effected, seeing how many of Owen's friends were in captivity. David's liberation, however, was by some means successfully accomplished, and he lived to fight and fall by the King's side at Agincourt, being knighted, some say, as he lay dying upon that memorable field.

When, in 1413, Prince Henry came to the throne, he issued a pardon to all Welsh rebels indiscriminately, not excepting Glyndwr. But, obstinate to the last, the old hero held to his mountains, refusing to ask or to receive a favour, striking with his now feeble arm, whenever chance offered, the English power or those who supported it. When Henry IV. succumbed to those fleshly ills which constant trouble had brought upon his once powerful frame, Glyndwr was still in the field and royal troops still stationed in the Welsh mountains to check his raids. Tradition has it that he was at last left absolutely alone, when he is supposed to have wandered about the country in disguise and in a fashion so mysterious that a wealth of legend has gathered around these wanderings.

"In 1415," says one old chronicler, "Owen disappeared so that neither sight nor tidings of him could be obtained in the country. It was rumoured that he escaped in the guise of a reaper bearing a sickle, according to the tidings of the last who saw and knew him, after which little or no information transpired respecting him nor of the place or name of his concealment. The prevalent opinion was that he died in a wood in Glamorgan; but occult chroniclers assert that he and his men still live and are asleep on their arms in a cave called Ogof Dinas in the Vale of Gwent, where they will continue until England is self-abased, when they will sally forth, and, recognising their country's privileges, will fight for the Welsh, who shall be dispossessed of them no more until the Day of Judgment, when the earth shall be consumed with fire and so reconstructed that neither oppression nor devastation shall take place any more, and blessed will he be who will see that time."

Carte says that Owen wandered down to Herefordshire in the disguise of a shepherd and found refuge in his daughter's house at Monnington.

It is quite certain that in 1415, Henry V., full of his French schemes and ambitions, and with no longer any cause to trouble himself about Wales, sent a special message of pardon to Glyndwr. Perhaps the young King felt a touch of generous admiration for the brave old warrior who had been the means of teaching him so much of the art of war and the management of men, and who, though alone and friendless, was too proud to ask a favour or to bend his knee. Sir Gilbert Talbot of Grafton, in Worcestershire, was the man picked out by Henry to accomplish this gracious act. Nothing, however, came of it immediately. Perhaps the great campaign of Poitiers interfered with a matter so comparatively trifling. But on the King's return he renewed it in February, 1416, commissioning this time not only Talbot but Glyndwr's own son, Meredith, as envoys. Whether or no it would have even now and by such a channel been acceptable is of no consequence, as the old hero was either dead or in concealment. Common sense inclines to the most logical and most generally accepted of the traditions which surround his last years, namely, the one which pictures him resting quietly after his stormy life at the home of one or other of his married daughters in Herefordshire. Monnington and Kentchurch both claim the honour of having thus sheltered him. Probably they both did, seeing how near they lie together, though the people of the former place stoutly maintain that it is in their churchyard his actual dust reposes.

At Kentchurch Court, where his daughter Alice Scudamore lived with her husband, and which still belongs to the family, a tower of the building is even yet cherished as the lodging of the fallen chieftain during part at any rate of these last years of obscurity. The romantic beauty of the spot, the survival of the mansion and of the stock that own it, would make us wish to give Kentchurch everything it claims, and more, in connection with Glyndwr's last days. Above the Court, which stands in a hollow embowered in woods, a park or chase climbs for many hundred feet up the steep sides of Garaway Hill, which in its unconventional wildness and entire freedom from any modernising touch is singularly in keeping with the ancient memories of the place. The deer brush beneath oaks and yews of such prodigious age and size that some of them must almost certainly have been of good size when Thomas Scudamore brought Alice, the daughter of Owen of Glyndyfrdwy, home as a bride; while just across the narrow valley, through which the waters of the Monnow rush swift and bright between their ruddy banks, the village and ruined castle of Grosmont stand conspicuous upon their lofty ridge. It must in fairness to the claims of Monnington be remembered that Grosmont was not precisely the object upon which Glyndwr, if he were still susceptible to such emotions, would have wished his fading eyesight to dwell long, since of all the spots in Wales (and it is just in Wales, the Monnow being the boundary) Grosmont had been the one most pregnant, perhaps, with evil to his cause. For it was the defeat of Glyndwr's forces there that may be said to have broken the back of his rebellion. And as we stand upon the bridge over the Monnow midway between England and Wales, the still stately ruins of the Norman castle that must often have echoed to Prince Henry's cheery voice crown the hill beyond us; while behind it the quaint village that rose upon the ashes of the town Glyndwr burnt, with all its civic dignities, looks down upon us, the very essence of rural peace.

Glyndwr's estates had long ago been forfeited to the Crown and granted to John, Earl of Somerset. Soon after his death Glyndyfrdwy was sold to the Salusburys of Bachymbyd and of Rûg near

Corwen, one of the very few alien families that in a peaceful manner had become landowners in North Wales before the Edwardian conquest. It is only recently indeed that there has ceased to be a Salusbury of Rûg. Owen's descendants, through his daughters, at any rate, are numerous. A few years after his death, Parliament, softening towards his memory, passed a special law for the benefit of his heirs, allowing them to retain or recover a portion of the proscribed estates. In consequence of this, Alice Scudamore made an effort to recover Glyndyfrdwy and Sycherth from the Earl of Somerset apparently without success, so far as the former went, in view of the early ownership of the Salusburys.

Of Griffith, the son who was so long a prisoner in the Tower in company with the young King of Scotland, we hear nothing more. But of Meredith this entry occurs in the Rolls of Henry V., 1421: "Pardon of Meredith son of Owynus de Glendordy according to the sacred precept that the son shall not bear the iniquities of the father." To another daughter of Glyndwr, probably an illegitimate one, Gwenllian, wife of Phillip ap Rhys of Cenarth, the famous bard, Lewis Glyncothi, wrote various poems, in one of which he says: "Your father was a potent prince, all Wales was in his council."

No intelligent person of our day could regret the failure of Glyndwr's heroic effort. That Welshmen of the times we have been treating of should have longed to shake off the yoke of the Anglo-Norman was but human, for he was not only a bad master, but a foreigner and wholly antipathetic to the Celtic nature. At the same time, the geographical absurdity, if the word may be permitted, of complete independence was frankly recognised by almost every Welsh patriot from earliest times. The notion of a suzerain or chief king in London, as I have remarked elsewhere, was quite in harmony with the most passionate of Welsh demands. Glyndwr perhaps had other views; but then the kingdom that he would fain have ruled, if the Tripartite Convention is to be relied on, stretched far beyond the narrow bounds of Wales proper and quite matched in strength either of the other two divisions which, under this fantastic scheme, Mortimer and Percy were respectively to govern. What was undoubtedly galling to the Welsh was the spectacle of a province to the north of the island, consisting, so far as the bulk of its power and civilisation was concerned, of these same hated Anglo-Normans, not only claiming and maintaining an entire independence on no basis that a Celt could recognise, but trafficking continuously with foreign enemies in a fashion that showed them to be destitute of any feeling for the soil of Britain beyond that part which they themselves had seized. To the long-memoried Welshman it seemed hard, and no doubt illogical, that these interlopers, one practically in blood and speech and feeling with their own oppressors, should thus be permitted to set up a rival independence within the borders of the island, while they on their part were forced to fuse themselves with a people who could not even understand their tongue and with whom they had scarcely a sentiment in common. It is difficult not to sympathise with the mediæval Welshman in this attitude or to refrain from wondering at the strange turn of fortune that allowed the turbulent ambition of some Norman barons to draw an artificial line and create a northern province, which their decendants, if they showed much vigour in its defence, showed very little aptitude for governing with reasonable equity.

Glyndwr, it is true, had thrown off the old British tradition and had called in foreigners from across the sea, as Vortigern to his cost had done nearly a thousand years before. He had also adopted a French Pope. Neither had done him much good, and Welshmen were soon as ready as ever to fight their late brief allies for the honour of the island of Britain. But Glyndwr from an early period in his insurrection had kept the one aim, that of the independence of his country, dream though it might be, consistently in view. No means were to be neglected, even to the ruining of its fields and the destruction of its buildings, to obtain this end. How thoroughly he carried out his views has been sufficiently emphasised; so thoroughly, indeed, as to cause many good Welshmen to refrain from wholly sharing in the veneration shown for his memory by the bulk of his countrymen. There can be but one opinion, however, as to the marvellous courage with which he clung to the tree of liberty that he had planted and watered with such torrents of human blood, till in literal truth he found himself the last leaf upon its shrunken limbs, and that a withered one. In the heyday of his glory his household bard

Copyright Mrs. Leather.

PORCH OF MONNINGTON CHURCH AND GLYNDWR'S REPUTED GRAVE.

and laureate wrote much extravagant verse in his honour, as was only natural and in keeping with the fancy of the period and of his class. But the Red Iolo himself, in all likelihood, little realised the prophetic ring in the lines he addressed to his master on the closing of his earthly course, though we, at least, have ample evidence of their prescience:

> "And when thy evening sun is set,
> May grateful Cambria ne'er forget
> Its morning rays, but on thy tomb
> May never-fading laurels bloom."

CHAPTER XII

CONCLUSION

AS I have led up to the advent of Glyndwr with a rough outline of Welsh history prior to his day, I will now cast a brief glance at the period which followed. English people have a tendency to underestimate, or rather to take into small consideration, the wide gulf which, not only in former days, but to some extent even yet, divides the two countries. They are apt to think that after the abortive rising of Glyndwr, provided even this stands out clearly in their minds, everything went smoothly and Wales became merely a geographical expression with an eccentric passion for maintaining its own language. As, in the introduction to this book, I had to solicit the patience of the general reader and crave the forbearance of the expert for an effort to cover centuries in a few pages, so I must again put in a plea for another venture of the same kind—briefer, but none the less difficult.

The ruin left by Glyndwr's war was awful. It was not only the loss of property, the destruction of buildings, the sterilisation of lands, but the quarrels and the blood-feuds which the soreness of these years of strife handed down for generations to the descendants of those who had taken opposing sides. And then before prosperity had fairly lifted its head, before bloody quarrels and memories had been forgotten, the devastating Wars of the Roses were upon the country, and it was plunged once more into a chaos not much less distracting than that in which the preceding generation had weltered.

Though, by a curious turn of events, she ultimately gave to England a Lancastrian king, Wales most naturally favoured the House of York. Edmund Mortimer, uncle to the young Earl of March, had shared the triumphs and the perils of Glyndwr's rising. The blood of Llewelyn ap Iorwerth flowed in the veins of the Mortimers, and their great estates lay chiefly in Wales and on the border. The old antagonism to Bolingbroke's usurpation, and the sympathy with Richard and his designated heir that half a century before accompanied it, were still remembered. The Yorkists, however, had no monopoly of Wales,—Welsh knights had fought victoriously in France under Henry V., and Marcher barons of Lancastrian sympathies could command a considerable following of Welshmen. The old confusion of lordship government still retained half Wales as a collection of small palatinates. Once more the castles that Glyndwr had left standing echoed to the bustle of preparation and the stir of arms, and felt the blows of an artillery that they could no longer face with quite the composure with which they had faced the guns of Henry the Fourth.

It was not so much the actual damage that was done, for this war was not so comprehensive, but rather the passions and faction it aroused among the Welsh gentry of both races, though this new faction no longer ran strictly upon racial lines. Nor, again, was it the amount of blood that was shed, for this compared to Glyndwr's war was inconsiderable, but the legacy, rather, of lawlessness that it left behind. Sir John Wynne of Gwydir, in the invaluable chronicle which he wrote at his home in the Vale of Conway during the reign of Elizabeth, draws a graphic picture of North Wales as Henry the Seventh found it. Sir John's immediate forbears had taken a brisk hand in the doings of those distracted times, and there were still men living when he wrote who had seen the close of the chaos with their own eyes, and whose minds were stored with the evidence of their fathers and grandfathers. Harlech in these wars stood once more a noted siege. It was held for the Lancastrians by a valiant Welshman against the Herberts, who made a somewhat celebrated march through the mountains to besiege it. The stout defence it offered inspired the music and the words of the Welsh national march, "Men of Harlech,"—as spirited an air of its kind, perhaps, as has ever been written. The Vale of Clwyd, the garden of North Wales, was burnt, says Sir John, "to cold coals." Landowners who had mortgaged their estates, he goes on to tell us, scarcely thought them worth redeeming, while the deer grazed in the very streets of Llanrwst. For two or three generations the country was infested by bands of robbers who found

 F. Frith & Co.

PEMBROKE CASTLE.

FROM A PHOTOGRAPH.

refuge in the mountains of Merioneth or the wild uplands of the Berwyn Range, and fought for the privilege of systematically plundering and levying blackmail on the Vale of Conway and the richer meadows of Edeyrnion. Sir John's grandfather found it necessary to go to church attended by a bodyguard of twenty men armed to the teeth. "The red-haired banditti of Mawddy" kept the country between the Dovey and Mawddach estuaries and inland nearly to Shropshire in a state of chronic terror. The Carnarvon squires cherished blood-feuds that almost resembled a vendetta, laid siege to one another's houses, and engaged in mimic battles of a truly bloodthirsty description. The first Wynne of Gwydir left West Carnarvonshire and preferred to live among the brigands of the Vale of Conway rather than among his own relatives, since he would "either have to kill or be killed by them." To try and combat these organised bands of robbers, Edward IV. instituted, in 1478, the Court of the President and Council of the Marches of Wales, with summary jurisdiction over all breakers of the peace—provided always that they could catch them! The legal machinery of the lordships was wholly ineffectual, for though each petty monarch had the power of life and death, the harbouring of thieves and outlaws became a matter purely of personal rivalry and jealousy.

But this epoch of Welsh history ended with the advent of the Tudors, which is in truth an even more notable landmark than the so-called conquest of Edward I. Wales since that time had been governed as a conquered country, or a Crown province —she had been annexed but not united, nor had she been represented in Parliament, while outside the Edwardian counties justice was administered, or more often not administered, by two or three score of petty potentates. One must not, however, make too much of what we now call union and patriotism. Cheshire had been till quite recently an independent earldom, with similar relations to the Crown as the lordship, say, of Ruthin or of Hay. As regards national feeling, it is very doubtful if the sentiments that had animated the heptarchy had been eradicated from that turbulent palatinate who boasted the best archers in England and were extremely jealous of their licentious independence.

But it was a pure accident that in the end really reconciled the Welsh to a close union with the hated Saxon. Steeped as they were in sentiment, and credulous to a degree of mysticism and prophecy, and filled with national pride, the rise of the grandson of Owen Tudor of Penmynydd to the throne of Britain was for the Cymry full of significance. The fact, too, that Henry was not merely a Welshman but that he landed in Wales and was accompanied thence by a large force of his fellow-countrymen to the victorious field of Bosworth was a further source of pride and consolation to this long-harassed people. It would be hard indeed to exaggerate the effect upon Wales and its future relationship with England, when a curious chain of events elevated this once obscure princeling to the throne of England. It was strange, too, that it should be a Lancastrian after all whose

Copyright W. H. Bustin.

KENTCHURCH COURT, WITH GLYNDWR'S TOWER.

accession caused such joy and triumph throughout a province which had shed its blood so largely upon the opposing side. The bards were of course in ecstasies; the prophecy that a British prince should once again reign in London—which had faded away into a feeble echo, without heart or meaning, since the downfall of Glyndwr—now astonished with its sudden fulfilment the expounders of Merlin and the Brut as completely as it did the audience to whom they had so long foretold this unlikely consummation. Not for a moment, however, we may well believe, was such a surprise admitted nor the difference in the manner of its fulfilment. But who indeed would carp at that when the result was so wholly admirable? It is not our business to trace the tortuous ways by which fate removed the more natural heirs to the throne and seated upon it for the great good of England as well as of Wales the grandson of an Anglesey squire of ancient race and trifling estate.

That the first Tudor disappointed his fellow-countrymen in some of their just expectations, and behaved in fact somewhat meanly to them, is of no great consequence since his burly son made such ample amends for the shortcomings of his father. The matrimonial barbarities of Henry the Eighth and his drastic measures in matters ecclesiastical have made him so marked a personage that men forget and indeed are not very clearly made to understand what he did for Wales, and consequently for England too.

By an Act of Parliament in 1535 the whole of the Lordship Marcher system was swept away, and the modern counties of Denbigh, Montgomery, Monmouth, Glamorgan, Brecon, and Radnor were formed out of the fragments. It is only possible to generalise within such compass as this. The precise details belong rather to antiquarian lore and would be out of place here. It will be sufficient to say that the Welsh people of all degrees, after waiting with laudable patience for their first King to do something practical on their behalf, petitioned Henry the Eighth to abolish the disorders under which half their country groaned and to grant that representation in Parliament as yet enjoyed by no part of the Principality, and without which true equality could not exist. The King appointed a commission to carry out their wishes. The sources from which the new counties took their names, though following no rule, are obvious enough. Glamorgan, the old Morganwg, had been practically a County Palatine since Fitzhamon and his twelve knights seized it in Henry the First's time, that is to say, the inferior lordships were held in fealty, not each to the King as elsewhere, but to the heirs of Fitzhamon, who for many generations were the Clares, Earls of Gloucester, having their capital at Cardiff, where higher justice was administered. Pembroke was something of the same sort, though the Flemish element made it differ socially from Glamorgan. Nor must it be forgotten that that promontory of Gower in the latter palatinate was a Flemish lordship. But Pembroke was the actual property of the Crown and its earls or lords were practically constables. The rest of the Marches (for this term signified all Wales outside the Edwardian counties) had no such definitions. That they followed no common rule was obvious enough. Brecon took its name from the old lordship of Brecheniog that Bernard de Newmarch had founded in Henry the First's time. The old Melynydd, more or less, became Radnor, after its chief fortress and lordship. Montgomery derived its shire name from the high-perched castle above the Severn, Monmouth from the town at the Monnow's mouth. Large fragments of the Marches, too, were tacked on to the counties of Hereford and Shropshire, the Welsh border as we know it to-day being in many places considerably westward of the old line. All the old lordship divisions with the privileges and responsibilities of their owners were abolished, and the castles, which had only existed for coercive and defensive purposes, began gradually from this time to subside into those hoary ruins which from a hundred hilltops give the beautiful landscape of South Wales a distinction that is probably unmatched in this particular in northern Europe. County government was uniformly introduced all over Wales and the harsh laws of Glyndwr's day, for some time a dead letter, were erased from the statutes. Parliamentary representation was allotted, though only one knight instead of two sat for a shire and one burgess only for all the boroughs of a shire; and the two countries became one in heart as well as in fact. Till 1535 the eldest son of English Kings, as Prince of Wales, had been all that the name implies. Henceforth it became a courtesy title; and one may perhaps be allowed a regret, having regard to the temperament of a Celtic race in this particular, that our English monarchs have allowed it to remain so wholly divorced from all Welsh connection. The last actual Prince of Wales was Henry the Eighth's elder brother Arthur, who died at the then official residence of Ludlow Castle a few weeks after his marriage with Catherine of Aragon.

This reminds me too that one peculiarity remained to distinguish the administration of Wales from that of England, namely that famous and long-lived institution, the "Court of the Marches." This has already been mentioned as introduced by Edward the Fourth, who was friendly to Wales, for the suppression of outlaws and brigands. It was confirmed and its powers enlarged by Henry the Eighth's Act, and with headquarters at Ludlow, though sitting sometimes at Shrewsbury and Chester, it was the appeal for all important Welsh litigation. Nor was it in any sense regarded as a survival of arbitrary treatment. On the contrary, it was a convenience to Welshmen, who could take cases there that people in North Yorkshire, for instance, would have to carry all the way to Westminster. For a long time, curiously enough, its jurisdiction extended into the counties of Worcester, Gloucester, Hereford, and Salop. It consisted of a president and council with a permanent staff of subordinate officials. The presidency was an office of great honour, held usually by a bishop or baron of weight in the country, associated with the two justices of Wales and that of Chester. The arrangement seems to have caused general satisfaction till the reign of William the Third, when the growth of industry and population made it advisable to divide Wales into circuits.

The petitions addressed from the Welsh people to Henry praying for complete fusion with England are instructive reading. Marcher rule at the worst had been infamously cruel, at the best inconvenient and inequitable. It was a disgrace to the civilisation of the fifteenth century, which is saying a great deal. To bring criminals to justice was almost impossible when they had only to cross into the next lordship, whose ruler, being unfriendly perhaps to his neighbour, made it a point of honour to harbour those who defied him. The still martial spirit of the Welsh found vent when wars had ceased in petty quarrels, and with such a turbulent past it did them credit that they recognised how sorely even-handed justice was wanted among them.

Lordship Marchers themselves were too often represented by deputies, and something like the abuses that were familiar in Ireland in more recent times owing to middlemen added to the confusion. According to local custom the humbler people of one lordship might not move eight paces from the road as they passed through a neighbouring territory. The penalty for transgression was all the money they had about them and the joint of one finger. If cattle strayed across the lordship boundary they could be kept and branded by the neighbouring lord or his representatives.

In the aforesaid petitions sent up to Henry VIII. the petitioners dwell upon their loyalty to the throne and the unhappy causes that had alienated them from it in the past. They remind him of how they fought in France for Edward III., and of their loyalty to Richard II., which was the sole cause, they declare, of their advocacy of Glyndwr. They indignantly declare that they are not "runaway Britons as some call us," but natives of a country which besides defending itself received all those who came to it for succour at the period alluded to. Resenting the imputation of barrenness sometimes cast on their country, they declare that "even its highest mountains afford beef and mutton, not only to ourselves, but supply England in great quantity." They recall the fact that they were Christians while the Saxons were still heathen. They combat those critics who describe their language as uncouth and strange and dwell on its antiquity and purity. If it is spoken from the throat, say these petitioners, "the Spanish and Florentines affect that pronunciation as believing words so uttered come from the heart." Finally, with presumably unconscious satire, they allude to the speech of the northern part of the island as "a kind of English."

Henry accomplished these great reforms in the teeth of the baronial influence of the whole Marches, and if the slaughter of the Wars of the Roses had made his task somewhat easier, he should have full credit for achieving a piece of legislation whose importance as an epoch-marking event could hardly be exaggerated, not only as affecting Wales but the four powerful counties that adjoined it.

To create and organise six new counties out of

chaos, to enfranchise and give representation to twelve, to permanently attach one of the three tributary kingdoms to the British Crown, is a performance that should be sufficient to lift the reign of a monarch out of the common run. Every schoolboy is familiar with the figure of Henry VIII. prancing in somewhat purposeless splendour on the Field of the Cloth of Gold. But who remembers the assimilation of Wales to England which was his doing?

Wales, though small in population, was numerically much greater in proportion to England than is now the case. To-day she is a twentieth, then perhaps she was nearly a seventh, of the whole. It was of vital importance that her people should be satisfied and well governed. The accession of the Tudors and the common sense of their second monarch achieved without difficulty what might have been a long and arduous business.

The palmy days of Elizabeth saw Wales, like England, advance by leaps and bounds. The native gentry, the tribesmen, the "Boneddigion," always pressing on the Norman aristocracy, now came again in wholesale fashion to the front. The grim castle and the fortified manor developed into the country house. Polite learning increased and the upper classes abandoned, in a manner almost too complete, the native tongue. The higher aristocracy, taking full and free part in English life, became by degrees wholly Anglicised, and the habit, though very gradually, spread downwards throughout the whole gentry class. The Reformation had been accepted with great reluctance in Wales. The people were conservative by instinct and loyal to all such constituted authorities as they held in affection. They would take anything, however, for that very reason, from the Tudors, and swallowed, or partly swallowed, a pill that was by no means to their liking. In Elizabeth's time the Bible and Prayer-Book were translated into Welsh, which marked another epoch in the history of Wales much greater than it at first sounds. It was not done without opposition: the desire in official circles to stamp out the native language, which became afterward so strong, had already germinated, and it was thought that retaining the Scriptures and the Service in English would encourage its acquisition among the people. The prospects, however, in the actual practice did not seem encouraging, and in the meantime the souls of the Welsh people were starving for want of nourishment. The Welsh Bible and Prayer-Book proved an infinite boon to the masses of the nation, but it did more than anything else to fix the native tongue.

Wales readily transformed its affection for the Tudors into loyalty for the Stuarts. The Church, too, was strong—the bent of the people being averse to Puritanism, and indeed nowhere in Britain did the survivals of popery linger so long as among the Welsh mountains. Even to-day, amid the uncongenial atmosphere that a century of stern Calvinism has created, some unconscious usages and expressions of the peasantry in remoter districts preserve its traces. The Civil War found Wales staunch almost to a man for the King. There were some

Roundheads in the English part of Pembroke, as was natural, and a few leading families elsewhere were found upon the Parliamentary side. Such of the castles as had not too far decayed were furbished up and renewed the memories of their stormy prime under circumstances far more injurious to their masonry. Harlech, Chirk, Denbigh, Conway, and many others made notable defences. The violent loyalty of Wales brought down upon it the heavy hand of Cromwell, though himself a Welshman by descent. The landed gentry were ruined or crippled, and the prosperity of the country greatly thrown back. It is said that the native language took some hold again of the upper classes from the fact of their poverty keeping them at home, whereas they had been accustomed to flock to the English universities and the border grammar schools, such as Shrewsbury, Chester, or Ludlow. Welsh poetry and literature expended itself in abuse of that Puritanism which in a slightly different form was later on to find in Wales its chosen home. But in all this there was of course little trace of the old international struggles. The Civil War was upon altogether different lines. The attitude of Wales was, in fact, merely that of most of the west of England somewhat emphasised.

Smitten in prosperity, the Principality moved slowly along to better times in the wake of England, under the benevolent neutrality of the later Stuarts and of William and Anne. It still remained a great stronghold in outward things, at any rate, of the Church, and kept alive what Defoe, travelling there in Anne's reign, calls "many popish customs," such as playing foot-ball between the services on Sunday, and retiring to drink at the public house, which was sometimes, he noted, kept by the parson, while even into the eighteenth century funeral processions halted at the crossroads and prayed for the soul of the dead. The Welsh landowning families were numerous and poor, proud of their pedigrees, which unlike the Anglo-Norman had a full thousand years for genealogical facts or fancies to play over. At the beginning of the eighteenth century there were very few wealthy landowners in Wales who stood out above the general level, which was perhaps a rude and rollicking one. There was no middle class, for there were neither trade nor manufactures worth mentioning, and little shifting from one class to another. Hence the genealogy was simple, and consequently, perhaps, more accurate than in wealthier societies. The mixture of English blood over most of the country was almost nil among the lower class, and not great even among the gentry.

The peasantry still submitted themselves without question to their own social leaders, and the latter, though they had mostly abandoned their own language, still took a pride in old customs and traditions, were generous, hospitable, quarrelsome, and even more addicted to convivial pleasures than their English contemporaries of that class. Defoe was at a cocking match in Anglesey and sat down to dinner with forty squires of the island. "They talked in English," he says, "but swore in Welsh." That the Welsh gentleman of the present day, unlike his prototype of Scotland or Ireland, shows no trace worth mentioning of his nationality is curious when one thinks how much farther removed he usually is in blood from the Englishman than either. It should be remembered, however, that there were no seats of learning in Wales such as Ireland and Scotland possessed. The well-to-do young Welshman went naturally to England for his education, even in days when difficulties of travelling were in favour of even indifferent local institutions.

Surnames became customary in Wales about the time of the Tudor settlement; previously only a few men of literary distinction had adopted them, such as Owen Cyfylliog, Prince of Upper Powys, Dafydd Hiraethog, etc. The inconvenience of being distinguished only by the names of his more recent ancestors connected by "ab" or "ap" was found intolerable by the Welshman and his English friends as life got more complex. It is said that Henry VIII. was anxious for the Welsh landowners to assume the name of their estates in the old Anglo-Norman fashion, and it is a pity his suggestion was not followed, in part at any rate. But the current Christian name of the individual was adopted instead and saddled for ever on each man's descendants. So a language full of euphonious place-names and sonorous sounds shows the paradox of the most inconveniently limited and perhaps the poorest family nomenclature in Europe.

In 1735, just two hundred years after its complete union with England, began the movement that was in time to change all Wales, I had almost said the very

Welsh character itself. This was the Methodist revival. All Welshmen were then Church people. The landed families for the most part supplied the parishes with incumbents, grouping them no doubt as much as possible so as to create incomes sufficient for a younger son to keep a humble curate and ruffle it with his lay relatives over the bottle and in the field. The peasantry may have been cheery and happy, but they were sunk in ignorance. They seem, however, to have been good churchgoers—the old instinct of discipline perhaps surviving—but the spiritual consolation they received there was lamentably deficient, and the Hanoverian régime was making matters steadily worse. Its political bishops rarely came near their Welsh dioceses. All the higher patronage was given to English absentees, for the poor Welsh squires could be of little political service and had no equivalent wherewith to pay for a deanery or a canon's stall. To be a Welshman, in fact, was then, and for more than a century later when the landed class had nearly ceased to enter the Church, of itself a bar to advancement. The mental alertness and religious fervour, however, of the Welsh people had only lain dormant under circumstances so discouraging, and were far from dead. They presented a rare field for the efforts of the religious reformer, though it seems more than likely that the beauty and ritual of an awakened Anglican Church would have appealed to their natures more readily even than the eloquence of the Calvinistic school that eventually led them captive. The Welsh people were imaginative, reverential, musical. Their devotion to the old faith in both its forms was sufficiently shown by the pathetic fidelity with which they clung to their mother churches till, both physically and mentally, they tumbled about their ears.

The Methodist revivalists of the eighteenth century were, as everyone knows, for the most part Churchmen. Many of them were in orders, valiant and devoted men, who not only preached in the highways and hedges, but founded schools all over Wales, whose peasantry at that time were almost without education. They suffered every kind of persecution and annoyance from the Church, while the country clergy headed mobs who treated them with physical violence. No effort was made to meet this new rival upon its own grounds,—those of ministerial energy and spiritual devotion,—but its exponents were met only with rotten eggs. The bishops were not merely absentees for the most part, but from 1700 to 1870 they were consistently Englishmen, ignorant of the Welsh tongue, and regarded in some sort as agents for the Anglicising of Wales. Men who with some exceptions were destitute of qualifications for their office found themselves in positions that would have taxed abilities of the highest order and all the energies of a modern prelate. The holders of Welsh sees laid neither such slender stocks of ability nor energy as they might possess under the slightest contribution on behalf of Welsh religion. With the funds of the Church, however, they observed no such abstention, but saddled the needy Welsh Establishment with a host of relatives and friends. As for themselves, with a few notable exceptions they cultivated a dignified leisure, sometimes at their palaces, more often in London or Bath. One prelate never saw his diocese at all, while another lived entirely in Westmoreland. With the Methodist revival one could not expect them to sympathise, nor is it surprising that their good wishes were with the militant pot-house parsons who were in favour of physical force. One must remember after all, however, that this was the Hogarthian period; that in all these features of life England was at its worst; and that the faults of the time were only aggravated in Wales by its aloofness and its lingual complications. The Welsh Methodist, it is true, did not formally leave the Church till 1811, but by that time Calvinism had thoroughly taken hold of the country, and the Establishment had not only made no spiritual efforts to stem the tide, but was rapidly losing even its social influence, as the upper classes were ceasing to take service in its ranks. The Welsh parson of indifferent morals and lay habits had hitherto generally been of the land-owning class. Now he was more often than not of a humbler grade without any compensating improvement in morals or professional assiduity. The immense development of dissent in Wales during the last century is a matter of common knowledge. The purifying of the Welsh Church and clergy in the latter half of it and the revival of Anglican energy within the last quarter are marked features of modern Welsh life. We have nothing to do here with the probabilities of a success so tardily courted. But it is of pertinent interest to consider the immense changes that have come over Wales since, let us say, the middle of the Georgian period; and by this I do not merely mean those caused by a material progress common to the whole of Great Britain. For there is much reason to think that the character of the Welsh peasantry has been steadily altering, particularly in the more thoroughly Welsh districts, since they fell under the influence of Calvinistic doctrines. There is much evidence that the old Welshman was a merry, light-hearted person, of free conversation and addicted to such amusements as came in his way; that he still had strong military instincts,* and cherished feudal attachments to the ancient families of Wales even beyond the habit of the time among the English. This latter instinct has died hard, considering the cleavage that various circumstances have created between the landed gentry and the peasantry. Indeed it is by no means yet dead.

The drift of the native tongue, too, since Tudor times has been curious. Its gradual abandonment by the landed gentry from that period onwards, with the tenacity with which their tenants for the most part clung to it, is a subject in itself. The resistance it still offers in spots that may be fairly described as in the very centre of the world's civilisation is probably the most striking lingual anomaly in Europe. Its disappearance, on the other hand, in regions intensely Welsh is worthy of note. Radnorshire, for instance, penetrating the very heart of the Principality, populated almost wholly by Cymry, forgot

* Recent events have demonstrated that this spirit is still far from extinct.

its Welsh before anyone now living can remember. Bits of Monmouth, on the other hand, long reckoned an English county, still use it regularly. It is the household tongue of villagers in Flint, who can see Liverpool from their windows, while there are large communities of pure Celts in Brecon and Carmarthen who cannot even understand it.

The great coal developments in South Wales have wholly transformed large regions and brought great wealth into the country, and replaced the abundant rural life of Glamorgan and its ancient families, Welsh and Norman, with a black country that has developed a new social life of its own. Slate quarrying has proved a vast and profitable industry among the northern mountains, while thousands of tourists carry no inconsiderable stream of wealth across the Marches with every recurring summer. But neither coal-pits, nor quarries, nor tourists make much impression on the Welsh character such as it has become in the North, more particularly under the influence of Calvinism, and very little upon the language which fifty years ago men were accustomed to regard as doomed.

The history of Welsh land since the time of the Tudor settlement is but that of many parts of England. Wales till this century was distinguished for small properties and small tenancies. There were but few large proprietors and few large farmers. In the matter of the former particularly, things have greatly altered. The small squires who lived somewhat rudely in diminutive manor-houses have been swallowed up wholesale by their thriftier or bigger neighbours, but the general and now regretted tendency to consolidate farms scarcely touched Wales, fortunately for that country. Save in a few exceptional districts it is a land of small working farmers, and in most parts the resident agricultural labourer as a detached class scarcely exists.

Few countries in the world contain within the same area more elements of prosperity and happiness than modern Wales, and fewer still are so fortunately situated for making the most of them. Coal, iron, slate, and other minerals in great abundance are vigorously exported and give work and good wages to a large portion of the population. In the rural districts a thrifty peasantry are more widely distributed over the soil, to which they are peculiarly attached, than in almost any part of Britain, and occupied for the most part in the more hopeful and less toilsome of the two branches of agriculture, namely, that of stock-breeding. Surrounded on three sides by the sea, there are ready facilities for the trader, the sailor, or the fisherman. The romantic scenery of the country is another valuable asset to its people and brings an annual and certain income that only one small corner of England can show any parallel to. Education is in an advanced state, while the humbler classes of society have resources due to their taste for music and their sentiment for their native language, which have no equivalent in English village life.

Even those strangely constituted minds that like to dig up racial grievances from the turmoil of the Middle Ages, when right and might were synonymous words the world over, and profess to judge the fourteenth century by the ethics of the nineteenth, must confess that the forced partnership with England has had its compensations. The reasonable Welshman will look back rather with much complaisance on the heroic and prolonged struggle of his ancestors against manifest destiny, remembering always that the policy of the Norman kings was an obvious duty to themselves and to their realm.

Had the Ireland of that day, with its larger fighting strength and sea-girt territory, possessed the national spirit and tenacious courage of Wales, who knows but that she might have vindicated her right to a separate nationality by the only test admissible in mediæval ethics, that of arms? Geography at any rate in her case was no barrier to an independent existence, and there would have been nothing illogical or unnatural in the situation. But geography irrevocably settled the destiny of Wales, as it eventually did that of Scotland. If the conditions under which Wales came into partnership were different and the date earlier, that, again, was partly due to its propinquity to the heart of England. Yet with all these centuries of close affinity to England, the Welsh in many respects—I had almost said in most—have preserved their nationality more successfully than the Celts of either Ireland or the North, and in so doing have lost nothing of such benefits as modern civilisation brings.

APPENDIX

THE BARDS

THE Bards as a class were so deeply interwoven with the whole life of ancient Wales and, though long shorn of most of their official glory, played so prominent a part in the rising of Glyndwr, that it seems desirable that a chapter touching on the subject should be included in this book. Within such limits the subject can only be treated in the most general and elementary manner. Yet such treatment is excusable from the fact that the slenderest and most inefficient description of Welsh song and Welsh singers must contain matter unknown to most English readers. I imagine that few of these would resent being asked to divest their minds of the time-honoured notion that the teaching of the Druids was nothing but a bloodthirsty and barbarous superstition. At any rate, Bardism and Druidism being practically the same thing, one is obliged to remind those readers who may never have given the matter any attention at all, that among the ancient Britons of the Goidel stock who inhabited most of Wales and the West previous to the Cymric immigration, Druidism was the fountain of law, authority, religion, and, above all, of education. The Druids, with their three orders, were a caste apart for which those who were qualified by good character and noble birth to do so, laboriously trained themselves. They decided all controversies whether public or private, judged all causes, from murder to boundary disputes, and administered both rewards and punishments. Those who ventured to defy them were excommunicated, which was equivalent to becoming moral and social lepers.

The three orders were known as Druids, Bards, and Ovates. The first were priests and judges, the second poets; the third were the least aristocratic, practised the arts and sciences, and were, moreover, a probationary or qualifying order through which candidates for the other two, who were on the same level of dignity, had to pass. As everyone knows, there was an Arch-Druid of the Isle of Britain who had his sanctuary in Anglesey. But it is a matter of much less common knowledge how close was the connection between the Druids and Christianity in the Roman period and even afterwards. The Romans, with conquest foremost in their minds, most naturally aimed at the native rulers of the people and made these bardic orders the objects of their special attack. Their slaughter on the banks of the Menai as described by Tacitus, and the destruction of the Sacred Groves of Mona, are among our familiar traditions.

The Druid orders fled to Ireland, Brittany, and elsewhere. But in time, when the Romans, strong in their seats, grew tolerant, the exiles returned and quietly resumed, in West Britain at any rate, something like their old positions.

When Christianity pushed its way from the West into the island, the bardic orders, unable to resist it, seem by degrees to have accepted the situation and to have become the priests of the new faith, as they had been the custodians and expounders of the old. This transition was the less difficult seeing that the Druids preached all the ordinary tenets of morality, and the immortality of the soul. To what extent the early Christianity of western Britain was tainted with the superstition of the Druids is a question upon which experts have written volumes, and it need not detain us here. A notable effort was made in the fourth century to merge Christianity, so to speak, in the old British faith, and Morgan or Pelagius, "sea-born," of Bangor Iscoed was the apostle of this attempted reaction. He left the island about A.D. 400, and his converts in what we now call Wales were numerous and active. The movement is historically known as the "Pelagian heresy" and has some additional importance from the number of ecclesiastics that came from over the sea for the purpose of denouncing it.

But all this is rather the religious than the secular side of Bardism, the leading feature of whose teaching in pre-Roman days had been the committal to memory of its literature, both prose and verse. Writing was discountenanced, as the possession of these stores of learning thus laboriously acquired were a valuable asset of the initiated. Three was the mystic number in the recitation of all axioms and precepts, for many of these were committed to writing later on in the seventh and tenth centuries, and are now familiar as the Welsh "Triads."

The bards, as a lay order, remained of great importance. In the laws of Howel Dda (tenth century) the royal bard stands eighth among the officers of the State. The fine for insulting him was six cows and twenty silver pennies. His value was 126 cows, his land was free, and he had the use of a house. His noblest duty was to sing "The Monarchy of Britain" at the head of his chieftain's army when victorious. The number of songs he had to sing to the King and Queen respectively during the social hours was clearly defined, as were his claims upon each. Among the latter was a specified portion of the spoils of war, a chessboard made from the horn of a sea-fish from the King, and a ring from the Queen. It was the business of the bards, moreover, to preserve genealogies, and they were practically tutors to the rising generation of the aristocracy. Every family of position in Wales had its domestic bard, while below these there were a great number of strolling minstrels who visited the dwellings of the inferior people, from whom they exacted gifts of money ("cymmorthau") as well as free quarters.

In treating of individual and well-known bards one naturally turns for a beginning to the sixth century, when that famous quartet, Taliesin, Merddyn, Aneurin, and Llywarch Hên, flourished. Several poems either actually their work or purporting to be so are extant. To linger over a period so dim, however great the names that adorn it, would be out of place here. That all four were great kings of song in their time is beyond doubt. The legends that distinguish them are comparatively familiar: how Taliesin was found floating in a leather bottle in Prince Elphin's salmon weir near Aberdovey, how Merddyn as a boy astonished the advisers of Vortigern and became his good angel, and how Llywarch Hên, at a hundred and fifty years of age, witnessed the slaughter of the last of his four-and-twenty sons in battle against the Saxons. His poem on the death of Cynddylan, Prince of Powys, seizes the imagination, not so much from the description the poet-warrior gives of the death of his friend and his own sons in a decisive combat which he himself took part in, but from the almost certain fact that from the top of the Wrekin he saw the Saxons destroy and sack Uriconium ("the white town"), whose ruins are such a striking feature among the sights of Shropshire.

From these four giants until 1080 there is little left whereby to judge of the merits of the bards, and no great record of their names. That they sang and played and gave counsel and kept genealogies is beyond question, but it was not till after the Norman conquest of England that they began to leave much behind them in the way of written documents.

When Prince Griffith ap Kynan returned from Ireland to Wales and the poet Meilir arose to sing his triumphs and good qualities, a new era in bardic history may be said to have commenced. The intellectual and religious revival that distinguished the twelfth century in Western Europe was conspicuous in Wales. The bards were no longer singing merely of battles, but of nature and kindred subjects, with a delicacy that showed them to be men of taste and culture. In the twelfth, thirteenth, and fourteenth centuries, in spite of war and conquest, the age was a golden one in Welsh song. Between eighty and ninety bards of this period have left poems behind them as a witness of their various styles and merits, while there are no literary remains whatever of very many who are known to have been quite famous in their day. Thousands, too, of popular songs must have existed that the jealousy of the composers or, more probably, the price of parchment consigned to oblivion.

"When the literary revival of this period reached Wales, its people," says Mr. Stephens in the *Literature of the Kymri*, "were better prepared than their neighbours for intellectual effort." "An order of bards existed, numerous and well disciplined; a language in all its fullness and richness was in use among all classes of people, and as a necessary consequence their literature was superior, more copious, and richer than that of any contemporaneous nation. The fabulous literature so prized by others was in no great repute, but gave way to the public preference for the more laboured and artistic productions of the bards."

Several Welsh Princes of commanding character and unusual ability came to the front in the long struggle with the Norman power, and were no unworthy sources of bardic inspiration. Many of them aspired themselves to literary as well as martial fame, of whom Owain Cyfeiliog, Prince of Upper Powys, was the most notable. Poetry was in high repute. Eisteddfodau were held periodically with much ceremony and splendour, and were sometimes advertised a year in advance, not only throughout Wales but in Ireland and other portions of the British Islands. Not poetry alone but literature generally and music, of course, both vocal and instrumental, were subjects of competition, while Rhys ap Tudor, a long-lived and distinguished Prince of South Wales, revived, after a sojourn in Brittany, the system of the Round Table. To Englishmen the long list of bards who adorned the period between the Norman arrival and Glyndwr's rising would be mere names, but even to those who may only read the works of the most notable in translations, they are of great interest if only as a reflection of life and thought at a time when England and English were still almost silent.

Gwalchmai, the son of a distinguished father, Meilir, already mentioned, was among the first of the revived school, whose work is regarded by Celtic scholars as of the first quality. His love of nature is prominent in many of the poems he has left :

"At the break of day, and at evening's close,
I love the sweet musicians who so fondly dwell
In dear, plaintive murmurs, and the accents of woe ;
I love the birds and their sweet voices
In the soothing lays of the wood."

Owain Gwynedd was the hero-king of Gwalchmai's day. His repulse of an attack made by Henry the

Second's fleet under the command of an unpatriotic Prince of Powys in Anglesey is the subject of the bard's chief heroic poem:

"Now thickens still the frantic war,
The flashing death-strokes gleam afar,
Spear rings on spear, flight urges flight,
And drowning victims plunge to-night
Till Menai's over-burthened tide,
Wide-blushing with the streaming gore,
And choked with carnage, ebbs no more;
While mail-clad warriors on her side
In anguish drag their deep-gash'd wounds along,
And 'fore the King's Red chiefs are heap'd the
mangled throng."

Owain Cyfeiliog, a Prince of Powys in the end of the twelfth century, though a noted warrior, is a leading instance of a royal bard. His chief poem, *The Hirlâs Horn* (drinking-cup), is famous wherever Welsh is spoken:

"This horn we dedicate to joy;
Then fill the Hirlâs horn, my boy,
That shineth like the sea,
Whose azure handles tipped with gold
Invite the grasp of Britons bold,
The sons of liberty."

This is one of the longest poems of the twelfth century. The scene is the night after a battle, and the Prince with his warriors gathered round him in the banqueting-hall sends the brimming cup to each of his chieftains successively and enumerates their respective deeds. A leading incident in the poem is when Owen, having eulogised the prowess of two favourite warriors in glowing terms, turns to their accustomed seats, and, finding them vacant, suddenly recalls the fact that they had fallen in the battle of the morning:

"Ha! the cry of death—And do I miss them!
O Christ! how I mourn their catastrophe!
O lost Moreiddig—How greatly shall I need thee!"

A most suggestive poem by another Prince is a kind of summary of his progress through his dominions from the Ardudwy mountains,

"Fast by the margin of the deep
Where storms eternal uproar keep,"

to the hills above Llangollen where he proposes "to taste the social joys of Yale." This is Howel, the illegitimate son of Owain Gwynedd, who seized and held for two years his father's kingdom. Though so strenuous a warrior, his poems are rather of love and social life. He sings with much feeling of the joys of Wales; her fair landscape, her bright waters and green vales, her beauteous women and skimming seagulls, her fields clothed with tender trefoil, her far-reaching wilds, and plenteousness of game. Himself a successful stormer of castles, there is something richly suggestive in the action of a man laying down the torch and bloody sword and taking up the pen to describe his havoc:

"The ravens croaked and human blood
In ruddy streams poured o'er the land;

There burning houses war proclaimed;
Churches in flames and palace halls;
While sheets of fire scale the sky,
And warriors 'On to battle!' cry."

Then the author wholly changes his mood:

" Give me the fair, the gentle maid,
Of slender form, in mantle green;
Whose woman's wit is ever staid,
Subdued by virtue's graceful mien.
Give me the maid, whose heart with mine
Shall blend each thought, each hope combine;
Then, maiden fair as ocean's spray,
Gifted with Kymric wit's bright ray,
Say, am I thine?
Art thou then mine?
What! silent now?
Thy silence makes this bosom glow.
I choose thee, maiden, for thy gifts divine;
'T is right to choose—then, fairest, choose me thine."

There is much misunderstanding as to the fashion in which the bards were treated by Edward the First. During war the leading minstrels were naturally identified with the patrons whose banners they followed and whose praises they sang; but the statement that they were put to death as bards rests on wholly secondary authority and seems doubtful. Stringent laws were certainly made against the lower order of minstrels who wandered homeless through the country, but they seem to have been devised as much for the protection of the common people, who were called on to support them, as against the men themselves, who were regarded by the authorities as mendicants and idlers. The superior bards, who kept strictly to the houses of the great, were probably not often interfered with. These, though they had regular patrons and fixed places of abode, made extended tours from time to time in which there seems to have been no special distinction between North and South Wales. The hatred of the bards towards England was a marked feature of their time, and was so consistent that though many Welsh princes, in their jealousy, lent their swords, as we have seen, to the invader, no bards, so far as one knows, turned against their countrymen. For generations they prided themselves in being intellectually superior to the Saxon. They also saw, after the Norman conquest, the English race despised and held down by their conquerors, and a species of serfdom in use among the Saxons which had no prototype in their own country. The ordinary bards, however, had beyond all doubt sacrificed much of their old independence and become the creatures of their patrons and ready to sell their praises for patronage. Even the respectable Meilir confesses:

> "I had heaps of gold and velvet
> From frail princes for loving them."

Llewelyn the Great, the second, that is to say, of the three Llewelyns, aroused the enthusiasm of Bardic literature and was the subject of much stirring eulogy:

> "None his valour could withstand,
> None could stem his furious hand.

Like a whirlwind on the deep,
See him through their squadrons sweep.
Then was seen the crimson flood,
Then was Offa bathed in blood,
Then the Saxons fled with fright,
Then they felt his royal might.

Dafydd Benvras, the author of this stanza, left many poems, and later on Griffith ap Yr Ynad Goch wrote what is regarded as among the finest of Welsh odes, on the death of the last Llewelyn, laying the blame of that catastrophe on the wickedness of his countrymen:

" Hark how the howling wind and rain
In loudest symphony complain;
Hark how the consecrated oaks,
Unconscious of the woodman's strokes,
With thundering crash proclaim he 's gone,
Fall in each other's arms and groan.
Hark! how the sullen trumpets roar.
See! how the white waves lash the shore.
See how eclipsed the sun appears,
See! how the stars fall from their spheres,
Each awful Heaven-sent prodigy,
Ye sons of infidelity!
Believe and tremble, guilty land.
Lo! thy destruction is at hand."

After the Edwardian conquest in 1284 the note of the bards sensibly softened and attuned itself much more generally to love and nature. The song-birds particularly were in great request as recipients of poetic addresses and confidences.

"And thoù, lark,
Bard of the morning dawn,
Show to this maid
My broken heart."

While the same singer, Rhys Goch, describes thus the light tread of his ladylove:

"As peahens stride in sun-ray heat,
See her the earth elastic tread ;
And where she walks, neath snow-white feet
Not e'en a trefoil bends its head.

The latter part of the 14th century was extremely prolific in poetry which, with some notable exceptions, is regarded rather as showing a good general level than as producing any masterpieces. Dafydd ap Gwilym, the Welsh Ovid, is of course a striking exception. Over 250 of his poems are preserved, while Lewis Glyncothi, Gutyn Owain, Iolo Goch, Glyndwr's bard, and two or three more have left behind them something like 300 others. Dafydd ap Gwilym, who was buried at Strata Florida, holds one of the highest places in Cymric literature. It is as a love poet that he is chiefly distinguished, but his love of nature and his own beautiful country finds sole expression in many of his productions. His ode to Fair Glamorgan, written from "the heart of wild, wild Gwynedd," asking the summer to be his messenger, is regarded as one of his best. In translation it is interesting as a contemporary picture, though a poetic one, of the richest Welsh province.

"Radiant with corn and vineyards sweet,
And lakes of fish and mansions neat,

With halls of stone where kindness dwells,
And where each hospitable lord
Heaps for the stranger guest his board,
And where the generous wine-cup swells,
With trees that bear the luscious pear,
So thickly clustering everywhere.
Her lofty woods with warblers teem,
Her fields with flowers that love the stream,
Her valleys varied crops display,
Eight kinds of corn and three of hay;
Bright parlour with her trefoiled floor!
Sweet garden, spread on ocean shore."

Quotations have already been made in the body of this book from Iolo Goch's ode to Glyndwr, and throughout the Wars of the Roses Lewis Glyncothi, Gutyn Owain, and Tudor Aled continued to sing of contemporary events.

The leading charge against Cymric poetry is that it is too prone to elaborate the mere art of versification at the expense of fire and animation. Alliteration was of course the chief method of ornament, though the rhyming of the terminal syllable was by no means always ignored. But, speaking generally, skill in the arrangement of words according to certain time-honoured conventions occupied more than an equitable share in the making of Welsh verse. A tendency to put mere sound above feeling and emotion did much to cramp it, and often forced it into mannerisms and affectations that would rather destroy than enhance the intrinsic merits of a composition.

"Beyond all rhetorical ornaments," says Giraldus Cambrensis, "they preferred the use of alliteration and that kind more especially which repeats the first letters or syllables of words. They made so much use of this ornament in every finished discourse that they thought nothing elegantly spoken without it."

Mr. Stephens, by way of illustration, points out poems by the greater bards which from the first line to the last commence with the same letter. He also attributes the extraordinary elaboration in structure with which fashion was prone to cumber Welsh poetry to a desire for increasing the difficulties of composition and in consequence the exclusiveness of the bardic order. It is not surprising that in a country where war was the chief business of life it should be by far the favourite subject of the minstrel, particularly when one remembers that the celebration of his employer's exploits or intended exploits was the chief source of the domestic poet's livelihood. The wars of Glyndwr stirred again the old fighting note which after the Edwardian conquest had given way in a great measure to gentler themes. The old laws against the bards, enunciated by Edward I., now for long a dead letter, were renewed, but after this final submission of Wales it is doubtful if they continued to have much meaning, particularly amid the chaos of the ensuing Wars of the Roses, when the bards most certainly did their full share of singing.

I have said nothing of the music which both in early and mediæval Wales played such a prominent part in the national life. The harp was always the true national instrument, though the pipe or bagpipe was well known and in frequent use; but it was never really popular, as in Ireland and Scotland, and this was surely a valuable testimony to the superior culture of the Welsh musicians. Griffith ap Kynan, King of North Wales about 1100, already mentioned, introduced it into the Eisteddfod as the result of his Irish education. The pipes had hitherto been forbidden, and the result at the celebrated Eisteddfod at Caerwys was that Griffith's prize of a silver pipe went to a Scotsman. The Welsh, in short, despised the instrument. Lewis Glyncothi has left an amusing satire on a piper. He finds himself in Flint at an English marriage, where the guests would have none of him or his harp, but "bawled for Will the Piper, low born wretch" who comes forward as best he may, "unlike a free enobled man."

"The churl did blow a grating shriek,
The bag did swell, and harshly squeak,
As does a goose from nightmare crying,
Or dog crushed by a chest when dying,
This whistling box's changeless note
Is forced from turgid veins and throat;
Its sound is like a crane's harsh moan,
Or like a gosling's latest groan."

Giraldus, half Welshman himself, writing after his extended tour through Wales, about 1200, with Archbishop Baldwin, says:

"The strangers who arrived in the morning were entertained until evening with the conversation of young women and with the music of the harp, for in this country almost every house is provided with both. Such an influence had the habit of music on the mind and its fascinating powers, that in every family or in every tribe, they esteemed skill in playing on the harp beyond any kind of learning. Again, by the sweetness of their musical instruments they soothe and delight the ear. They are rapid yet delicate in their modulation, and by the astonishing execution of their fingers and their swift transitions from discord to concord, produce the most pleasing harmony."

The part-singing of the Welsh seems also to have greatly struck Giraldus in contrast to the unison in which he heard the musicians of other nations perform.

To draw the line between the bard and musician would be of course impossible. Many writers of verse could only declaim; some could sing to their own accompaniment. The mass of musicians, how ever, we may take it, belonged to the lower grade of wandering bards, who played first, as we have seen, upon the national instrument, the harp, as well as upon the pipe and "crwth" (a kind of rude violin).

The tone of morality was certainly not high among the mediæval Welsh bards. They had long lost all touch with the order of the priesthood, and indeed monks and poets had become almost as a matter of course inimical to one another. The latter, too, maintained a steady hatred of the Saxon that was almost creditable, seeing how often their masters, for the sake of interest or revenge, took up arms against their fellow-countrymen.

It is sufficiently difficult merely to touch, and that in the slightest manner, so vast a subject as this. In recognising the insufficiency of such an attempt,

I am almost thankful that the period of Glyndwr and the succeeding turmoil of the Wars of the Roses puts a reasonable limit to my remarks. For it goes without saying that when Wales settled down under the Tudors to its happy and humdrum existence, the martial attitude of the bards as feudal appanages and national firebrands altogether ceased. Welsh poets hereafter were private individuals, their song ceased for the most part to be of war; nor was the Saxon or the Lloegrian any longer an object of invective. The glory of this new United Britain to which they belonged was not without its inspiration, but it has been by no means a leading note in Welsh verse, which, speaking generally, has since in this particular sung upon a minor key.

INDEX

H

Printed in the United Kingdom by
Lightning Source UK Ltd., Milton Keynes
139568UK00001B/158/P

9 781409 766254